BUSINESS INTELLIGENCE AND DATA ANALYSIS IN THE AGE OF AI

BUSINESS INTELLIGENCE AND DATA ANALYSIS IN THE AGE OF AI

Arshad Khan

MERCURY LEARNING AND INFORMATION
Boston, Massachusetts

MERCURY LEARNING AND INFORMATION
121 High Street, 3rd Floor
Boston, MA 02110
info@merclearning.com

A. Khan. *Business Intelligence and Data Analysis in the Age of AI.*
ISBN: 978-1-5015-2425-7

The publisher recognizes and respects all marks used by companies, manufacturers, and developers as a means to distinguish their products. All brand names and product names mentioned in this book are trademarks or service marks of their respective companies. Any omission or misuse (of any kind) of service marks or trademarks, etc. is not an attempt to infringe on the property of others.

Library of Congress Control Number: 2024952581

242526321   This book is printed on acid-free paper in the United States of America.

Our titles are available for adoption, license, or bulk purchase by institutions, corporations, etc.

All of our titles are available in digital format at various digital vendors.

CONTENTS

PREFACE

Welcome to *Business Intelligence and Data Analysis in the Age of AI*. This book embarks on a journey through the evolving landscape of business intelligence (BI) and data analysis, exploring the intersection of traditional methodologies with cutting-edge artificial intelligence (AI) technologies.

As organizations increasingly harness the power of data to drive decision-making and gain competitive advantage, understanding the fundamentals of BI and data analysis has become essential. Each chapter delves into critical aspects of modern data management, from the foundational concepts of analytics processes and tools to the complexities of big data, data integration, and quality.

The book begins with an introduction to BI, then explores the analytics process and essential tools. Chapters on understanding data, big data, and data integration provide insights into managing and effectively leveraging vast amounts of information. Additionally, topics such as governance, security, privacy, and ethics shed light on the ethical considerations and regulatory frameworks surrounding data usage.

As we delve deeper, we explore the intricacies of data warehousing, data lakes, extraction, transformation, and loading (ETL) and data design. We will introduce you to the benefits and application of programming languages like R, SQL, and Python, which are extensively used for data manipulation and analysis.

The journey continues with chapters dedicated to reporting in BI, cloud computing, and data visualization, emphasizing the importance of presenting data in meaningful and accessible formats. Furthermore, we explore predictive analytics, unlocking the potential to forecast future trends and outcomes based on historical data.

In the latter part of the book, we examine advanced topics such as fundamental and advanced insights in data analysis. We also learn about the integration of AI into BI and data analysis, discussing its potential, risks, ethical considerations, and future implications.

Whether you are a seasoned data professional or a novice navigating the world of BI and data analysis, this book serves as a comprehensive guide to understanding, implementing, and leveraging AI in the age of data-driven decision-making. Join us on this enlightening journey as we unravel the intricacies of BI and data analysis in the era of AI.

CHAPTER 1

INTRODUCTION TO BUSINESS INTELLIGENCE

OVERVIEW

The primary objective of business intelligence (BI) is to empower organizations with actionable insights derived from their data, fostering informed decision-making and strategic planning. By systematically collecting, processing, and analyzing data, BI enables enterprises to gain a comprehensive understanding of their internal processes, market dynamics, and customer behavior. The overarching goal is to transform raw data into meaningful information, providing stakeholders at all levels with the tools needed to identify trends, uncover patterns, and respond swiftly to emerging opportunities or challenges. Ultimately, BI serves as a guiding compass, enhancing organizational efficiency, optimizing resource allocation, and facilitating a data-driven culture that propels businesses toward sustained success in an ever-evolving landscape.

Definition

The term *business intelligence* was popularized and defined by Howard Dresner in 1989. Dresner (founder and CRO of Dresner Advisory Services), who was working at the Gartner Group during that time, used the phrase to describe a set of concepts and methods to improve business decision-making by utilizing fact-based support systems. His early definition laid the groundwork for the field of business intelligence, which has since evolved into a crucial component of modern business strategies, involving data analysis, reporting, and the use of technology to provide actionable insights for organizations.

Evolution

The evolution of BI traces a transformative journey from its early roots to its current sophisticated state. Beginning in the late twentieth century, BI emerged as a concept for improving decision-making processes by leveraging data-driven insights. Initially focused on reporting and querying, BI evolved with the advent of data warehousing, extract, transform, load (ETL) processes, and multidimensional analysis.

In the 2000s, a shift toward more user-friendly interfaces and interactive dashboards occurred, making BI accessible to a broader audience. The rise of big data and cloud computing in the following decade further propelled BI, enabling organizations to handle larger datasets and facilitate real-time analytics. Today, BI incorporates advanced analytics, machine learning, and AI, providing predictive and prescriptive capabilities for more proactive decision-making. The evolution of BI reflects a continuous adaptation to technological advancements, expanding its capabilities and impact on organizational strategies.

Concept

Business intelligence is like having a smart assistant for business data. Imagine having a treasure chest full of information about a company—sales numbers, customer feedback, and more. BI is the tool that helps to unlock the secrets hidden in that treasure chest. It organizes all that information into clear charts, graphs, and reports, making it easy for individuals to understand what is happening in their business. Therefore, instead of drowning in a sea of numbers, BI helps to see trends, identify opportunities, and make smarter decisions. It is like having a friendly guide that turns data into insights, helping steer the business in the right direction.

Importance

Business intelligence holds paramount importance in the contemporary business landscape, as it serves as the linchpin for informed decision-making. In an era where organizations are inundated with vast amounts of data, BI plays a pivotal role in transforming raw information into actionable insights. By leveraging advanced analytics, reporting tools, and data visualization techniques, BI empowers businesses to comprehensively understand their operations, market dynamics, and customer behavior. This insight, in turn, enables executives and decision-makers at all levels to make strategic and timely choices, optimize resource allocation, enhance operational efficiency, and stay agile in a rapidly evolving marketplace.

The ability to glean meaningful patterns from data not only fosters a proactive approach to challenges but also positions businesses to capitalize on emerging opportunities, ultimately driving sustained success in today's data-driven business environment.

Application

Business intelligence applications encompass a diverse array of functionalities that cater to different aspects of data-driven decision-making. These applications play a crucial role in transforming raw data into actionable insights, offering a comprehensive suite of tools for organizations across various industries.

One category of BI applications is operations reporting, which furnishes information pertaining to routine business operations and facilitates benchmarking. This serves as a foundational layer for organizations to understand and optimize their day-to-day activities. On a more strategic level, strategic reporting focuses on aligning BI tools, such as online analytical processing (OLAP) and data visualization, with the overarching goals of the enterprise. Multidimensional analysis, through techniques like slicing and dicing, provides a nuanced insight into data at different levels of granularity, aiding in more comprehensive decision-making.

Analytics is another integral category, encompassing a range of techniques, including predictive analysis and statistical analysis, which enable the optimization of decision-making processes. Based on the extrapolation of historical data, forecasting provides organizations with estimates and insights into future trends. Correlation, often achieved through data mining, delves into the relationships between various variables. Dashboards offer a consolidated view of reports and key performance indicators (KPIs), allowing users to grasp critical information at a glance and drill-down to explore underlying data. Collaboration tools within BI applications enable different functional areas, both within and outside the company, to collaborate seamlessly, fostering a collective approach to decision-making.

The spectrum of BI applications extends beyond these categories to cover managed reporting, ad hoc reporting, interactive data visualizations, predictive analysis, data integration, business performance management, text mining, information widgets, customer profiling, market segmentation, and insights into revenue, sales, and profitability. Collectively, these applications empower organizations to harness the full potential of their data, enabling them to make informed decisions, enhance operational efficiency, and gain a competitive edge in today's data-driven business landscape.

USAGE

The usage of BI empowers organizations to transform raw data into actionable insights, driving strategic decisions and operational efficiency. The following sections discuss various ways in which BI can be used.

Decision-Making

Business intelligence plays a pivotal role in strategic decision-making by transforming raw data into meaningful insights, offering a comprehensive view of organizational performance. Through the utilization of advanced analytics, reporting tools, and data visualization, BI empowers decision-makers to discern patterns, identify trends, and extract actionable information from vast datasets. This process enables businesses to make well-informed decisions, optimize resource allocation, and navigate complexities in real time.

The strategic significance of BI lies in its ability to serve as a guiding compass for decision-makers. It provides the necessary tools not only to understand the past and present but also to anticipate and shape the future. In doing so, BI fosters agility and sustained success in today's dynamic business landscape. The insights derived from BI are instrumental in aligning organizational goals with strategic decision-making processes. BI acts as a bridge between data and strategy, facilitating a proactive approach to challenges and opportunities.

It is essential to integrate BI processes into the broader strategic framework to align BI with organizational goals. This involves defining clear objectives, KPIs, and metrics that align with the overarching goals of the organization. BI tools should be configured to deliver insights that directly contribute to achieving these objectives. Regular assessments and refinements ensure that BI remains aligned with evolving organizational priorities.

Moreover, fostering a culture of data-driven decision-making within the organization is critical. This entails promoting BI literacy among stakeholders and encouraging the use of BI insights in day-to-day operations. Training programs, clear communication of BI findings, and collaborative efforts between BI teams and decision-makers are essential components of this cultural shift.

In conclusion, BI not only provides the means to analyze and inter-pret data but also serves as a strategic enabler. By aligning BI with organizational goals, businesses can harness their power to navigate complexities, make informed decisions, and position themselves for success in an ever-evolving business landscape.

Usage Categorization

The versatility of business intelligence enables it to find applications across various domains, each of which is categorized to fulfill specific business needs. One of the most prevalent forms is business operations reporting, which serves as the backbone of BI usage. This category involves the analysis of actual performance against predefined goals, often materializing in standard weekly or monthly reports crucial for organizational assessment.

Another critical facet is forecasting, where BI acts as both a science and an art. Forecasting necessitates predicting future outcomes and acknowledging the uncertainties that come with unforeseen events, such as competitors' strategic moves or unexpected market fluctuations. It combines historical data extrapolation with a nuanced understanding of potentially influencing factors.

Dashboards, as a BI category, are designed for quick informa-tion absorption without the need for in-depth data exploration. The emphasis lies on presentation and ease of use, providing a snapshot of critical metrics at a glance. Multidimensional analysis, however, involves the intricate "slicing and dicing" of data, offering detailed insights at a granular level. This requires a robust data warehousing infrastructure and skilled analysts who are experienced in interpreting complex datasets.

Delving even further into the BI landscape is the category of finding correlations among different factors. Here, the focus is on understand-ing the intricate relationships between diverse factors and identify-ing significant time trends that can be leveraged or anticipated. This advanced level of BI requires a thorough understanding of business dynamics and the ability to uncover hidden correlations that may influ-ence decision-making.

In essence, the diverse categories within BI underscore its adapt-ability to meet varied business requirements, ranging from routine reporting to sophisticated analyses that examine the complexities of correlation and forecasting. Each category uniquely empowers organizations by providing the insights needed for informed decision-making and strategic planning.

User Diversity

User needs within business intelligence vary significantly, reflecting individuals' diverse information requirements and technical proficiencies. Users may seek simple, easy-to-use queries and reports with minimal parameters depending on their technological aptitude. Others may require the generation of periodic reports for in-depth analysis of variances, while some users aim to actively engage with data by crunching numbers, slicing and dicing information, and manipulating data to derive meaningful insights. Additionally, users may have specific needs related to accessing and navigating dashboards, as well as executing embedded reports.

The diversity in user requirements becomes even more apparent when considering different classes of users. A savvy analyst, for instance, may delve into sophisticated analysis involving statistical methods and data mining. On the other end of the spectrum, an information subscriber may simply receive reports executed by another user or the system. Executives typically seek summarized strategic results, while a report writer is adept at building complex reports. With a need for daily operational insights, managers often require the ability to drill-down into detailed data to facilitate more granular decision-making. This broad range of user needs underscores the flexibility and adaptability that effective BI solutions must offer to cater to the diverse roles within an organization.

TECHNOLOGY

Techniques

Business intelligence encompasses a range of resources and techniques for gathering, transforming, storing, and analyzing data. These include various processes, technologies, applications, data quality considerations, skills, practices, and risk management. The technologies involved in BI cover a spectrum, such as data warehousing, OLAP for multidimensional analysis, data mining, analytical and statistical tools, querying and reporting tools, as well as data visualization, dashboards, and scorecards. These technologies collectively facilitate data and information tasks, including collection, integration, analysis, interpretation, and presentation.

BI holds distinct perspectives for its primary user groups—business and IT. While IT often perceives BI as a tool, the business sees it as a source of valuable information. It is crucial to note that although the term *business intelligence* is sometimes used interchangeably with "competitive intelligence" due to their shared focus on decision-making support, BI specifically utilizes technologies, processes, and applications to mainly analyze internal, structured data and business processes. In contrast, competitive intelligence involves gathering, analyzing, and disseminating all-source information and data, both structured and unstructured, focusing predominantly on external sources and also incorporating internal data to support decision-making processes.

Tool Categories

Business intelligence tools form a diverse ecosystem, each category catering to distinct facets of data analysis and reporting. At the forefront are data visualization tools, exemplified by Tableau and Microsoft Power BI, designed to create interactive visual representations facilitating a comprehensive understanding of complex datasets. Reporting tools, such as SAP Crystal Reports and IBM Cognos Reporting, focus on structuring and presenting data in a clear and organized format, which is crucial for conveying critical business information effectively.

The landscape extends to encompass OLAP tools like Microsoft Analysis Services, which empower users to explore datasets from various perspectives. Data mining tools, represented by RapidMiner and KNIME, delve into advanced analytics, unveiling patterns and relationships within large datasets for predictive insights.

Self-service BI tools, including Tableau and Microsoft Power BI, empower nontechnical users to craft their own reports and visualizations, fostering a culture of decentralized data-driven decision-making. These categories, among others, contribute to a dynamic BI environment by adapting to the evolving needs of organizations seeking to harness the power of their data for informed decision-making and strategic planning.

CORE COMPONENTS

Business intelligence comprises several core components that collectively enable organizations to gather, analyze, and transform data into meaningful insights. The key BI components are described in the following subsections.

Data Sources

Data sources form the bedrock of BI, constituting the diverse repositories and systems that facilitate the collection of valuable information. They range from structured databases and data warehouses to spreadsheets and external sources, providing organizations with a comprehensive array of data to derive insights and support strategic decision-making.

Data Integration

Data integration plays a pivotal role in the data analytics landscape. It orchestrates the seamless amalgamation of information from disparate sources into a cohesive and unified view, thereby guaranteeing not only the consistency and accuracy of the data but also its ready availability for in-depth analysis and meaningful interpretation.

Data Warehousing

Data warehousing involves the storage of large volumes of structured data collected from different sources. Data warehouses serve as centralized repositories that facilitate efficient querying and reporting.

Extract, Transform, Load (ETL)

ETL processes are integral to BI and involve the extraction of data from source systems, transforming it into a usable format, and loading it into a target data repository such as a data warehouse.

Data Modeling

Within the realm of business intelligence, data modeling goes beyond mere structuring. It serves as the architectural blueprint, intricately defining the organization and relationships among various data elements and meticulously crafting the schema that acts as the backbone for organizing and optimizing data for comprehensive analysis.

Reporting and Querying

Business intelligence tools empower users with the ability to retrieve, visualize, and create reports and queries, covering a wide range of simple tables to complex visualizations. This flexibility accommodates diverse analytical needs and preferences.

Data Analysis

BI tools offer a multifaceted approach to data analysis, employing statistical analysis, OLAP, and data mining techniques. These collectively enable the extraction of meaningful trends, patterns, and insights from the data, empowering organizations with a comprehensive understanding of their information landscape.

Data Visualization

Data visualization involves presenting data in graphical formats such as charts, graphs, and dashboards. Visualizations make it easier for users to interpret complex information and derive actionable insights.

Performance Management

BI systems often include performance management components that focus on tracking and measuring KPIs. These metrics help organizations monitor their progress toward strategic objectives.

Metadata Management

Metadata, or data about the data, is crucial for understanding and managing the information within a business intelligence system. Metadata management involves documenting and organizing metadata to ensure the accuracy and reliability of the data.

Security and Access Control

BI systems prioritize security by implementing robust measures to control access to sensitive information, incorporating practices such as user authentication, authorization, and encryption. These measures not only safeguard the integrity of the data but also ensure the confidentiality of sensitive information, reinforcing the overall security of the BI environment.

These core components work collaboratively to create a robust business intelligence infrastructure, empowering organizations to make informed decisions and gain a competitive advantage through the strategic use of data.

TYPES

Operational BI

Business intelligence has traditionally concentrated on strategic decision-making and analytics. The evolving landscape introduces the concept of operational business intelligence, or operational BI, which shifts the focus toward providing real-time to multiyear insights specifically tailored for day-to-day operations. Unlike the historical emphasis on strategic decisions, operational BI is geared toward empowering users to make timely decisions that directly impact immediate business operations.

This approach proves invaluable to a diverse user base, enabling them to efficiently run, manage, or optimize time-sensitive business processes within minutes or a few hours. The evolution toward operational BI underscores a dynamic shift in leveraging intelligence not only for long-term strategy but also for enhancing the agility and efficiency of day-to-day business functions.

Differences Between Enterprise BI and Operational BI

Enterprise BI concentrates on strategic decision-making at an organizational level, offering insights derived from diverse data sources to support executives in long-term planning and trend identification. It deals with historical and aggregated data, providing a comprehensive view of the overall business landscape.

Operational BI focuses on day-to-day operations, providing real-time or near-real-time data for immediate action. It caters to users at the operational level, facilitating efficient decision-making in ongoing business processes. Operational BI involves more granular, transactional data, enabling quick, tactical decisions that impact immediate operations. Both enterprise and operational BI play distinct roles in providing decision-makers with the necessary insights tailored to their specific organizational responsibilities.

BENEFITS

Drive Business Value

Business intelligence serves diverse purposes, encapsulated by the acronym MARCKM, each contributing to creating business value. The first pillar, measurement (M), involves creating a hierarchical structure of performance metrics and benchmarking to inform business leaders about the progress toward organizational goals. This program, also known as business process management, establishes a foundation for understanding and optimizing business processes.

Analytics (A), the second key component, encompasses quantitative processes that aid businesses in making optimal decisions and undertaking business knowledge discovery. This program often employs advanced techniques such as data mining, statistical analysis, predictive analytics, predictive modeling, and business process modeling. It serves as a critical tool for organizations seeking to extract actionable insights from their data.

Reporting (R), specifically enterprise reporting, forms the third pillar, focusing on building infrastructure for strategic reporting to serve the needs of strategic management rather than operational reporting. This program involves elements such as data visualization, executive information systems, and OLAP, providing a robust framework for strategic decision-making. The fourth component, collaboration (C), centers on fostering cooperation among different areas, both within and outside the business, through data sharing and electronic data interchange.

Finally, knowledge management (KM), the fifth pillar, is a program designed to make companies data-driven by implementing strategies and practices for identifying, creating, representing, distributing, and enabling the adoption of insights and experiences that constitute true business knowledge. Knowledge management is foundational to learning management and regulatory compliance. Collectively, these BI applications form an indispensable suite of tools for organizations striving to leverage their data for informed decision-making and strategic advancement.

Support Decision-Making Processes

Business intelligence is a transformative force that offers many advantages that significantly shape an organization's strategic and operational dimensions. These benefits encompass a wide range of functionalities, all of which are geared toward fostering informed decision-making, optimizing processes, and elevating overall business performance.

At the heart of BI's impact lies its ability to support both strategic and operational decision-making processes. BI systems ensure timely information delivery, seamlessly integrating data and processes across internal and external spheres of operation. This integrated approach spans various functions and accommodates historical and current data to establish a single, reliable source of truth. This empowers decision-makers with cohesive insights and robust decision-support tools.

Facilitate Data Analysis

BI facilitates effortless data analysis across different periods and streamlines business processes, contributing to more efficient operations. It also provides a comprehensive view of business trends and opportunities, creating a competitive edge through enhanced knowledge about the business and its market counterparts. This strategic advantage can lead to new revenue streams, cost reductions via improved processes, and an overall bottom line enhancement. BI's impact on customer relations is equally significant, helping organizations increase and retain customers, elevate customer service, and boost overall satisfaction.

In summary, with its suite of analytical tools, BI transcends traditional technological implementations. It has emerged as a strategic partner in an organization's decision-making processes, offering the essential tools for understanding, adapting to, and thriving in the dynamic landscape of contemporary business.

Beneficiaries

Business intelligence applications have undergone a transformative evolution, extending their reach to a diverse spectrum of users across every echelon of the corporate hierarchy. What once started as a tool limited to business reporting for a select few has now evolved into a democratized resource accessible to the masses. This broad user base encompasses a myriad of roles, reflecting the inclusive nature of BI adoption in contemporary business environments.

Strategic and operational users find BI indispensable for making informed choices. Managers at all levels, including top executives, middle management, and junior-level managers, leverage BI to gain comprehensive insights. Line managers and front-tier workers benefit from BI's ability to distill complex data into actionable information, aiding in day-to-day decision-making. Business analysts and information workers utilize BI for in-depth analysis and interpretation, while novice and casual users find user-friendly interfaces accommodating.

Power users, often referred to as super users, harness the advanced capabilities of BI applications for more intricate analyses and strategic planning. IT professionals and developers play a pivotal role in implementing and customizing BI solutions to align with organizational needs. Beyond internal stakeholders, BI extends its utility to external parties, including customers, partners, and suppliers, by fostering collaboration and transparency throughout the business ecosystem.

In essence, BI has evolved into a universal tool, breaking down traditional barriers and empowering a wide array of users with the ability to extract valuable insights. This democratization of BI aligns with the contemporary ethos of data-driven decision-making, where access to actionable intelligence is not confined to a select few but extends to all those who play a role in the success and growth of the organization.

LEADING BI VENDORS

The following is an overview of leading vendors in various categories.

Self-Service BI

Tableau is renowned for its intuitive data visualization capabilities, providing users with a seamless experience in creating visually compelling reports and dashboards. Its user-friendly interface empowers individuals to explore and communicate data insights effectively. Microsoft Power BI stands out for its user-friendly interface and strong integration with other Microsoft tools, making it a preferred choice for those already within the Microsoft ecosystem. Power BI enables users to harness the power of data visualization for impactful decision-making within familiar Microsoft environments.

Enterprise BI

Microsoft Power BI extends its capabilities to enterprise-level solutions, offering a comprehensive suite for large-scale data analytics. Its scalability and integration with other Microsoft products make it a robust solution for organizations with complex analytical needs. SAP BusinessObjects is recognized for its extensive BI tools suite, catering to the complex needs of enterprise-level data analysis and reporting. With a focus on providing a broad range of BI functionalities, SAP BusinessObjects is a leading choice for organizations seeking a holistic approach to enterprise BI.

Cloud-based BI

Tableau Online provides cloud-based access to Tableau's powerful analytics, allowing users to leverage the benefits of the cloud for scalable and collaborative BI. It facilitates seamless collaboration and data sharing in a cloud environment. Now part of Google Cloud, Looker focuses on cloud-native BI, emphasizing data exploration in a cloud environment. Looker's integration with Google Cloud enhances its scalability and accessibility, providing users with a flexible and efficient cloud-based BI solution.

Open-Source BI

Business intelligence and reporting tools (BIRT) is an open-source software project for creating data visualizations and reports, providing a flexible and cost-effective solution. Its open-source nature enables customization and adaptation to specific organizational needs. Pentaho, now part of Hitachi Vantara, offers open-source BI and data integration solutions, making it a preferred choice for those seeking customizable and open solutions. Pentaho's open architecture supports organizations in tailoring their BI and data integration processes to unique requirements.

Big Data BI

Domo excels in handling large volumes of data, offering insights from various sources for comprehensive big data analysis. Its robust capabilities make it suitable for organizations dealing with extensive datasets and diverse data sources. QlikView stands out for its associative data modeling approach, which provides a robust solution for analyzing and visualizing vast datasets. QlikView's emphasis on associative data relationships enhances the depth of analysis for organizations dealing with complex big data scenarios.

Mobile BI

Tableau Mobile provides a mobile extension for Tableau's BI capabilities, allowing users to access and interact with data on the go. Its mobile-friendly design ensures that decision-makers can stay connected and informed anytime and anywhere. MicroStrategy Mobile specializes in mobile BI solutions, emphasizing security and scalability for mobile data access and analytics. MicroStrategy Mobile's focus on security makes it a trusted choice for organizations prioritizing secure mobile access to BI insights.

Predictive Analytics

IBM Watson Analytics seamlessly integrates predictive analytics into BI, enabling users to gain advanced insights and make data-driven predictions. Its incorporation of predictive analytics enhances the depth of analysis, allowing organizations to anticipate trends and make proactive decisions. SAS Business Intelligence is renowned for its advanced analytics and predictive modeling capabilities, providing a comprehensive solution for organizations requiring predictive analytics in their BI processes. SAS BI's emphasis on advanced analytics caters to organizations looking to harness the power of predictive modeling for strategic decision-making.

Collaborative BI

Domo facilitates collaboration and sharing of insights across teams, fostering a collaborative environment for data-driven decision-making. Its collaborative features promote teamwork and knowledge sharing, enhancing collective intelligence within organizations. Microsoft Power BI allows collaboration through shared dashboards and reports, enhancing teamwork and knowledge sharing within organizations. The collaborative features of Power BI enable seamless communication and collaboration among users, promoting a culture of shared insights.

Embedded BI

Looker is recognized for its embedded analytics solutions, integrating BI seamlessly into applications and platforms. Its embedded BI solutions allow organizations to integrate analytics directly into their existing workflows and applications. Sisense provides embeddable BI solutions, making it a preferred choice for organizations looking to integrate BI capabilities directly into their existing applications. Sisense's embeddable BI solutions cater to the specific needs of organizations seeking to enhance their applications with analytics capabilities.

Real-Time BI

Sisense offers real-time data analytics for quick decision-making, enabling organizations to access and analyze data as it happens. Its real-time capabilities empower organizations to make informed decisions based on the most up-to-date information. Qlik Sense specializes in real-time data exploration and visualization, providing users with up-to-the-minute insights for informed decision-making. Qlik Sense's real-time features support organizations in gaining a competitive edge by responding swiftly to dynamic data changes.

It is crucial to conduct thorough research and consider specific business requirements when selecting a BI vendor. Additionally, market dynamics can change, and new vendors may emerge; therefore, staying updated with the latest industry reports and reviews is recommended.

FUTURE OF BUSINESS INTELLIGENCE

In the dynamic landscape of business intelligence and analytics, staying abreast of the latest trends is crucial for organizations aiming to derive actionable insights and maintain a competitive edge. From the integration of advanced technologies such as AI to evolving approaches in data visualization and privacy governance, the realm of BI is witnessing transformative shifts.

The following sections delve into prominent trends shaping the current BI and analytics landscape, unraveling the innovative methodologies and technologies reshaping how businesses harness data for informed decision-making.

Augmented Analytics

The increased integration of machine learning and AI is expected to transform BI through augmented analytics, harnessing their power to automate tasks such as data preparation, pattern identification, and the generation of actionable insights. This entails automating data preparation, discovering insights, facilitating decision-making processes, and enhancing the capabilities of traditional BI tools by leveraging advanced algorithms to provide more intelligent and context-aware insights. These technologies streamline the analytics process, making it more efficient and accessible for users by automating complex tasks and staying at the forefront of BI trends.

Natural Language Processing

The future of BI involves a growing reliance on natural language processing (NLP) interfaces, revolutionizing analytics platforms by enabling users to interact using natural language queries. This approach reduces the barrier for nontechnical users to engage with complex datasets, fostering a more intuitive and accessible approach to data analysis. NLP enhances accessibility by allowing users to receive insights in a conversational manner, thus making data analysis more intuitive and user-friendly.

Explainable AI

Explainable AI is gaining importance, particularly within the realm of BI, as it emphasizes the development of transparent models and interpretable algorithms. This approach ensures that AI-driven decisions made within BI systems are not only accurate but also understandable and trusted by users. By providing insight into how decisions are reached, explainable AI promotes transparency and accountability in the decision-making process, enabling stakeholders to have greater confidence in the insights and recommendations provided by BI systems. This emphasis on transparency ultimately enhances the effectiveness and adoption of AI-driven analytics within BI environments, as users can better understand and validate the rationale behind the decisions made by AI algorithms.

Data Democratization

The trend of data democratization will continue, with BI seeking to empower nontechnical users across organizations by fostering a culture of data-driven decision-making and making data and analytics accessible to a broader audience. This involves providing user-friendly interfaces, accessible training, and self-service analytics tools to enable users to independently access, analyze, and interpret data, thereby reducing dependence on IT teams.

Advanced Data Visualization

The evolution of data visualization techniques is poised to offer more immersive and interactive experiences, with BI tools expected to explore augmented and virtual reality applications. This pivotal trend incorporates immersive technologies such as virtual and augmented reality (AR) for interactive data experiences, fostering a more engaging and insightful exploration of complex datasets beyond conventional charting.

Edge Analytics

BI increasingly explores edge analytics, processing data closer to IoT sources, reducing latency, and enabling real-time decision-making. This trend is vital for extracting insights from IoT-generated data that are tightly integrated with IoT adoption. Edge analytics enhances efficiency and responsiveness in distributed environments, which is crucial for timely decision-making. As the trend continues, it underscores the importance of processing data at the edge to maximize the benefits of IoT implementations.

Embedded BI

Embedded BI solutions are gaining traction, integrating analytics directly into other business applications. This streamlines workflows by providing users with seamless access to analytics within familiar tools. The integration of BI into existing applications enhances user adoption and facilitates decision-making within the context of daily operations.

Continuous Intelligence

The future of BI emphasizes continuous intelligence, focusing on real-time or near-real-time analytics. This approach enables organizations to respond promptly to changing conditions, leveraging up-to-the-minute insights for agile decision-making. Continuous intelligence supports dynamic business environments and enhances adaptability.

Blockchain Integration

BI is exploring blockchain integration to enhance data security, integrity, and traceability, leveraging its decentralized and tamper-resistant nature. This integration aims to fortify data governance and mitigate data manipulation risks, ensuring data transparency and immutability. Organizations are increasingly adopting blockchain to secure data used in analytics processes, ensuring a tamper-proof foundation for analysis.

Cloud-Based BI

Cloud-based BI continues to gain prominence, leveraging the scalability and flexibility of cloud platforms, which organizations utilize to handle large datasets, enable seamless collaboration, and provide a scalable infrastructure for BI processes. Organizations leverage the scalability and flexibility of cloud platforms to utilize cloud-based solutions for these purposes, further emphasizing the importance of cloud-based solutions in the BI landscape.

Hybrid and Multicloud Deployments

The future of BI involves the increasing adoption of hybrid and multicloud architectures. This strategic shift provides organizations with flexibility, scalability, and redundancy in their BI deployments. By leveraging a combination of on-premises and cloud-based solutions, businesses can optimize their BI infrastructure to meet evolving requirements.

Ethical and Responsible AI

As AI plays a more prominent role in analytics, the emphasis on ethical and responsible AI practices is growing. BI stakeholders are becoming more aware of potential biases in AI algorithms and are focusing on ethical considerations. This involves ensuring fairness, transparency, and accountability in AI-driven decision-making processes.

Predictive and Prescriptive Analytics

BI is witnessing continued growth in the application of predictive and prescriptive analytics, with a growing emphasis on machine learning models for predicting future trends and automating decision-making. Beyond forecasting future trends, these advanced analytics approaches aim to recommend specific actions to optimize outcomes, empowering organizations to proactively address challenges and capitalize on opportunities based on predictive insights.

Data Governance and Privacy

The landscape of BI is evolving to address data governance and privacy concerns, with a key focus on ensuring compliance with regulations, enhancing data quality, and building trust in BI outputs. Organizations are establishing robust frameworks to comply with regulations and ensure ethical data use, integrating privacy by design principles to safeguard sensitive information and enhance trust in BI insights. This evolution addresses data integrity, privacy, and security concerns, contributing to the reliability and credibility of BI output.

Collaborative BI

Fostering real-time collaboration among teams, this trend enables simultaneous work on dashboards, reports, and data analyses within BI tools. Emphasizing interactive features like commenting and annotation facilitates effective communication and enhances collaboration within the BI environment.

Self-Service BI

Marked by user-friendly interfaces and tools tailored for individuals with varying technical expertise, this trend emphasizes providing users with autonomy to independently create reports and dashboards, thereby minimizing reliance on IT support.

CHALLENGES AND PITFALLS

Implementing business intelligence systems involves many challenges, pitfalls, and mistakes, which are described in the following sections.

Challenges

Business intelligence initiatives, while immensely valuable, are not without their challenges. One significant challenge is the complexity of data integration. Organizations often grapple with the amalgamation of data from diverse sources, which may involve different formats and structures. Ensuring data consistency, accuracy, and timeliness is a substantial hurdle. Additionally, the sheer volume of data generated in today's digital age can overwhelm BI systems, making it challenging to handle and analyze large datasets efficiently. This necessitates robust data governance practices to maintain data quality and integrity throughout the BI process.

Another challenge lies in the alignment of BI with organizational goals. It is common for BI implementations to face difficulties in translating data insights into actionable strategies. This may be due to a lack of clarity in defining KPIs or a disconnect between BI findings and the overarching business objectives. Effective BI requires collaboration between the business and IT teams to ensure that BI solutions are not only technically proficient but also strategically aligned. Overcoming these challenges demands a holistic approach that addresses both technical complexities and the need for a well-defined strategic framework.

Common BI Pitfalls and Mistakes

Implementing business intelligence initiatives can be highly beneficial, but organizations should be aware of common pitfalls, some of which are identified in the following subsections.

Lack of Clear Objectives

Failing to define specific business goals and KPIs can lead to ambiguity in measuring success. Clear objectives are crucial for aligning BI efforts with overall organizational strategies.

Poor Data Quality

BI relies heavily on accurate and reliable data. Poor data quality, including incomplete or inaccurate information, can result in flawed analysis and misguided decision-making, highlighting the necessity of robust data quality management.

Neglecting Data Governance

Proper data governance is essential for addressing issues such as inconsistent definitions, lack of data ownership, and security concerns. Establishing strong data governance practices ensures data integrity, compliance, and effective management throughout the BI process.

Ignoring User Adoption

Effective BI tools require user engagement and adoption. Neglecting user training and communication can lead to low adoption rates, diminishing the impact of BI solutions on decision-making processes.

Overemphasizing Technology

Overemphasis on BI technology without considering underlying business processes and organizational culture can result in a misalignment between technology and business needs. Maintaining a balance is crucial for ensuring that BI solutions meet both technical and strategic requirements.

Complexity Overload

Creating overly complex BI solutions can overwhelm users. Balancing sophisticated analytics with user-friendly interfaces is essential for encouraging user adoption and ensuring the effectiveness of BI tools.

Inadequate Planning

Insufficient planning, including a lack of scalability considerations, can result in challenges as data volumes increase. A well-designed BI strategy, including future scalability requirements, is essential for long-term success.

Ignoring Change Management

BI implementations often lead to changes in workflows and decision-making processes. Failure to manage these changes effectively can lead to resistance and hinder the successful integration of BI into daily operations.

Failure to Iterate and Improve

Regular review and refinement of BI strategies are crucial. Organizations that do not continuously optimize their BI initiatives may miss opportunities for improvement and enhanced outcomes.

Relying Solely on Historical Data

Focusing exclusively on historical data without incorporating predictive analytics limits the ability to respond proactively to future trends and opportunities. Integrating predictive analytics enhances the proactive nature of decision-making.

Siloed BI Initiatives

Fragmented BI initiatives across different departments or business units can result in duplicate efforts and inconsistent reporting standards. A cohesive, enterprise-wide BI approach ensures consistency and maximizes the impact of BI across the organization.

CHAPTER 2

ANALYTICS PROCESS AND TOOLS

This section explores the systematic steps and essential technologies used to collect, analyze, and interpret data for informed decision-making.

OVERVIEW

Analysis

In the context of analytics, analysis is the pivotal phase in which raw data is transformed into meaningful insights. This process involves deploying various techniques to uncover patterns, trends, and relationships within the data to extract actionable information. Analysts employ statistical methods, mathematical models, and often advanced machine learning algorithms to scrutinize datasets, explore correlations, identify outliers, and gain a comprehensive understanding of the underlying information.

The analysis phase involves not only interpreting past occurrences but also predicting future trends and making informed decisions based on the derived insights. Effective analysis is fundamental to the success of the entire analytics process, as it forms the basis for data-driven decision-making and strategic actions within an organization.

Analytics

Analytics is a systematic and scientific approach for extracting valuable insights from data, primarily aiming to improve decision-making processes. This multifaceted process involves transforming raw data into meaningful patterns and communicating these patterns to enhance understanding.

At its core, analytics relies on the concurrent application of statistics, computer programming, and operations research. Statistics provide the foundational framework for analyzing and interpreting data, while computer programming facilitates the automation of complex analytical processes. Alternatively, operations research contributes optimization techniques for enhancing decision-making efficiency.

One key aspect of analytics is its emphasis on data visualization. Instead of overwhelming decision-makers with raw data, analytics leverages visual representations to communicate insights effectively. This can include charts, graphs, and other visual aids that make complex information more accessible and digestible.

In essence, analytics is a dynamic and interdisciplinary field that transforms data into actionable intelligence. It empowers organizations to uncover patterns, trends, and correlations within their data, ultimately guiding strategic decisions and fostering a data-driven culture.

Analytics versus Analysis

Analytics, a multidimensional discipline at the intersection of mathematics, statistics, and descriptive techniques, serves as a powerful tool for extracting valuable insights from data. It goes beyond mere individual analyses, encompassing an entire methodology that enables decision-making within a business context. In a broader business setting, the term *analytics* is often utilized to underscore this comprehensive perspective, emphasizing its role in guiding actions and decisions.

Advanced analytics is at the center stage within the realm of analytics, delving into the technical intricacies of predictive modeling, machine learning techniques, and neural networks. This specialized branch of analytics empowers organizations to harness the full potential of data for informed decision-making and strategic planning.

Application

Illustrating the application of analytics, marketing optimization stands out as a prime example. The evolution of marketing from a creative process to a data-driven endeavor showcases the transformative impact of analytics. Marketers use analytics to assess campaign outcomes, guide investment decisions, and effectively target consumers. Web analytics, exemplified by tools such as Google Analytics, enables the collection of user interactions with a Web site. This includes tracking the referrer, searching keywords, IP addresses, and visitor activities, and providing marketers with crucial insights to enhance campaigns, refine Web site content, and optimize layout.

Another facet where analytics proves invaluable is in portfolio analysis. This application involves scrutinizing portfolios from both a value and risk perspective. For lenders, portfolio analysis becomes instrumental in striking a balance between the return on loan and the associated risk of default, whether considering an individual loan or the entire portfolio. This exemplifies how analytics becomes an indispensable tool for financial decision-makers, offering a nuanced understanding of the risk-return dynamics inherent in lending practices.

In conclusion, analytics emerges as a dynamic and all-encompassing discipline that seamlessly integrates mathematical rigor, statistical methodologies, and descriptive techniques to obtain meaningful insights from data. Its transformative influence extends beyond singular analyses, shaping the entire decision-making methodology within a business framework. Analytics, whether it is optimizing marketing strategies or conducting portfolio analyses, stands at the forefront of empowering organizations to navigate the complexities of data-driven decision-making.

UNLOCKING INSIGHTS WITH ANALYTICS

Unlocking insights with analytics enables organizations to transform data into meaningful, actionable knowledge that drives decision-making. By applying advanced analytical techniques, businesses can uncover patterns, predict trends, and gain a deeper understanding of their operations and market dynamics.

Unraveling Insights

With analytics, a myriad of questions can be unraveled, guiding both human decisions and fueling automated processes. Through techniques such as querying, reporting, and OLAP, analytics addresses fundamental queries such as determining what happened, quantifying occurrences, identifying patterns in frequency, pinpointing problem areas, and outlining necessary actions. This foundational layer of analytics lays the groundwork for extracting valuable insights that span the spectrum from historical occurrences to proactive predictions and strategic foresight.

Advanced Business Analytics

Delving deeper into the expansive realm of business analytics, the focus shifts toward answering more complex questions that examine the "why" and "what if" scenarios. Business analytics has become the compass that navigates inquiries, such as understanding the root causes behind occurrences, projecting future trends and outcomes, predicting potential scenarios, and determining optimal courses of action. It transcends the descriptive layer, evolving into a predictive and prescriptive force that not only interprets data but also shapes strategies for the future.

Unlocking the Power of Analytics in Decision-Making

The benefits of embracing analytics as a cornerstone of decision-making processes are diverse and impactful. From expediting decision-making processes to fostering better alignment with overarching strategies, analytics serves as a catalyst for transformative change. It reduces costs, enhances responsiveness to user data needs, improves competitiveness, and generates a unified view of enterprise information.

Synchronizing financial and operational strategies, increasing revenues, sharing information across a broader audience, fostering innovation in products and services, aligning resources strategically, and finding applications across diverse industries, underscoring the versatility and profound impact that analytics can deliver. In essence, analytics is not merely a tool; it is a dynamic force that propels organizations toward smarter, more informed, and strategically aligned decision-making.

WEB ANALYTICS

Web analytics is the process of collecting, measuring, and analyzing website data to understand user behavior and optimize online performance.

Unveiling Online Insights

In the dynamic realm of the Internet, understanding user behavior and optimizing Web usage has become paramount for businesses seeking to thrive in the digital landscape. Web analytics has emerged as the linchpin, encompassing the measurement, collection, analysis, and reporting of Web data with the overarching goal of revealing insights and enhancing online interactions. At its core, Web analytics is a strategic tool designed to delve into Web traffic and usage patterns, providing a comprehensive picture of a Web site's performance and popularity.

The fundamental objective of Web analytics is rooted in the meticulous collection and scrutiny of data pertaining to Web site visitors, page views, and overarching traffic trends. It not only quantifies the volume of visitors but also serves as a sentinel, deciphering the ebb and flow of user interactions. Beyond mere statistical metrics, Web analytics serves as a multifaceted instrument capable of offering invaluable insights into user behavior, preferences, and the overall effectiveness of a Web site.

Impact

Web analytics transcends mere statistical inquiry; it has emerged as a robust tool for business and market research. By scrutinizing and interpreting Web data, businesses can make informed decisions to enhance their online presence and strategic positioning. Web analytics applications extend beyond the digital realm, providing a means to assess and optimize the effectiveness of traditional advertising campaigns. For instance, it becomes a beacon, illuminating how Web site traffic fluctuates in response to the launch of new advertising initiatives, bridging the gap between the virtual and physical realms of marketing.

Web Data: Sources and Significance

The mosaic of Web data, crucial for obtaining insights through Web analytics, primarily originates from four distinct sources. Direct HTTP request data forms the backbone, emerging directly from HTTP request messages encapsulating crucial details found in request headers. Network level and server-generated data associated with HTTP requests, although not part of the request itself, play a pivotal role in successful data transmission, including the essential IP addresses of requesters.

Moreover, intricately woven through programs such as JavaScript, PHP, and ASP.Net, application-level data provides nuanced information such as session details and referrals, often captured through internal logs. External data, the final strand in this intricate tapestry, augment on-site data by incorporating elements such as IP addresses correlated with geographic regions, Internet service providers, email engagement metrics, direct mail campaign data, and historical sales and lead information.

In essence, Web analytics transcends mere numerical summaries, evolving into a strategic compass for businesses navigating the complexities of the digital landscape. It not only quantifies Web interactions but also empowers businesses with the tools to optimize, strategize, and thrive in the ever-evolving world of online presence and engagement.

DATA ANALYSIS PROCESS

Data analysis is the process of obtaining raw data and converting it into information that is useful for decision-making. It involves procedures for analyzing data, cleaning, transforming, and modeling data with the goal of discovering useful information. It helps interpret the results, suggests conclusions, and supports decision-making. Data analysis has multiple facets and approaches, encompassing diverse techniques under a variety of names in different business, science, and social science domains.

The following sections explain the different steps involved in the data analysis process.

Identify What the Business Needs

The first step is to understand what the business would like to improve or what problem it wants to solve. To address these issues and meet the business goals, relevant data, which will drive the scope of data collection and analysis, is identified by the business users, subject matter experts (SMEs), and business analysts.

The data should be able to answer the key questions for which answers are sought. It should be able to answer key questions such as "Which data are available?," "How can we use it?," and "Is it easily available?" It can also identify the need for process improvement. For this to be meaningful, the right questions must be asked. They should be measurable, clear, and concise. The questions should be designed to either qualify or disqualify potential solutions to the specific problem or opportunity.

If data is required for driving decision-making, there needs to be a measurable way to determine if the business is advancing toward its goals. Therefore, key metrics or performance indicators must be identified early in the process. Identifying the goals and metrics provides direction and avoids meaningless data analysis.

Collect the Data

In the next step, the data required for the analysis is collected from a variety of sources. The requirements may be communicated by analysts to data custodians, such as IT personnel, who play a crucial role in facilitating communication between analysts and data sources. The data may also be collected from existing databases, online sources, and sensors (such as monitoring devices, satellites, and recording devices).

Since so much data is available, there needs to be limits on how much data is collected. The data can be real-time, hourly, daily, monthly, or quarterly. The volume of data collected directly impacts the processing requirements, tools/processes to be used for data collection and processing, and file storage. The data obtained must be processed or organized for analysis. For example, data may be placed into rows and columns in a table format for further analysis, such as within a spreadsheet or statistical software.

More data, especially from diverse sources, enables finding better correlations, building better models, and finding more actionable insights.

Review and Clean the Data

This step ensures that the data used is of high quality and can be used for analysis. This process involves cleaning the data, resolving missing data issues, removing duplicates, removing outliers (values that lie outside the other values), developing new variables (from existing ones), and so on. Removing outliers is important as they can impact the model and the accuracy of results. The results of data cleaning can lead to the initiation of steps to prevent the repeating of errors.

This is the most critical step in the data value chain. Even with the best analysis, junk data will generate incorrect results and mislead the business. After the data has been cleaned, the analyst will try to make better sense of the data using a variety of techniques, such as plotting the data using scatter plots to identify possible correlations or nonlinearity and descriptive statistics (such as mean, mode, median, and standard deviation).

Model the Data

In this step, mathematical formulas or models, called algorithms, are applied to the data to identify relationships among the variables, such as correlation or causation. In general terms, models may be developed to evaluate a particular variable in the data based on other variable(s) in the data. For example, regression analysis may be used to model whether a change in advertising (independent variable X) explains the variation in sales (dependent variable Y). In mathematical terms, Y (sales) is a function of X (advertising). Analysts may attempt to build models that are descriptive of the data to simplify the analysis and communicate the results.

Data scientists build models that correlate the data with the business outcome. Their unique expertise, correlating the data and building models that predict business outcomes, becomes critical for business success. Data scientists must have a strong background in statistics and machine learning, enabling them to build scientifically accurate models and avoid the traps of meaningless correlations and models that rely only on existing data and, therefore, fail in predictive analysis. Statistical background is not sufficient; data scientists need to understand the business well enough that they will be able to recognize whether the results of the mathematical models are meaningful and relevant.

Analyze the Data

In this step, cleaned data is analyzed through a variety of techniques to explore and extract meaningful insights. Analysts manipulate the data via statistical analysis, employing tools like Excel for tasks such as creating pivot tables and sorting data. Descriptive statistics, including averages and medians, are generated to enhance the understanding of the data. Data visualization, a key method within the analytical process, is employed to present graphical representations, offering an additional layer of insight.

During this step, analysts perform a simple regression analysis to assess the predictive capabilities of the data. The exploration process involves slicing and dicing the data, making different comparisons, and deriving actionable insights. This stage may prompt additional data cleaning, requests for further data, or a revision of the initial question, highlighting the iterative nature of data analysis.

Specific guidelines are followed to ensure a thorough understanding of the quantitative data. Analysts check for anomalies, redo important calculations, confirm main totals, and assess relationships between numbers. Additionally, they normalize numbers for easier comparisons and break down problems into component parts by analyzing contributing factors.

Throughout this stage, data analysis tools and software play a crucial role, facilitating efficient and effective exploration. This comprehensive approach to analyzing cleaned data underscores the dynamic and evolving nature of the analytical workflow, where insights are continuously refined and improved.

Interpret the Results

The interpretation of results is a critical step following data analysis, and key questions must be posed to ensure the validity and applicability of the findings. Analysts must ask whether the data effectively address the original question, how they contribute to defending against potential objections unexplored angles, or whether there are any limitations on the conclusions that are drawn.

Thorough scrutiny of these questions ensures the robustness of the data interpretation. If the results withstand this scrutiny, a meaningful and productive conclusion can be drawn. The final step involves leveraging the outcomes of the data analysis process to determine the best course of action.

By emphasizing the importance of following a systematic data analysis process, this approach guarantees that decisions are underpinned by meticulously collected and analyzed data. As practitioners gain experience, the efficiency and accuracy of data analysis improves, empowering organizations to make better-informed decisions for effective operational management.

Predict and Optimize

The predict and optimize stage is a crucial step in the data analysis process where the analyst employs predictive techniques such as decision trees and neural networks. These techniques investigate the data, revealing patterns and relationships and uncovering hidden evidence of influential variables. Subsequently, the predicted values are compared with the actual values, and the computed predictive errors provide valuable insights.

The data value chain, being a repeatable process, undergoes continuous improvement, benefiting both the business and the data value chain itself. Multiple predictive models are commonly used, and the best-performing model is selected based on predefined constraints and limitations. The analyst's expertise in choosing the optimal solution, considering factors such as the lowest error and alignment with strategic goals, plays a pivotal role.

Upon selecting the model, the business implements changes to driving levers, and the data science team measures the outcomes. Based on these results, the business decides on further actions while the data science team refines data collection, clean-up, and models. This iterative process allows the business to make swift course corrections, extracting value from the data. Through multiple iterations, the model evolves to generate accurate predictions, aiding the business in reaching predefined goals. The resulting data value chain becomes a valuable asset for ongoing monitoring, reporting, and tackling future business challenges.

Communicate

The communication phase becomes pivotal after the data analysis, bridging the analytical findings and their impact on decision-making. Once the data have been meticulously examined, the results are presented in various formats tailored to the diverse audience of the analysis. This communication can take the form of reports, presentations, or dashboards, ensuring that the insights are comprehensible to a wide range of stakeholders.

User feedback plays a crucial role in this phase, potentially leading to additional rounds of analysis. The iterative nature of the analytical cycle allows for continuous refinement based on user input. Data visualization is a key component of this communication process, leveraging visual elements such as tables and charts to effectively convey the key messages embedded in the data. Visual representation not only enhances understanding but also facilitates more meaningful discussions and collaborative decision-making among stakeholders with varying levels of technical expertise.

FEATURES AND TOOLS

This section explores the essential functionalities and tools that empower businesses to effectively manage, analyze, and visualize their data for strategic decision-making.

Analysis Functions

Analysts perform a variety of essential data analysis functions to extract meaningful insights, including retrieving values, applying filters, computing derived values, identifying data with extreme attributes, sorting data, determining value spans within a set, characterizing distributions, detecting anomalies, identifying clusters of similar attribute values, and establishing correlations. These functions collectively contribute to the process of uncovering patterns, trends, and valuable information within datasets.

Legacy Tool

Excel has traditionally served as the go-to legacy tool for data analysts, offering a robust set of functions that cater to diverse analytical needs. It encompasses essential features such as sorting, filtering, pivot tables, conditional formatting, and charting capabilities. Excel's functionality extends to advanced operations such as concatenation for merging data from multiple cells, what-if analysis, trend analysis, and the application of data tables to model real-world problems and analyze extensive datasets.

Additionally, Excel supports simulations and incorporates Solver, an invaluable tool for modeling practical problems and finding solutions by iterating through numerous possibilities. The Analysis ToolPak, as an Excel add-in program, enriches the platform with specialized data analysis tools tailored for financial, statistical, and engineering data analysis.

Tools for Analytics

Analytics users can leverage a variety of robust tools to enhance their data analysis capabilities. Several noteworthy options in the analytics toolkit include Tableau, OpenRefine (formerly GoogleRefine), RapidMiner, Google Fusion Tables, NodeXL, Import.io, Google Search Operators, Solver, WolframAlpha, Infogram, Many Eyes, Statwing, BigML, KNIME, and Data Applied. These tools span a spectrum of functionalities, providing users with diverse features for efficient and insightful data analysis across different domains and applications.

CHALLENGES

The implementation of BI systems is fraught with complexities, especially pertaining to data. Effectively navigating these challenges is critical for maximizing the value of BI initiatives and ensuring sustainable success.

Unstructured Data

In the dynamic landscape of BI, the integration of unstructured data sources such as emails, documents, and log files introduce a paradigm shift, augmenting the complexity and richness of the data landscape. Unstructured data, distinguished by its diverse formats and complexity, poses challenges in storage within traditional relational databases, necessitating substantial data transformation efforts.

Unlocking Insights from Unstructured Data

Analyzing unstructured data presents a myriad of challenges, starting with the fundamental task of understanding the intricacies of varied data formats and content. The expansion of these datasets across massive, complex, and ever-changing landscapes demands the use of advanced analytical tools to extract meaningful insights. Challenges include ensuring data quality, displaying meaningful results, addressing outliers, and meeting the demands of speed and real-time analytics.

Multifaceted Nature of Challenges

Building a data-driven culture emerges as a pivotal challenge, requiring a transformative shift in organizational mindset and practices. Data integration complexities arise as structured and unstructured data amalgamation necessitates robust frameworks. Processing vast data volumes seamlessly, managing solution costs, adapting to mobile trends, and addressing the scarcity of quantitative talent highlight the multifaceted nature of challenges encountered within the expansive landscape of unstructured data in the BI domain.

CHAPTER 3

UNDERSTANDING DATA

D ata serves as the foundation for any successful business intelligence initiative. Gaining a deep understanding of data, including its sources, structure, and quality, is essential for generating meaningful insights and driving informed decision-making.

TYPES OF DATA SOURCES

Impact of Big Data on Data Analytics

In data analysis, a fundamental classification distinguishes between two main types: structured and unstructured data. Historically, the analytical focus has predominantly revolved around structured data due to the lack of infrastructure and tools designed to unravel the complexities of unstructured data. The rigidity of structured data, organized in predefined formats such as tables, facilitated traditional analysis methods. It is important to note that the landscape of data analytics underwent a revolutionary transformation with the advent of big data technologies, notably exemplified by the introduction of Hadoop. This technological breakthrough ushered in a new era, rendering feasible what was once deemed unthinkable—the analysis of unstructured data on a large scale.

The dichotomy between structured and unstructured data is no longer an insurmountable barrier to comprehensive data analysis. The evolution of big data technologies has opened avenues for delving into the rich tapestry of unstructured data, unlocking a wealth of insights that were previously elusive. The accessibility and capabilities afforded by technologies such as Hadoop have propelled data analytics into uncharted territories, empowering organizations to harness the full spectrum of data, whether structured or unstructured and derive actionable insights that propel them into a new era of informed decision-making.

Structured Data

Structured data is characterized by a high degree of organization, typically arranged in databases and spreadsheets, where information is stored in easily manageable columns and rows. This structured arrangement streamlines the efficient organization and processing of data, allowing for easy integration into databases or well-structured file formats such as XML. Despite its organized nature, structured data constitutes only a fraction of the available data, estimated at approximately 20%. In contrast, the majority, approximately 80%, comprises unstructured data, primarily in the form of text.

Although structured data is outnumbered by its unstructured counterpart, its significance in the realm of data analytics remains paramount. By acting as the backbone of organizational operations, structured data provides the foundation upon which businesses run their critical processes. It plays a crucial role in data analytics, acting as a prerequisite for effectively analyzing unstructured data. Without the structured data framework, extracting meaningful insights from the vast landscape of unstructured data has become a challenging endeavor.

Structured data examples span various categories, including machine-generated and human-generated data. Machine-generated examples encompass sensory data from GPS systems, manufacturing sensors, medical devices, and point-of-sale data such as credit card information and call detail records. Human-generated structured data include input data, such as information manually entered into a computer, covering aspects such as age, zip code, and gender.

Unstructured Data

Unstructured data represents raw and disorganized information lacking a predefined data model or a predetermined organizational structure. It encompasses various forms such as emails, word processing files, PDFs, digital images, videos, audio, social media content (from platforms such as X and Facebook), presentations (such as PowerPoint and SlideShare), and messaging data (instant messages and text messages).

Compiling unstructured data is challenging due to the lack of an inherent structure, making the process time-consuming. Converting this type of data into structured formats or developing data analysis mechanisms capable of extracting meaningful insights becomes crucial for organizations seeking substantial returns. Efficient tools for analyzing unstructured data can yield insights that structured data alone might not capture.

While some unstructured data can be transformed into structured formats, the process often incurs high costs and time investments, and not all types of unstructured data can be easily converted into structured models. For instance, while emails have standard fields such as time sent, subject, and sender, the contents of messages are more challenging to break down and categorize, potentially introducing compatibility issues with relational database systems.

Despite their differences, both structured and unstructured data offer valuable insights and should be integral components of an organization's analytics strategy.

DATA STORAGE

Efficient data storage is a cornerstone of business intelligence, ensuring that vast amounts of structured and unstructured data are securely housed and easily accessible. Modern storage solutions must balance scalability, performance, and security to support advanced analytics and real-time decision-making.

Scalable Storage Solutions

In the ever-evolving landscape of data analytics, efficient and scalable storage solutions play a pivotal role in enabling organizations to harness the full potential of their data. As data volume, variety, and velocity continue to surge, the demand for robust storage infrastructure has become more critical than ever. Storage not only serves as a repository for vast datasets but also underpins the speed, accessibility, and reliability required for meaningful analytics.

From structured databases to unstructured repositories, the storage architecture forms the backbone that supports the entire analytics workflow, facilitating data retrieval, processing, and analysis. In this dynamic realm, optimizing storage strategies is essential for organizations seeking to derive actionable insights, make informed decisions, and navigate the complexities of the data-driven landscape.

Data Storage Volume

Storage volumes are driven by the requirements, such as the period for which the data must be made available for analysis. For example, the storage required for three years of data will be quite different compared to twenty years of historical data.

In the case of real-time analysis, the data storage requirements are dependent on the data being generated and the type of analysis needed. The storage options, which can be quite different, are driven by business requirements. For example, data can be stored for a specific period and then discarded or overwritten if shorter time frames are needed. In extreme cases, most of the generated data is stored for longer periods, so historical analysis can be performed and patterns can be easily determined.

Data Storage Levels

For efficient retrieval, data is stored at three levels:

- Current detailed data: Contains transaction-level data
- Lightly summarized data: Contains aggregated data, such as revenues by week or by sub-region
- Highly summarized data: Contains aggregated data, such as revenues by month or by region

Each data level targets a different type of user, ranging from senior executives to operational users. While an inventory clerk may need to review the available inventory for a specific item, which requires the availability of detailed data, a CFO will typically be more interested in reviewing the performance of a business unit or region, which would require the availability of highly summarized data.

Current Detailed Data

Current detailed data constitutes the predominant portion within most storage systems, representing the data at the lowest level of granularity. The duration for which organizations maintain current detailed data can vary significantly. Typically, entities store such data for two to five years to meet their immediate analytical needs. A notable aspect of contemporary data management practices is the diversity across organizations.

Many entities opt for extended retention periods, preserving the current detailed data for as long as twenty to twenty-five years. Various factors, including industry-specific regulations, business requirements

for historical analysis, or adherence to comprehensive data governance policies can influence this extended duration. Understanding the
nuanced considerations behind these diverse retention practices provides valuable insights into how organizations manage and leverage
their detailed data over time.

Lightly Summarized Data

Lightly summarized data refers to data that has been rolled up for particular dimensions or attributes. For example, detailed sales data can
be stored at the daily level, while lightly summarized sales data can
be stored at the monthly level. The requirement for light data summarization is based on the fact that most users run queries that repeat-
edly access and analyze the same data elements at a summarized level.
Therefore, by storing summarized data, there can be considerable
improvement in the performance and storage requirements.

Highly Summarized Data

Highly summarized data refers to data that has been rolled up to an
even higher level than lightly summarized data. Instead of monthly
data summarization referred to in the previous example, data can be
summarized at a higher level—at the annual sales level. The sources
for highly summarized data can be lightly summarized data or current
detailed data. The primary users of highly summarized data are senior
executives and strategic users. While their needs are primarily limited
to this level, they can also access detailed data at lower levels through a
drill-down process if needed.

Aggregated Data

Frequently accessed data, such as monthly or annual sales, can be
aggregated or accumulated along predefined attributes. For example,
car sales data can be aggregated by geography and model by adding
the sales dollars for each model within a specific geography. Similarly,
overall sales can be cumulated for a week, month, quarter, or year. The
data to be stored in an aggregated format are determined by a number
of factors, including the frequency and complexity of queries.

   The objective of creating aggregates is to improve performance by
reducing the amount of data to be read by a query. When a query is run
against aggregated data, the response is faster because less data needs
to be accessed (since it is already aggregated). Aggregates enable faster
navigation as well as faster query run times. While aggregates reduce

the retrieval cost by reducing the amount of data to be retrieved, there is a cost associated with updating them. The reason is that aggregate rollup is required whenever new data is loaded. Therefore, dependent aggregates need to be recalculated whenever there are changes to the detailed data, master data, or hierarchies.

Effect of Granularity

Granularity is an important design issue because it affects the volume of data to be stored and the type of query that can be executed. If data is highly granular and has a very high level of detail, the data volume will be enormous. For example, a highly granular data warehouse will contain very detailed data, which can include every captured transaction, such as individual sales orders and purchase requisitions. A less granular data warehouse will contain a higher level of data, such as total purchase orders issued for each month or total monthly sales by region.

If stored data is very granular, practically any type of query can be run against it. If the data is less granular, the types of queries that can be executed will be limited. Usually, senior executives and decision-makers require less granular data, as they work with summarized and aggregated data, while operational staff require more granular and detailed data. In recent years, however, this distinction has been blurred as the needs and requirements of these two types of users have started to overlap due to changes in the decision-making levels and empowerment of lower-level employees.

Data Archiving

The decision regarding which data to archive and the frequency of archiving are contingent upon the intended use of the data. Operational support requirements can often be fulfilled by retaining data for a more immediate two-year period. When the data serves a strategic purpose, organizations lean toward considerably longer retention periods, spanning from five to twenty-five years. This determination is shaped by a variety of factors, including compliance with industry regulations, adherence to data governance policies, and recognition of the potential value embedded in historical data for activities such as trend analysis.

Compliance considerations may dictate the need for extended data retention to meet specific regulatory requirements governing specific industries. Additionally, a meticulous approach to data governance might influence decisions around archiving, ensuring that data are managed in alignment with organizational policies and industry standards. Moreover, recognizing the value of historical data for uncovering patterns, predicting trends, and informing strategic decisions can lead to a more extensive archival strategy.

By examining these factors, organizations can formulate a comprehensive approach to data archiving that not only satisfies immediate operational needs but also aligns with long-term strategic objectives. This approach ensures that archived data, whether at the same granularity as current detailed or aggregated data, is a valuable and well-managed asset for the organization.

Database Design Process

The design of a database is a meticulous process that involves a series of structured steps, each playing a pivotal role in shaping a robust and effective information management system. The journey begins with planning and analysis, a phase in which the organizational landscape is carefully scrutinized. By identifying data requirements, analyzing user needs, and delineating the scope of the database, this initial step lays the groundwork for subsequent design phases. A nuanced understanding of business processes and objectives is critical at this stage, as they act as a guiding compass for the entire design endeavor.

A data model takes shape from the conceptualization to the conceptual design phase. This model, often represented through an entity relationship diagram, encapsulates the abstract essence of the data. Unlike delving into the specifics of how data will be stored, this phase focuses on what data will be stored. Entities, attributes, and relationships are delineated to create a conceptual framework that aligns with the organizational vision.

As the design journey progresses, the focus shifts to the logical design phase. Here, the conceptual model metamorphoses into a logical structure ready for implementation using a database management system (DBMS). This involves defining tables, establishing relationships, and specifying constraints to create a blueprint that ensures data integrity and supports efficient querying. The subsequent physical design step delves into the implementation intricacies, determining how the logical design translates into a tangible database on chosen hardware and software platforms. Decisions on indexing, partitioning, and storage optimization come to the fore, aiming to enhance performance and scalability while minimizing storage requirements.

The culmination of this intricate process is the Implementation phase, where the database takes its tangible form based on the meticulously crafted design. Database administrators bring the design to life by creating tables, establishing relationships, defining data types, and implementing security measures. As the database is populated with relevant data, the fruition of the design is realized, meeting the intended objectives and providing a structured framework for effective information management. By navigating through these well-defined steps, organizations can establish a resilient database that aligns with their operational needs, ensuring that the data is not only stored but also leveraged strategically.

DATA CHALLENGES IN ANALYTICS

Data challenges in analytics often stem from issues like data quality, integration, and scalability, which can hinder the generation of accurate insights. Overcoming these challenges is essential to unlocking the full potential of analytics and driving informed, data-driven decisions.

Understanding Data Sources

Source data, often referred to as the lifeblood of information management, constitutes the primary reservoir from which organizations draw insights, make informed decisions, and propel their operational processes. The spectrum of data sources is diverse, ranging from conventional databases and datasets to familiar spreadsheets or even hard-coded data snippets embedded within applications.

Major enterprise-level applications, exemplified by industry giants such as Oracle, Salesforce, and SAP, rely on databases as their bedrock data sources. These robust databases provide structured storage, streamlined retrieval, and intricate data management capabilities. While stalwarts like Oracle favor specialized database systems, some applications, such as Microsoft Access, can adeptly harness other types of databases. The choice often hinges on factors such as scalability, reliability, and the specific requirements of the application.

In certain scenarios, a series of spreadsheets emerges as an alternative, albeit less common, data source. The stability of such an approach diminishes as the size of spreadsheets burgeons, posing challenges of corruption and data integrity. Unlike databases, spreadsheets lack the systematic backup and maintenance mechanisms that are integral to large-scale data management.

Databases, which are integral components of broader data backup systems, distinguish themselves as more efficient and resilient data sources. The meticulous maintenance afforded by databases not only enhances their stability but also positions them as preferred choices, especially in contexts where data integrity and reliability are paramount. In essence, the selection of a data source is a strategic decision intricately woven into the fabric of an organization's data management strategy, balancing considerations of stability, scalability, and long-term maintenance.

Source Data Problems

Source data imported into an analytics system often present challenges stemming from its inherent dirtiness and inconsistency, a scenario commonly observed in diverse data sources within the same organization. For instance, a single entity such as a vendor may be referred to as IBM, International Business Machines, or IBM Global Services across three different sources, introducing variations that can lead to inaccuracies in results during analysis within the analytics system.

The spectrum of problems associated with source data is extensive, covering various issues such as field data not aligning with the field description, data files from diverse sources adopting different formats, variations in the spelling of names across systems, discrepancies in addresses from different sources, multiple names residing in the same field, coexistence of name and address in a single field, inconsistent use of special characters, and data truncation. Missing zip codes in addresses, absent area codes in phone numbers, inconsistent spacing, and other anomalies further contribute to the complexity. Addressing these issues is a critical task in every analytics system project, necessitating thorough checks and validations to ensure the accuracy and consistency of the imported data.

Data Selection

A crucial first step marks the initiation of the data migration process: the meticulous identification of source systems that will act as the reservoir for data flowing into the analytics system. Given the pervasive issue of data duplication and the potential existence of shared data elements across multiple sources, a thorough analysis of the source systems becomes imperative. The goal is to discern the optimal source for importing data—a source that not only proves reliable and accurate but also ideally aligns with the required format or necessitates minimal transformation for seamless import.

Undertaking the task of source identification is a nuanced endeavor, demanding a significant investment of time and effort. The intricacies and potential anomalies among various source databases present challenges that require careful navigation. Analyzing diverse source systems to pinpoint the most suitable data source involves delving into the intricacies of each, evaluating their reliability, and ensuring accuracy in the context of the intended analytical objectives. This intricate process is foundational to the success of the data migration journey, setting the stage for subsequent phases that hinge on the robustness of the identified source systems.

Data Import

In the realm of data-driven decision-making, the quality of the data under scrutiny is paramount. The characteristics of data that render it suitable for analysis are numerous and nonnegotiable. A comprehensive checklist includes the prerequisites of being clean, consistent, accurate, complete, reliable, relevant, current, and timely. These attributes collectively lay the foundation for a robust and trustworthy analytical process.

The journey to data quality commences before data is imported into the analytical ecosystem. Rigorous checks and validations are imperative to ensure that the data is not only properly structured but also accurate and complete. The importance of accuracy and reliability cannot be overstated; any compromise in these aspects results in a loss of credibility, rendering the data futile for analytical purposes. When inaccurate data infiltrates decision-making processes, the ramifications are significant, potentially compromising the integrity of organizational decisions.

Concrete and proactive steps must be taken to maintain data quality when initiating data clean-up. Often, this necessitates intricate cleaning procedures to rectify discrepancies and inconsistencies. Failing to address data quality at its source can have severe consequences, ranging from project failure and disruptions in business operations to the generation of incorrect reports and flawed analyses. Thus, prioritizing data quality is not merely a best practice; it is an indispensable prerequisite for meaningful and reliable data-driven insights.

Data Loading

The process of data loading is essential for any analytical endeavor, drawing upon both internal and external data sources. This source data undergoes a migration process to be imported into the target data storage system. Often, this data requires conversion to ensure compatibility with the target system's format and structure. Initial data loads can be substantial, particularly when importing historical data spanning several years. Subsequent loads are typically incremental, capturing only the changes or additions since the last load, which may or may not necessitate conversion depending on the system's design and requirements.

Data Volume

Data volumes play a crucial role in analytics, influencing every stage of the analytical process. The sheer volume of data generated and collected by organizations has experienced exponential growth in recent years, driven by the proliferation of digital interactions, connected devices, and the advent of big data technologies. The scale of the data has a profound impact on the storage infrastructure, computational requirements, and overall efficiency of the analytical processes. As data volumes escalate, organizations grapple with the challenges of managing, processing, and extracting meaningful insights from vast datasets.

Consideration of data volumes is integral to designing robust storage solutions, implementing scalable processing frameworks, and optimizing analytics workflows. Moreover, the magnitude of the data also influences decision-making time frames, with real-time analytics demanding rapid processing capabilities to derive timely insights. Understanding, assessing, and effectively managing data volumes are essential components of a comprehensive analytics strategy, ensuring that organizations harness the full potential of their data resources to make informed and strategic decisions.

Detailed and External Data

Relying solely on summarized data as the cornerstone for analysis is a strategic misstep, as the true value often resides in the granular intricacies of detailed transaction data. Summarized data, by its very nature, provides an overview that sacrifices the richness of individual transactions. This limitation not only constrains the flexibility of analyses but also imposes restrictions on the breadth and depth of insights that can be gleaned. To unlock the full potential of analytics, it is imperative to embrace the wealth embedded in detailed transactional data.

Moreover, the scope of data utilization should extend beyond internal sources, incorporating a holistic approach that integrates both external and internal data sources. Disregarding the wealth of external data is a missed opportunity, as it can bring unique perspectives, market trends, and contextual information that enrich the analytical landscape. A comprehensive analytical strategy entails tapping into all available data reservoirs to extract valuable insights, fostering a more robust and informed decision-making process. In essence, to maximize benefits, organizations should adopt an inclusive approach, leveraging the full spectrum of potentially beneficial data sources at their disposal.

Historical Data

The richness and utility of an analytics system are intricately tied to the volume and diversity of the data at its disposal. Historical data, in particular, holds immense value in enhancing the capabilities of the analytics system. The availability of extensive historical data provides a temporal dimension to the analyses, enabling organizations to discern trends, patterns, and anomalies that may not be apparent in a narrower time frame. This historical context empowers users to make more informed decisions by understanding the evolution of variables and performance metrics over time.

To harness the full potential of historical data, organizations are encouraged to import as much relevant historical data as possible. This encompasses a wide spectrum of information, ranging from past transactional data and customer interactions to operational records and market dynamics. The goal is to create a comprehensive repository that captures the historical footprint of the organization's activities. This endeavor should be approached judiciously, considering both feasibility and cost-effectiveness. Striking the right balance ensures that the analytics system is not overwhelmed by unnecessary data while still reaping the benefits of a robust historical dataset that enriches the analytical capabilities and strategic foresight of the organization.

Data Import Cost

Considerable effort and time are invested in the ETL task before analytics tools import and utilize data. This intricate process involves several key tasks. First, a comprehensive data analysis is conducted to gain insights into its structure and relevance to both technical and business requirements. Next, data extraction is executed meticulously from various sources to ensure the integrity and accuracy of the transferred information. The source data then undergoes conditioning and transformation to align with specific technical and business needs, effectively bridging the gap between the raw data and the requirements set by analytics tools. Finally, the processed data is loaded into the target system for optimal utilization.

Despite the availability of numerous ETL tools equipped with advanced automated functions, the data migration task still requires a substantial manual effort. The overall effort expended in the ETL task can notably impact the cost of migration. This consideration becomes more pronounced when organizations choose to implement custom ETL programs, where development and maintenance demand a dedicated investment of financial resources and human capital.

Several database vendors provide alternative solutions with embedded ETL tools to address this challenge. These tools not only simplify the data migration task but also contribute to cost-effectiveness. By leveraging predefined mappings that come integrated with the tools, organizations can streamline the process, which reduces the manual effort required and mitigates the associated costs. This integrated approach not only enhances efficiency in data migration but also proves to be a more economically viable solution for organizations seeking to optimize their analytics endeavors.

DATA CONVERSION

Data conversion involves transforming data from one format or structure into another to ensure compatibility and usability across systems. This process is vital for integrating diverse data sources and enabling seamless analytics workflows.

Complexity and Significance

Data conversion is the essential process of transforming data from one format to another. For instance, conversion becomes imperative when migrating data from mainframe or flat files to a relational database due to differences in storage types, data structures, and variations in data encoding across computer systems. Disparities in operating systems also come into play, as they adhere to distinct standards for data and file handling. Furthermore, the unique ways in which computer programs handle data contribute to the complexity of data conversion.

These conversions can range from simple to highly complex, impacting the degree of effort and cost involved in the extraction process. The intricacies of converting data underscore the importance of careful consideration and strategic planning when undertaking such tasks. Recognizing the multifaceted nature of data conversion is crucial for organizations to allocate resources effectively and ensure a seamless transition of information between diverse systems.

Techniques

Various techniques are employed for the conversion of data, reflecting the diverse nature of information processing in the digital landscape. Typically, the process involves reading a file, interpreting its contents, executing the necessary transformations, and generating output in a new file format. This intricate series of operations ensures that data seamlessly transitions from one representation to another.

Data conversion can be facilitated through dedicated data conversion programs specifically designed to handle various formats and intricacies involved in the transformation process. These specialized programs are instrumental in automating and streamlining the conversion workflow, providing efficiency and accuracy in handling diverse data types.

Alternatively, organizations may opt for custom computer programs developed in-house to address unique data conversion requirements. These solutions are tailored to the specific needs of the organization, offering a greater degree of control and customization over the conversion process. While requiring a more significant initial investment, in-house programs can prove to be invaluable for organizations with complex or highly specialized data conversion needs.

In addition to proprietary solutions, a plethora of third-party tools are available to cater to a wide range of data conversion tasks. These tools often include advanced features and support for various file formats, providing organizations with versatile and user-friendly options for handling their data conversion requirements. Leveraging third-party tools can be a cost-effective and time-efficient approach, especially for organizations with diverse data conversion needs but limited resources for in-house development.

In essence, the realm of data conversion is enriched by a spectrum of techniques, ranging from specialized programs to custom in-house solutions and third-party tools. The choice among these approaches depends on the specific requirements, complexity, and resources available to an organization, highlighting the flexibility inherent in the data conversion process.

DATA MIGRATION

Data migration refers to the process of transferring data between systems, formats, or storage environments. This critical step ensures that organizations can maintain data integrity and functionality while upgrading systems, consolidating platforms, or adapting to new technologies.

Overview of Data Migration

Data migration involves the intricate process of transferring data from an existing system to a new system, often exemplified by the transition to a data warehouse. This operation is executed through the utilization of either custom programs or third-party tools. These tools facilitate the automatic transfer of data, adhering to predefined rules that ensure accuracy and consistency during the migration.

The choice between custom programs and third-party tools is contingent upon several variables, highlighting the complex and nuanced nature of data migration. Factors such as the systems involved, data volume and complexity, data quality, cost considerations, and the availability of resources collectively influence the method selected for a particular migration project. This adaptability is crucial, allowing organizations to tailor their approach based on unique requirements and constraints.

The data migration process is inherently complex, primarily due to the substantial variations in the number, type, and quality of the data sources. Thorough analysis is a prerequisite because it precedes decision-making on how to implement the migration task effectively. This analysis encompasses a comprehensive examination of both the source data and the associated processes. Understanding the intricacies of the source data is essential for devising a migration strategy that aligns with the specific characteristics and challenges posed by the data at hand.

In essence, data migration is a multifaceted undertaking that demands careful consideration and strategic planning. The recognition of the diverse variables involved underscores the importance of a tailored approach to address the unique circumstances of each migration project. This process, while challenging, is indispensable for organizations seeking to seamlessly transition to new systems and leverage the benefits offered by advanced data management solutions such as data warehouses.

Data Migration Drivers

Data migration is motivated by four main factors: storage migration, database migration, application migration, and business process migration. Each of these facets presents distinct challenges and demands a tailored approach for successful execution. Storage migration involves transferring data to new storage systems, while database migration focuses on relocating data between databases. Application migration entails the movement of data to support the transition to new applications, and business process migration involves the realignment of data to accommodate changes in business processes. These diverse motivations for data migration underscore the complex and multifaceted nature of the processes involved.

In each of these migration scenarios, the environment is characterized by a set of challenges. Multiple data sources contribute to the complexity of the problem, and varying data quality also poses potential hurdles. Inconsistent nomenclature and definitions further complicate the migration process, as does dealing with inconsistent data. The existence of varying data models across databases necessitates careful handling, and consolidation requirements often arise when dealing with nonstandard aging legacy systems. Additionally, the lack of skilled legacy IT resources can impose a significant constraint, underscoring the importance of strategic planning and resource allocation in addressing the intricacies of data migration across diverse and complex environments.

Data Migration Process

Data migration involves a sequence of four fundamental steps. First, a comprehensive analysis is conducted on the source system, aiming to understand its data structure thoroughly. Following this, the data structure of the new system is meticulously determined, laying the groundwork for a seamless transition. Subsequently, a critical aspect involves mapping fields between the two systems. This process identifies common fields in both the old and new systems, ensuring that the data moved from the source system arrives at the proper location within the new system. This step is pivotal for maintaining data integrity and consistency during the migration process.

The final step in data migration involves defining the migration process itself. This step focuses on automating the actual import process, wherein data is extracted from the source system and then loaded into the new system. By establishing a well-defined migration process, organizations can streamline their overall operation, reducing manual intervention and potential errors. This automation not only enhances efficiency but also ensures a more reliable and accurate migration of data from the old to the new system.

Data Migration Complexity

The complexity of the data migration task is pronounced due to significant variations in the number, type, and quality of sources feeding into an analytics system. Analyzing both the source data and associated processes comprehensively is imperative before the extraction process can be efficiently designed and the data can be loaded into the target system. Within a data migration project, a substantial portion of time, ranging from 50% to 75%, is dedicated to critical tasks such as extracting data from the sources, conditioning and transforming source data to meet technical and business requirements and loading the data into the data warehouse. This underscores the resource-intensive nature of these pivotal steps in ensuring a successful data migration.

The migration of data from complex and disparate systems poses a formidable challenge that demands meticulous management. Failure to handle this complexity effectively can result in issues related to data quality or project delays. In extreme cases, inadequate management of data migration challenges may even lead to project failure. Recognizing the intricacies involved and allocating resources judiciously throughout the data migration lifecycle is crucial to mitigating risks and ensuring the seamless integration of data into the analytics system.

Data Volume to Be Migrated

The amount of data to be imported is usually driven by business requirements. Typically, the business wants the maximum volume of data, extending over many years, to be imported. Alternatively, IT wants to minimize the data volume to be imported due to the ETL effort involved, which can be very time-consuming and expensive, as well as the effort required to clean and validate the additional data to be imported. The final decision regarding the period for which data is to be imported usually falls somewhere between the IT and business requirements.

Importing insufficient data can limit the analysis that can be performed. Since highly granular data allows maximum analytical versatility, the import of transaction data should be maximized even though doing so significantly increases data volumes. In general, the usefulness and versatility of an analytics system increases as the volume of data stored in it increases. There is no doubt that sharing too much data, especially if it is irrelevant, can have a negative impact because of the extra effort required for the ETL and data validation tasks. Therefore, the amount and type of data to be imported should be limited to whatever is required to make the users effective and efficient.

Data Migration Tool Selection

A diverse array of third-party software tools is available to assist organizations in the intricate process of data migration. These tools exhibit remarkable versatility, offering functionalities that go beyond mere data transfer. They can validate names and addresses, which is particularly valuable when consolidating information from multiple sources, rectify errors in data elements, and create new data in formats compatible with the requirements of the target database. The strength of these tools lies in their ability to streamline the consolidation of disparate data sources, ensuring accuracy, standardization, and compatibility with the target system.

These third-party tools often encompass robust features for data cleansing and transformation, expanding on their capabilities. This includes the standardization of data, rectification of inconsistencies, and the seamless adaptation of information to align with the specific requirements of the target system. Moreover, their capacity to create new data in desired formats significantly enhances their adaptability to diverse database structures, adding to their effectiveness in managing complex migration projects.

The selection of an appropriate third-party tool poses a significant challenge. Balancing conflicting requirements such as ease of use, stringent data quality standards, speed, scalability, cost-effectiveness, alignment with application requirements, and future usability necessitates a meticulous evaluation process. Organizations must carefully weigh the features and capabilities of available tools against their unique needs and long-term goals. This strategic selection process is critical, ensuring that the chosen tool not only meets immediate migration requirements but also aligns with the organization's broader data management objectives.

In essence, third-party software tools emerge as invaluable companions in the data migration journey, providing a versatile toolkit to address complex challenges. The success of migration endeavors hinges on the thoughtful selection of a tool that effectively balances conflicting demands while laying the foundation for robust and sustainable data management practices.

Migration Effort Estimation

Underestimating the effort and difficulties associated with migrating data is a widespread problem for a number of reasons. The most common reason is that data quality is frequently far worse than expected, which can cause many problems and delay a critical task—validating the imported data. Additionally, designing the ETL processes for extracting data from multiple courses and loading them into a single target is one of the most difficult, challenging, and costly tasks in a migration project.

Data Migration Problems

Mitigating data migration problems requires a strategic approach encompassing several key considerations. First and foremost, it is crucial not to harbor unrealistic expectations regarding data quality. Acknowledging the possibility of encountering very dirty data is vital, as it sets a realistic foundation for addressing challenges. The task effort and duration should not be underestimated, necessitating a careful evaluation of project timelines. Building contingency in the project plan is essential for accommodating unforeseen issues that may arise during the migration process.

Furthermore, shortcuts in the ETL process should be avoided to maintain data integrity. Recognizing the intricate nature of data migration, organizations should prioritize a comprehensive and thorough ETL process to ensure accurate data transfer. To further mitigate challenges and risks, leveraging state-of-the-art tools for data transformation, cleansing, capture, and loading can be beneficial. These tools provide advanced functionalities to streamline and enhance the migration process, contributing to a more efficient and successful data migration project.

Ensuring Data Quality

Ensuring the quality of information provided to users is a critical success factor in the realm of analytics systems. The impact is profound, directly influencing a company's profitability. The analytics system is akin to a gold mine housing strategic data accessible to decision-makers across all hierarchy levels. If the data within the analytics system is inaccurate and unreliable, credibility will be lost, leading to user neglect. The consequences of using unreliable data for decision-making are severe, compromising the overall quality of decisions and potentially causing detrimental effects. Therefore, data imported into an analytics system must undergo rigorous checks and validation to guarantee proper structure, accuracy, and completeness. Characteristics such as consistency in format and data representation, along with accuracy, are paramount in maintaining the highest quality standards.

For data to be deemed of high quality, it must be accurate and consistent but also be clean, complete, reliable, relevant, understandable, current, and timely. This comprehensive approach to data quality underscores its significance in upholding the credibility of the analytics system and, subsequently, facilitating effective decision-making throughout the organization.

Data Migration versus Data Integration

The differentiation between data migration and data integration is crucial in understanding their distinct roles in the realm of information management. Data migration entails the focused task of relocating data from one environment or source system to another, often executed as a well-defined project that may culminate in retiring the source system. This meticulous process involves planning, execution, and validation, typically undertaken to upgrade systems or consolidate data repositories for improved efficiency.

Data integration is an ongoing and dynamic process rooted in the seamless flow of data across various sources and applications. Based on data flows within different data sources and applications, this process creates a unified view of the data, providing users with a comprehensive and cohesive perspective. In recent years, data integration has gained prominence, driven by the exponential growth in data volumes and the escalating need for organizations to share data internally and with external partners. This intricate process not only fosters collaboration but also enhances decision-making by ensuring that users have access to a harmonized and up-to-date representation of information. The integration of data from diverse sources is instrumental in navigating the complexities of modern data management and supporting informed decision-making across organizational landscapes.

CHAPTER 4

BIG DATA

B ig Data encompasses vast volumes of structured and unstructured data generated at high velocity from various sources. Leveraging Big Data effectively allows organizations to uncover patterns, trends, and insights that drive informed decision-making and innovation.

OVERVIEW

Evolution of Data Management

The evolution of data management can be traced through distinct waves, each representing a significant phase in the way organizations handle information. The first wave focused on establishing manageable data structures laying the groundwork for structured and organized data storage. The second wave introduced advancements in Web and content management, reflecting the changing landscape of data dissemination and accessibility. As organizations grappled with the increasing volume and complexity of data, the third wave emerged, emphasizing the management of big data. This wave underscored the need for scalable and sophisticated approaches to handle vast datasets, acknowledging the challenges and opportunities presented by the era of large-scale and diverse data sources.

What Is Big Data?

Big data refers to datasets or combinations of datasets that are characterized by their immense size, complexity, and speed at which they are generated or processed. These datasets exceed the capabilities of traditional data processing tools and technologies, such as relational databases, to capture, store, manage, and analyze the information within a reasonable time frame. The concept of big data is defined not only by the volume of data but also by the aspects of velocity (the speed at which data is generated and processed) and variety (the diverse types of data, including structured, semistructured, and unstructured data).

The goal of managing and analyzing big data is to extract valuable insights, make data-driven decisions, and uncover patterns or trends that may not be apparent with smaller or more traditional datasets. As technology evolves, the threshold for what is considered "big" continues to expand, making big data a dynamic and evolving field.

Big Data Sources

The complex nature of big data is driven by structured and unstructured data generated by modern technologies. These include Weblogs, radio frequency IDs (RFIDs), sensors embedded in devices, machinery, vehicles, Internet searches, social media such as Facebook and LinkedIn, portable computers, mobile devices, smartphones, GPS devices, call center records, scientific devices, and other inputs, as well as traditional data sources. To effectively utilize big data, it is often necessary to blend it with structured data from traditional business applications like enterprise resource planning (ERP) or customer relationship management (CRM) systems.

Contrasting Approaches to Data Management and Analysis

Big data and traditional data warehousing are two distinct paradigms for managing and analyzing vast volumes of data. Data warehousing has long been a staple for organizations to store and process structured data in a structured manner. It typically involves extracting, transforming, and loading data into a centralized repository optimized for complex queries and business intelligence. In contrast, big data encompasses a broader spectrum, dealing not only with structured data but also unstructured and semistructured data, often in real time.

Technologies such as Hadoop and NoSQL databases enable the storage and processing of diverse data types, fostering a more flexible and scalable approach. While data warehousing is well-suited for structured and historical data, big data solutions cater to the ever-growing volumes and varieties of data, offering more agility in handling complex analytics and uncovering insights from a wide array of sources.

In essence, while data warehousing provides a structured approach to traditional business intelligence, big data opens up new horizons by embracing the complexity and diversity inherent in modern data ecosystems.

BIG DATA CHARACTERISTICS

The characteristics of Big Data define its complexity and potential. Understanding these attributes is essential for organizations to effectively manage and extract actionable insights from their data assets.

Volume (Data at Rest)

Volume, in the context of data, refers to the sheer quantity of information generated. It plays a crucial role in determining the significance and potential of the dataset, thereby defining what constitutes big data. The term *big data* underscores the emphasis on size as a defining characteristic.

As discussed earlier, several factors contribute to the exponential growth in data volume. Historically, the challenge lay in managing large volumes of data due to storage limitations. With the declining storage costs, new challenges have emerged, such as identifying relevant information within vast datasets and leveraging analytics to derive value from this data.

The proliferation of online platforms, real-time data capture devices, and interconnected networks has fueled the expansion of big data volumes. This trend is expected to persist, with data volume continuing to escalate in the foreseeable future.

Velocity (Data in Motion)

Velocity refers to the speed of data generation and processing. When data is streaming in at an unprecedented speed, especially in real time, it must be dealt with in a timely manner. Streaming data may require milliseconds to seconds to respond. Examples include:

- Clickstreams and ad impressions that capture user behavior at millions of events per second
- High-frequency stock trading algorithms that reflect market changes within microseconds
- Machine-to-machine processes exchanging data between billions of devices

▪ Infrastructure and sensors generating massive log data in real-time

▪ Online gaming systems supporting millions of concurrent users

The volume to be processed may range from terabytes to exabytes of existing data.

Variety (Data in Many Forms)

Another characteristic of big data is variety. Currently, data is generated in structured and unstructured formats. These include but are not limited to, numeric data in traditional databases, data from business applications, stock market data, financial transactions, geospatial data, multimedia, 3D data, unstructured text documents, log files, social media, email, video, audio, and so on.

Organizations are struggling to manage and analyze different varieties of data. Big data helps address these problems and provides companies with the means to create tremendous business value.

Additional Big Data Characteristics

In addition to volume, velocity, and variety, three additional dimensions have been identified as big data characteristics: variability, complexity, and veracity.

Variability

In addition to the increasing velocities and varieties of data, data flows can exhibit high levels of inconsistency with periodic peaks, such as sudden increases in data volume when something is trending on social media. Daily peaks in e-commerce transaction data during peak shopping hours, seasonal spikes in sales data during holiday seasons, and event-triggered surges in Web site traffic data during product launches or promotional campaigns can be challenging to manage, especially where unstructured data is involved. Data variability or inconsistency is a characteristic that poses a challenge for analyzing data, as it hampers the process of effectively handling and managing data, leading to potential issues in data analysis and decision-making.

Complexity

Data management can become a highly complex process, particularly when dealing with large volumes of data imported from multiple sources. This data must be linked, matched, cleansed, and transformed across systems. Connecting and correlating relationships, hierarchies, and multiple data linkages is essential; otherwise, the data can quickly spiral out of control. This characteristic is referred to as the complexity of big data.

Veracity (Data in Doubt)

The quality of the data being captured can vary greatly. Uncertainty about the data can be due to data inconsistency and incompleteness, ambiguities, latency, and so on. The accuracy of the analysis depends on the veracity of the source data.

DRIVING TRANSFORMATION AND BENEFITS

The transformative power of Big Data lies in its ability to drive innovation and deliver significant benefits across industries. By leveraging its key characteristics, organizations can uncover insights that fuel efficiency, enhance decision-making, and create new growth opportunities.

Big Data: Transforming Insights

Big data is important because of its transformative potential for organizations across various industries. By harnessing the vast amounts of structured and unstructured data generated daily, businesses can gain valuable insights into customer behavior, market trends, and operational efficiency. The ability to analyze and interpret large datasets empowers organizations to make informed, data-driven decisions that can enhance strategic planning and boost overall performance. Moreover, big data facilitates the discovery of patterns and correlations that might not be apparent through traditional data analysis methods. This capability is particularly valuable in uncovering hidden opportunities, mitigating risks, and gaining a competitive edge in dynamic and fast-paced markets.

Big Data Benefits

The benefits of big data are far-reaching, involving aspects ranging from improved decision-making to enhanced customer experiences. With robust analytics, organizations can optimize processes, leading to increased efficiency and cost savings. Businesses can personalize customer interactions by leveraging data insights and tailoring products and services to meet individual preferences and needs. Big data analytics has contributed to advancements in patient care, disease prevention, and medical research in healthcare.

Additionally, big data fosters innovation, enabling the development of new products and services based on a deeper understanding of market demands. Overall, the effective utilization of big data translates into improved operational performance, strategic agility, and more competitive positioning in today's data-centric business landscape.

The key is not to just acquire large amounts of data. It is what one does with the data that counts. When big data is effectively and efficiently captured, processed, and analyzed, companies can gain a complete understanding of their business, customers, products, competitors, and so on. This can lead to efficiency improvements, increased sales, lower costs, better customer service, and improved products and services.

ANALYZING BIG DATA

Analyzing big data enables organizations to uncover patterns, trends, and insights hidden within vast datasets. By applying advanced analytical techniques, businesses can transform raw data into actionable intelligence, driving informed decision-making and innovation.

Big Data Analytics

Big data analytics is the process of examining and interpreting large and complex datasets to extract valuable insights, patterns, and trends. It involves the use of advanced analytical techniques, algorithms, and tools to uncover meaningful information from diverse data sources, including structured and unstructured data. The primary goal of big data analytics is to turn raw data into actionable intelligence that can inform decision-making and drive business strategies. By leveraging sophisticated analytical models and technologies, organizations can better understand customer behavior, market dynamics, and operational efficiency.

Big data analytics plays a crucial role in various industries, including finance, healthcare, retail, and manufacturing, offering the potential to optimize processes, enhance product development, and improve overall business performance. As organizations continue to accumulate massive volumes of data, the adoption of big data analytics becomes increasingly essential for remaining competitive, fostering innovation, and unlocking new opportunities for growth.

Analysis Process

The big data analysis process involves a systematic approach to extracting valuable insights from vast and varied datasets. The journey typically begins with data collection, during which organizations gather information from diverse sources, including structured databases, unstructured documents, and real-time streaming data. Once collected, the data undergoes preprocessing, including cleaning, transformation, and normalization, to ensure quality and compatibility.

The next crucial step is storage, often in distributed or cloud-based systems, to accommodate the sheer volume of data. Subsequently, the data is subjected to analysis using advanced techniques such as statistical analysis, machine learning, and data mining. This phase aims to unveil patterns, correlations, and trends within the data, providing actionable insights.

Finally, the results of the analysis are interpreted and communicated to stakeholders, enabling strategic decision-making. The iterative nature of the big data analysis process allows organizations to continuously refine their understanding of data, adapt to evolving business needs, and harness the full potential of the insights derived from the massive datasets at their disposal.

Technologies

With its extensive volume, velocity, variety, and complexity, big data demands a sophisticated technological ecosystem to effectively unlock its potential. At the heart of this ecosystem is Hadoop, an open-source framework meticulously designed for the distributed storage and processing of vast datasets. Hadoop serves as an open-source software framework, facilitating the distributed storage and processing of big data across large clusters of commodity hardware. Its core functionalities encompass massive data storage and accelerated processing.

Hadoop utilizes a distributed file system (HDFS) and the MapReduce programming model, enabling organizations to handle massive data processing tasks seamlessly. In tandem with Hadoop, Apache Spark has emerged as a powerful and fast cluster-computing framework that processes in-memory data. Spark is particularly valuable for real-time data processing and analytics because it offers enhanced speed and versatility compared to traditional approaches.

NoSQL databases have become pivotal components of the technological landscape to accommodate the diverse and dynamic nature of big data. Databases such as MongoDB, Cassandra, and Couchbase provide scalable and flexible storage solutions, addressing the limitations of traditional relational databases when confronted with vast and varied datasets. Data warehousing solutions, exemplified by platforms such as

Amazon Redshift and Google BigQuery, offer scalable architectures for storing and analyzing large datasets efficiently. These technologies help organizations in structuring their data, making it accessible and conducive to in-depth analysis.

Machine learning, discussed in Chapter 18, plays a crucial role in extracting meaningful insights from big data. Tools and libraries such as TensorFlow, PyTorch, and scikit-learn empower organizations to implement predictive modeling and pattern recognition, uncovering hidden trends within large datasets. Data integration tools, including Apache NiFi and Talend, streamline the process of extracting, transforming, and loading data from diverse sources into big data environments. Additionally, data visualization tools such as Tableau and Power BI enable organizations to communicate insights effectively, providing stakeholders with intuitive and interactive representations of complex data.

Cloud computing platforms, exemplified by Amazon Web Services (AWS), Microsoft Azure, and Google Cloud, offer scalable infrastructure and storage solutions, providing organizations with the flexibility to adapt to changing data requirements. Furthermore, stream processing platforms such as Apache Kafka and Apache Flink are indispensable for handling real-time streaming data, facilitating organizations in processing and analyzing the generated data. Containerization and orchestration technologies, such as Docker and Kubernetes, enhance the efficiency and scalability of big data applications, simplifying deployment and management processes.

In conclusion, the multifaceted nature of big data necessitates a diverse and sophisticated technological toolkit. From distributed frameworks such as Hadoop and Spark to advanced databases, machine learning tools, and cloud computing platforms, the synergy of these technologies forms the backbone of organizations seeking to unlock the insights embedded within vast and complex datasets. As big data continues to evolve, the integration of these technologies offers a dynamic and robust foundation for organizations striving to derive value and innovation from the wealth of information at their disposal.

OPERATIONAL VERSUS ANALYTICAL

Operational and analytical systems serve distinct yet complementary roles in Big Data management. While operational systems focus on real-time processing and managing day-to-day transactions, analytical systems are designed to extract insights and support strategic decision-making from large-scale data analysis.

Operational and Analytical Systems in Big Data

The big data landscape comprises two main types of technology: systems providing operational capabilities for real-time, interactive workloads and those offering analytical capabilities for retrospective and complex analysis that may involve most or all of the data. These technology classes often work together to meet the varied needs of handling large datasets.

Operational systems, such as NoSQL databases, focus on handling numerous concurrent requests with low-latency responses, especially when dealing with highly selective access criteria. These systems are geared toward real-time, transactional workloads, ensuring swift and responsive interactions.

In contrast, analytical systems prioritize high throughput and are designed to execute complex queries that may involve the majority, if not all, of the data in the system. These systems excel in retrospective analysis, allowing for in-depth examination of extensive datasets to derive meaningful insights.

Both operational and analytical systems typically operate across distributed clusters, managing substantial amounts of data spread across numerous servers. This distributed approach ensures scalability and the ability to handle large datasets, which are characteristic of the vast and dynamic nature of big data. The collaborative use of these systems reflects the comprehensive approach required to address the diverse challenges and opportunities within the big data landscape.

Operational Big Data Workloads

Operational big data workloads have witnessed a transformative shift with the emergence of NoSQL big data systems specifically designed to address a diverse array of applications. Architectures such as document databases, key-value stores, column family stores, and graph databases cater to specific use cases, demonstrating the versatility of NoSQL technologies. Notably, NoSQL systems have risen to prominence by overcoming the limitations of traditional relational databases in modern computing environments. They boast enhanced speed and scalability, outperforming relational databases and aligning seamlessly with the dynamic requirements of contemporary big data workloads.

A pivotal aspect of NoSQL big data systems is their adept integration with cloud computing architectures, which have evolved over the past decade. This integration is not merely incidental but rather a deliberate design choice, leveraging cloud features for scalability, cost-effectiveness, and efficiency in handling massive computations. By harnessing the power of cloud computing, NoSQL systems enable organizations to scale their operational workloads dynamically, ensuring that computing resources match the evolving demands of the data landscape. This strategic alignment with cloud technology translates into tangible advantages, offering organizations a cost-effective and efficient infrastructure for managing the complexities of large-scale data processing.

Furthermore, NoSQL systems contribute significantly to the ease of implementation in operational big data workloads. They streamline the management of data and expedite implementation processes, leading to notable reductions in both time and costs. Specific examples or statistics showcasing the reduced implementation times or cost savings would underscore the practical benefits of NoSQL systems. This ease of implementation not only enhances the efficiency of operational workloads but also contributes to the broader objective of making big data technologies more accessible and feasible for a diverse range of organizations. In essence, strategic integration with cloud computing architectures and streamlined implementation processes have made NoSQL systems instrumental in reshaping the landscape of operational big data workloads.

Analytical Big Data Workloads

Analytical big data workloads find effective solutions in massively parallel processing (MPP) database systems and MapReduce, playing pivotal roles in large-scale data analysis. These technologies bring scalability to the forefront, allowing organizations to seamlessly manage growing data volumes by distributing processing tasks across multiple nodes. The parallel processing capabilities inherent in MPP databases optimize computational efficiency, enabling faster data analysis and decision-making. Their proficiency in handling complex analytical tasks extends beyond simple aggregation, facilitating the execution of sophisticated algorithms.

MapReduce, once a cornerstone technology in the realm of big data processing, has witnessed a decline in usage with the emergence of newer, more advanced frameworks like Apache Spark. While MapReduce was indeed influential in the early days of big data processing, its usage has somewhat diminished due to limitations in performance and flexibility compared to newer technologies. Today, organizations are increasingly adopting Apache Spark and similar frameworks for their analytical workloads, as these frameworks offer superior speed, flexibility, and ease of use.

In addition to these advantages, organizations may experience certain limitations during the implementation of MPP database systems and MapReduce. Achieving optimal performance in scalable environments often demands a well-designed infrastructure, and users may encounter a learning curve due to the intricacies of the MapReduce programming model.

The landscape of analytical technologies within the big data realm is in constant evolution. Recent developments have witnessed the rise of advanced analytical tools and frameworks that surpass traditional MPP and MapReduce approaches. Machine learning algorithms, in-memory analytics, and real-time processing capabilities offer more sophisticated and agile solutions for deriving insights from data. Technologies such as Apache Spark have emerged as faster and more flexible alternatives, exemplifying the ongoing evolution in analytical methodologies.

Analytical big data workloads seamlessly integrate with data visualization tools, enhancing the interpretability and usability of analytical results. Visualization becomes a crucial conduit for translating complex findings into actionable insights. Tools such as Tableau, Power BI, and Apache Superset facilitate the creation of interactive and visually engaging representations of analytical outcomes, empowering organizations to make informed decisions with a clear understanding of their data.

In the pursuit of analytical insights, organizations must navigate the challenges of data security and privacy. Analytical workloads often involve processing sensitive information, necessitating robust measures to safeguard data integrity and confidentiality. Best practices include implementing encryption protocols, access controls, and anonymization techniques. Technologies such as differential privacy are gaining traction for preserving individual privacy while enabling effective analysis of large datasets.

In conclusion, the advantages and considerations associated with MPP database systems, MapReduce, and the evolving landscape of analytical technologies underscore the dynamic nature of big data analytics. Integrating analytical workloads with visualization tools and prioritizing data security and privacy are integral components of a comprehensive and responsible approach to deriving value from vast datasets.

Combining Operational and Analytical Technologies

New technologies such as NoSQL, MPP databases, and Hadoop have emerged to address the complexities of big data, empowering businesses to innovate and deliver cutting-edge products and services. A prevalent strategy for harnessing the capabilities of these systems involves seamlessly integrating a NoSQL database, such as MongoDB, with

Hadoop. This integration facilitated through existing APIs, empowers analysts and data scientists to delve into complex, retrospective queries for insightful big data analysis while preserving the efficiency and user-friendly attributes inherent in NoSQL databases.

The fluid connection between NoSQL databases and Hadoop is a pivotal feature streamlining the handling of vast datasets. This integration plays a crucial role in scalability and performance improvement. NoSQL systems, tailored to manage massive volumes of unstructured and semistructured data, enable horizontal scalability by distributing data across multiple nodes. This scalability is complemented by the parallel processing capabilities of MPP databases and Hadoop, allowing organizations to seamlessly scale their infrastructure to meet the growing demands of big data.

In the realm of scalability and performance, the integrated use of NoSQL, MPP databases, and Hadoop is pivotal. The inherent scalability of NoSQL databases, coupled with the parallel processing capabilities of MPP databases and Hadoop, effectively addresses the challenges posed by expanding datasets. This integrated approach not only enhances performance by distributing the workload but also mitigates the risks associated with vertical scaling, minimizing potential bottlenecks.

In essence, the symbiotic utilization of NoSQL, MPP databases, and Hadoop not only addresses the intricacies of big data but also serves as a robust solution for scalability and improved performance. This cohesive integration is especially useful for managing large datasets, providing organizations with a flexible and resilient framework for extracting valuable insights from their data.

CONSIDERATIONS FOR DECISION-MAKERS

Critical Dimensions in Big Data Technology

In navigating big data technology, decision-makers must consider several critical dimensions. While many technologies are mature for mission-critical use, the landscape remains nascent and requires thoughtful evaluation. The dimensions to be weighed include distinguishing between online and offline big data applications, implications of software licensing models (proprietary, open-source, and cloud service), community support, developer appeal, organizational agility through ease of use and flexibility, and the choice between general-purpose and niche solutions. These considerations guide decision-makers in adopting technologies aligned with organizational goals and the dynamic nature of data-related challenges.

Online versus Offline Big Data

Online big data refers to real-time data processing for operational applications, where low latency and high availability are crucial. Examples include social networking news feeds and real-time ad servers. Databases like MongoDB and other NoSQL solutions are commonly used for online big data tasks.

Alternatively, offline big data involves batch processing of large datasets, often for nonoperational purposes. Response times can be slower, ranging from hours to days, as these applications typically produce static outputs like reports or dashboards. Technologies like Hadoop, modern data warehouses, and ETL tools are typical choices for offline big data tasks.

Organizations should align their choice of big data technologies with their specific use cases. An operational data store (ODS) is essential for real-time operational needs, while offline solutions like Hadoop are suitable for long-running analytical processes. Some organizations may require both, and integrations between online and offline technologies, such as MongoDB's integration with Hadoop, can offer comprehensive solutions.

Software License Model

There are three general types of licenses for big data software technologies. Proprietary licenses involve a software product owned and controlled by a company, with the source code not available to licensees. Customers typically obtain perpetual licenses, allowing indefinite use, with annual maintenance fees for support and software upgrades. Examples of this model include databases from Oracle, IBM, and Teradata.

Open-source licenses provide freely available software products and source code. Companies monetize these products by selling subscriptions and additional components such as management tools and support services. Examples include MongoDB and Hadoop (by Cloudera and others).

Cloud service licenses involve hosting the service in a cloud-based environment outside of customers' data centers, delivered over the public Internet, with a predominant pay-per-use or subscription-based model. Examples include the Google App Engine and Amazon Elastic MapReduce.

Regulations and internal policies around data privacy often limit Fortune 1000 companies' ability to leverage cloud-based solutions.

Consequently, most big data initiatives are driven by onsite technologies, primarily open-source software developed by pioneering Web companies.

Community

Communities offer valuable opportunities for learning and collaboration, prompting organizations to assess the prevalence of initiatives utilizing similar technologies and aligning with comparable objectives. Evaluating a technology's adoption involves considering factors such as the number of users, the frequency and participation in local community-organized events, the health and activity of online forums such as Google Groups and StackOverflow, and the availability and attendance levels of conferences. This comprehensive approach allows organizations to gauge the robustness and engagement of a community, providing insights into the adoption and vitality of specific technologies within the broader landscape.

Developer Appeal

The market for big data talent is tight, with top engineers and data scientists opting to work for innovative companies such as Google and Facebook, where they are exposed to leading-edge technology. Organizations can attract the brightest talent by offering developers the opportunity to work on tough problems, and by using a technology that has strong developer interest, a vibrant community, and a bright long-term future,

Agility

Organizations seeking agility in big data endeavors should prioritize products that facilitate flexibility and streamline processes. The focus should be on technologies that empower teams to concentrate on extracting value from their data rather than grappling with the complexities of deploying new applications and infrastructure. Agility, in this context, encompasses three key components. First, ease of use is crucial, with accessible technology for developers fostering a quick learning curve and facilitating the prompt initiation of big data projects. Technologies with steep learning curves and limited educational resources pose challenges to project execution.

Second, technological flexibility is essential because it favors products that enable teams to swiftly adapt to changing requirements. This includes modifying data models, selecting data sources, and adjusting data processing methods as teams evolve their findings and respond to internal and external needs. Dynamic data models and scalability are pivotal capabilities to seek out. Third, licensing freedom plays a vital role, with open-source products offering easier adoption by allowing teams to commence projects swiftly with free community versions.

Additionally, open-source solutions are usually more scalable from a licensing perspective, enabling teams to expand as requirements increase. In contrast, proprietary software vendors often require significant upfront license purchases, hindering swift project initiation and future scalability.

General Purpose Versus Niche Solutions

Organizations are constantly trying to standardize on fewer technologies to reduce complexity, improve their competency in the selected tools, and make their vendor relationships more productive. Organizations should consider whether adopting big data technology helps them address a single or many initiatives.

If the technology is of general purpose, the expertise, infrastructure, skills, integration, and other initial project investments can be amortized across many projects. Organizations may find that while niche technology may be a better fit for a single project, a more general-purpose tool is the better option for the organization as a whole.

BIG DATA CHALLENGES

While the potential benefits of big data are real and significant, and many successes have already been achieved, many technical challenges remain that must be addressed to fully realize this potential. The sheer size of the data is a major challenge and is well recognized, as is the handling of data variety and velocity. We will now cover some other challenges.

Analytics Challenges in Big Data Management

It is a daunting task for most organizations that deal with big data to just understand the available data and determine the best use of that data based on the companies' industry, strategy, and tactics. Additionally, these types of analyses need to be performed on an ongoing basis as the data landscape changes at an ever-increasing rate and as executives develop a greater appetite for analytics based on all available information.

Navigating Emerging Big Data Technologies

Since much of the technology required to utilize big data is new to most organizations, it will be necessary for them to learn about these new technologies at an ever-accelerating pace and potentially engage with different technology providers and partners than they did in the past. Companies entering the world of big data need to balance business needs with the costs associated with capturing, storing, processing, and analyzing big data.

Security and Management Challenges in Data Centers

A new trend is for company data to be managed and stored in data centers. While these solutions include ERP and CRM applications, data warehouses, and many others, the common issue pertains to the security and management of such data. These solutions often offer companies tremendous flexibility and cost savings opportunities compared to more traditional onsite solutions. They also raise new dimensions related to data security and the overall management of an enterprise's big data.

Big Data Security: Privacy and Regulations

Given the volume and complexity of big data, it is challenging for most firms to manage and secure their data to prevent it from falling into the hands of unauthorized parties. The costs of a data privacy breach can be enormous. In the regulatory area, for instance, properly storing and transmitting personally identifiable information (PII), including that contained in unstructured data such as emails, can be problematic and necessitate new and improved security measures and technologies.

There are significant differences in privacy laws for global companies between the U.S. and other countries. Hence, there is a need to tightly integrate big data, data security/privacy, and regulatory functions.

Archiving and Disposal

Since big data will lose its value for current decision-making over time, and since it is voluminous and varied in content and structure, it is necessary to utilize new tools, technologies, and methods to archive and delete big data without sacrificing its effectiveness for meeting current business needs.

Demand for Skilled Big Data Professionals

Addressing the escalating demands of big data initiatives necessitates a substantial pool of skilled professionals. According to estimates, the industry faces a growing need for individuals with deep analytical expertise, approximately 140,000 to 190,000 workers. These skilled professionals play a pivotal role in extracting meaningful insights from the vast and complex datasets characteristic of big data.

Simultaneously, the demand for data-literate managers is projected to surge, with an estimated need for 1.5 million individuals. These managers, equipped with a profound understanding of data, are crucial for steering organizations through the strategic and operational implications of big data analytics. As companies increasingly recognize the transformative potential of data-driven decision-making, investing in retraining existing personnel or recruiting new talent becomes imperative to successfully implement robust and effective big data initiatives.

Implementation Challenges

While many organizations are only beginning to explore initial projects, they find that big data presents significant challenges. Companies often grapple with different definitions of big data, leading to varied expectations—from the anticipation of large immediate cost savings to mistaken notions about implementation costs. Furthermore, organizations hold differing views regarding data sources and uses, with valuable data sources sometimes omitted or overlooked. The varied perceptions about the scope and benefits of big data contribute to the complexity, including the belief that it demands an extremely substantial investment and unrealistic expectations about cost savings. Additionally, there is a tendency to believe that implementing big data across enterprises should occur in a big-bang (comprehensive, full-scale) manner.

In the realm of big data implementations, complexities arise in multiple dimensions, encompassing sizing, budget considerations, timing, in-house skills, and performance. These factors collectively contribute to the intricate nature of integrating and harnessing the potential of big data within organizational frameworks.

ANALYSIS CHALLENGES IN BIG DATA

Heterogeneity and Incompleteness

Machine analysis algorithms expect homogeneous data. Therefore, data must be carefully structured as a first step in (or prior to) data analysis. Computer systems work most efficiently if they can store multiple items that are all identical in size and structure. Efficient representation, access, and analysis of semistructured data require further work.

Even after data cleaning and error correction, some incomplete data and errors in the data are likely to remain. This incompleteness and these errors must be managed during data analysis. Doing this correctly is a challenge.

Scale

Managing large and rapidly increasing volumes of data has long been a significant challenge. Historically, this challenge was mitigated by the continuous improvement in processor speeds following Moore's law, which provided the computational resources needed to cope with expanding data volumes. It's important to note that a fundamental shift is now underway: data volume is scaling faster than computational resources, and CPU speeds have reached a plateau.

In recent years, processor technology has undergone a dramatic transformation. Instead of relying on increasing clock cycle frequencies every eighteen to twenty-four months, processors now incorporate a growing number of cores due to power constraints, resulting in stagnant clock speeds. These changes necessitate a reevaluation of how we design, build, and operate data processing components.

Simultaneously, there is a significant shift toward cloud computing, where various workloads with differing performance objectives are consolidated into large clusters. This extensive resource sharing on sizable and costly clusters demands novel approaches to efficiently managing and executing data processing tasks.

Furthermore, traditional hard disk drives (HDDs), which have served as the primary storage solution for decades, are being supplanted by solid-state drives (SSDs) and other emerging technologies. This transformation in the storage subsystem has profound implications for data processing across various aspects.

Timeliness

The flip side of size is speed. The larger the dataset to be processed, the longer it will take to analyze. The design of a system that effectively addresses size will also likely result in a system that can process a given dataset size faster. It is not just this speed that is usually meant when one speaks of velocity in the context of big data.

There are many situations in which the analysis results are needed immediately. For example, if a fraudulent credit card transaction is suspected, it should ideally be flagged before the transaction is completed, potentially preventing the transaction from occurring at all.

With new analyses that are desired using big data, there is a need to devise new index structures. Designing such structures becomes particularly challenging when the data volume is growing rapidly, and queries have tight response time limits.

Privacy

The privacy of data is another major concern, which is increasing in the context of big data. There are strict laws governing what can and cannot be done for electronic health records. For other data, regulations, especially in the United States, are less stringent. It's no secret that there is great public fear regarding the inappropriate use of personal data, particularly through linking data from multiple sources.

Managing privacy is effectively both a technical and a sociological problem, which must be addressed jointly from both perspectives to realize the promise of big data.

Human Collaboration

Despite tremendous advances made in computational analysis, there remain many patterns that humans can easily detect, but computer algorithms have difficulty determining them. CAPTCHA exploits this fact to separate human Web users from computer programs. Ideally, analytics for big data will not be all computational. Rather, it will be designed explicitly to have a human in the loop.

The new subfield of visual analytics is attempting to do this, at least with respect to the modeling and analysis phase in the pipeline. There is a similar value to human input at all stages of the analysis pipeline. In today's complex world, multiple experts from different domains are often needed to really understand what is going on. A big data analysis system must support input from multiple human experts and share results.

CHAPTER 5

DATA INTEGRATION AND QUALITY

Effective data integration and quality management are fundamental to ensuring reliable insights in analytics. By seamlessly
combining data from diverse sources and maintaining its accuracy, organizations can build a solid foundation for informed decision-
making and operational efficiency.

TECHNIQUES FOR INTEGRATING DATA

Data Integration: Overcoming Challenges and Strategies

Data integration, the process of consolidating and harmonizing data
from diverse sources, is vital for organizations aiming to extract valuable insights from extensive datasets. This endeavor presents several
challenges. A significant obstacle is the diversity of data formats and
structures across sources, including various databases, file formats, and
unstructured data. Addressing data quality issues such as inconsistencies and inaccuracies is also crucial to ensure reliable analyses and
decision-making.

To tackle these challenges, organizations implement strategic
approaches. Data cleansing and normalization refine raw data to adhere
to standardized formats, rectifying errors and ensuring consistency. ETL
processes extract data from source systems, transform it into a common
format, and load it into a destination system. Cloud-based solutions offer
scalable infrastructures for seamless integration across distributed environments. Additionally, data governance frameworks establish standards
and policies, addressing security and compliance concerns. The following
sections briefly explain the common challenges in data integration.

Data Format and Structure Variability

One of the common challenges in data integration is dealing with diverse data formats and structures across different sources. Variability in storing, representing, and organizing data can complicate the integration process, requiring efforts to standardize and normalize the data for meaningful analysis.

Data Quality Issues

Inaccuracies, inconsistencies, and incomplete data are persistent challenges in data integration. Poor data quality can lead to erroneous conclusions and decisions. Addressing data quality issues involves thorough data cleansing, normalization, and validation processes to ensure the accuracy and reliability of integrated datasets.

Incompatible Systems and Technologies

Organizations often use a mix of legacy and modern systems, each with its own technology stack. Integrating data from incompatible systems can be a significant challenge. Bridging the gap between different technologies, databases, and software applications requires careful planning and using middleware or transformation layers.

Scalability and Performance

As data volumes grow, scalability and performance become challenges in data integration. Efficiently processing and moving large volumes of data in a timely manner can strain systems and impact overall performance. Scalable architectures and optimized integration processes are essential for handling increasing data loads effectively.

Advances in Data Integration Technologies

In recent years, remarkable advancements have been made in data integration technologies, revolutionizing how organizations manage and leverage vast and diverse datasets. One of the significant breakthroughs is the widespread adoption of cloud computing for data integration. Cloud-based solutions offer unparalleled scalability, flexibility, and accessibility, allowing organizations to integrate data seamlessly across geographically dispersed systems. With cloud services, companies can harness the power of distributed computing to process and integrate data efficiently, reducing the need for extensive on-premises infrastructure.

Machine learning and AI have also emerged as game-changers in the field of data integration. These technologies enable intelligent automation in the data integration process, from identifying patterns and relationships within the data to automating data mapping and transformation tasks. ML algorithms can learn from historical integration patterns and adapt to evolving data structures, enhancing the adaptability and efficiency of integration workflows.

Additionally, AI-driven data integration tools can automate the discovery and classification of data, making it easier to understand and manipulate. These advancements not only streamline the data integration process but also contribute to more accurate and insightful analyses by revealing hidden patterns and trends within integrated datasets. As organizations continue to explore the potential of these cutting-edge technologies, the landscape of data integration is poised for further innovation and efficiency gains.

Real-Time Data Integration

Real-time data integration has become a critical component of the modern data landscape, enabling organizations to make timely and informed decisions based on up-to-the-minute information. Unlike traditional batch processing, real-time data integration involves the immediate processing and transfer of data as it is generated, allowing organizations to respond swiftly to changing conditions. This capability is particularly crucial in industries such as finance, e-commerce, and healthcare, where decisions are often time-sensitive and require the most current data available. Real-time data integration is achieved through the implementation of event-driven architectures and stream processing technologies, which enable the continuous flow of data from source to destination in near real time.

The benefits of real-time data integration extend beyond timely decision-making. Organizations can gain a competitive edge by providing customers with dynamic and personalized experiences based on their current interactions and behaviors. For example, in the realm of online retail, real-time integration allows instant updates on product availability, pricing changes, and customer preferences. Moreover, industries such as logistics and supply chain management benefit from real-time insights into inventory levels and shipment status, enabling more efficient operations and reducing the risk of disruptions. While real-time data integration poses technical challenges, such as managing data consistency and ensuring low-latency processing, its advantages in terms of agility and responsiveness make it an indispensable strategy for organizations operating in today's fast-paced business environment.

Governance, Security, and Privacy

Data governance and security are crucial aspects of successful data integration initiatives. Data governance involves establishing policies, standards, and procedures for managing data throughout its lifecycle. It ensures data quality, defines ownership and responsibilities, and enforces consistency across disparate sources. Robust data governance frameworks mitigate the risk of errors and inconsistencies, ensuring compliance with regulatory requirements and safeguarding sensitive information.

Security is paramount in data integration to protect against unauthorized access and ensure the confidentiality of integrated datasets. Encryption protocols, access controls, and authentication mechanisms are essential components of a secure data integration strategy. Access should be granted based on the principle of least privilege to limit exposure to sensitive data.

Monitoring and auditing data access and integration processes are essential to detect and respond to unauthorized activities promptly. With the increasing prevalence of cyber threats, maintaining a robust security framework is indispensable to safeguard data integrity and instill confidence in stakeholders.

Overall, effective data governance and security measures are essential for successful data integration, ensuring reliability, confidentiality, and compliance while protecting against potential risks and threats.

TOOLS, PROCESSES, AND FRAMEWORKS

The right combination of tools, processes, and frameworks is essential for harnessing the full potential of data analytics. These elements provide the structure and capabilities needed to streamline workflows, ensure accuracy, and drive actionable insights effectively.

Data Profiling and Cleansing Tools

Data profiling tools can be used to analyze and understand the characteristics of data from various sources. Data cleansing tools can be implemented to address inconsistencies, inaccuracies, and missing values. By proactively identifying and rectifying data quality issues, organizations can enhance the overall integrity of integrated datasets.

Standardization and Normalization Processes

Standardized data formats and normalization processes should be established to handle variability in data structures. Common data models and mapping rules should be defined to ensure consistency across disparate sources. This approach facilitates smoother integration by providing a unified framework for handling diverse data formats.

Middleware and Integration Platforms

Investment should be made in middleware solutions and integration platforms that support interoperability between different systems and technologies. These platforms often include prebuilt connectors and adapters for popular data sources, simplifying the integration process. They also provide tools for data transformation and mapping, making it easier to bridge the gap between incompatible systems.

Data Governance Frameworks

Comprehensive data governance frameworks should be implemented to manage data throughout its lifecycle. Data ownership and policies for data usage and enforcement of data quality standards should be established. A well-defined data governance strategy helps organizations maintain control over their data assets and ensures that integrated datasets adhere to established standards.

Security Protocols and Access Controls

Robust security measures should be implemented to safeguard data during the integration process. Encryption should be utilized for data in transit and at rest. Access controls based on the principle of least privilege should be implemented, and regular security audits should be conducted. Addressing security concerns is essential for maintaining the confidentiality and integrity of integrated data, especially when dealing with sensitive information.

Scalable Architectures and Performance Tuning

Scalable architectures that can handle growing data volumes should be designed. Consider distributed computing frameworks and cloud-based solutions for elasticity and flexibility. Additionally, integration processes can be optimized through performance tuning, caching mechanisms, and parallel processing to ensure efficient handling of large datasets in real-time or batch scenarios.

DATA QUALITY

Ensuring data quality is fundamental to the success of any analytics or business intelligence initiative. High-quality data provides a reliable foundation for insights, enabling accurate decision-making and fostering organizational trust in analytical outcomes.

Key Principles and Challenges

Achieving reliable and effective information within systems necessitates adherence to key principles and addressing various challenges. Data quality stands as a cornerstone, encompassing principles such as accuracy, completeness, relevance, trustworthiness, and timeliness, crucial across the entire system architecture. Common data quality issues such as missing data, incorrect types, duplicates, inconsistent values, and flawed relationships undermine these principles.

Neglected data cleaning processes result in inaccurate reports, eroding trust in system outputs and diminishing confidence, thereby affecting the credibility and usability of the analytics infrastructure. Corrupted data introduces risks, leading to flawed decision-making and increased maintenance costs. Notably, data redundancy exacerbates inefficiencies and confusion, while legal and compliance issues may arise, posing additional risks.

Various factors contribute to data quality problems, spanning technical and nontechnical realms. Technical challenges encompass inadequate control or management of databases and applications, poor design, errors in the ETL processes, and procedural deficiencies. Nontechnical factors include business changes such as mergers and acquisitions, organizational restructuring, alterations in business rules, and a lack of ownership and control over data.

Moreover, the integration of systems and applications over time, changes in applications, modifications in processes, workarounds, absence of standards, violations of business rules, data entry errors, incorrect population of fields, data purging, and system conversions over time add to the complexity of data quality challenges.

Addressing these issues requires data quality accountability and implementing application validity checks to mitigate technical and nontechnical factors. Recognizing and mitigating these challenges are crucial in establishing robust data quality management practices.

In summary, by acknowledging the importance of adhering to key principles and addressing the myriad challenges, organizations can pave the way for more reliable and effective data within their systems, thereby enhancing decision-making processes and overall operational efficiency.

Characteristics of Good Quality Data

Quality data embodies various attributes, collectively defining its excellence. Numerous characteristics contribute to this definition. Some attributes consistently associated with good quality data include accuracy, which ensures precision and error-free information. Completeness signifies the presence of all required data. Conformity emphasizes adherence to established standards and formats. Consistency is essential for maintaining uniformity and coherence throughout the dataset. Integrity reflects reliability and accuracy in data relationships.

Timeliness and availability underscore the importance of up-to-date and readily accessible data. Moreover, auditability allows for traceability and examination of data changes. Relevance ensures alignment with the intended purpose. Being understood and trusted by users highlights the necessity for end-users to have clarity and reliability. A lack of duplication prevents redundant entries, and presentation quality ensures that the data is presented in a clear and comprehensible manner. These individual characteristics collectively contribute to the overall quality of data, playing a pivotal role in its effectiveness and utility.

In an era where organizations increasingly rely on data-driven decision-making, adhering to these quality characteristics becomes imperative for maintaining the integrity and value of the information within datasets.

Data Quality Improvement Benefits

Improving data quality yields a multitude of benefits that positively impact various aspects of organizational operations. These advantages encompass enhanced confidence in the accuracy and integrity of the data, fostering a greater sense of trust and reliance on the information at hand. Higher reliability is a direct outcome, ensuring that the data can be consistently counted on for decision-making and strategic planning. This, in turn, contributes to reduced risk, as decision-makers can make informed choices based on dependable data.

In addition to these reliability and risk reduction benefits, improved data quality leads to decreased maintenance efforts. The need for extensive data clean-up and correction activities is minimized, allowing resources to be allocated more efficiently. Higher productivity ensues as employees can devote their time and effort to value-adding tasks rather than addressing data quality issues. This, coupled with reduced risk and improved reliability, contributes to overall customer satisfaction.

Furthermore, streamlined data quality positively impacts reconciliation processes, requiring less time and effort to align and verify discrepancies in the data. The ultimate goal of achieving "one version of the truth" is thereby advanced, fostering a cohesive and unified understanding of organizational data across all stakeholders.

IMPROVING DATA QUALITY

Improving data quality is essential for maximizing the effectiveness of analytics and decision-making processes. By addressing inconsistencies, inaccuracies, and gaps, organizations can ensure their data is trustworthy, actionable, and aligned with business objectives.

Data Cleansing

The preparation of source data for integration into the target system involves a crucial phase known as data cleansing or scrubbing. This preparatory task is imperative for eliminating errors commonly present in source systems and ensuring the integrity and accuracy of the data in the target system. The data cleansing process encompasses several essential steps, including identifying redundant data, correcting or deleting inaccurate or corrupt records, rectifying erroneous values in fields, populating fields with missing values, and standardizing formats. The techniques employed in this process span parsing, data transformation, elimination of duplicates, and the application of statistical methods to enhance the overall data quality.

The efficiency of data cleansing directly influences the occurrence of loading errors during the transition from the source to the target database. A noteworthy correlation exists between the amount of effort invested in data cleansing and the subsequent reduction in expected errors. Generally, a more substantial investment in data cleansing efforts results in a lower incidence of errors during the data migration process, emphasizing the pivotal role of meticulous data preparation in achieving accurate and reliable outcomes in the target system.

Fostering Data Quality Excellence

Improving data quality encompasses a range of strategies and initiatives. This involves emphasizing the critical significance of data quality within an organization and ensuring the active involvement of management in endorsing and supporting data quality efforts. The establishment of data standards and procedures plays a pivotal role, providing a structured framework for maintaining consistency and accuracy. Initiating performance evaluation criteria helps gauge and incentivize efforts toward enhancing data quality. Assigning data ownership ensures accountability and responsibility for data integrity.

Using appropriate tools and techniques, such as data cleansing and validation tools, is instrumental in effectively addressing quality issues. Providing comprehensive training equips personnel with the necessary skills and knowledge to contribute to data quality improvements. Collaboration between business and IT stakeholders is essential for aligning data quality efforts with organizational objectives. Conducting regular data audits helps identify and rectify discrepancies. Employing a methodology that prioritizes data-driven decision-making reinforces a culture of data quality. Leveraging new data-oriented technologies, such as master data management (MDM), contributes to more advanced and holistic approaches to managing data quality challenges.

Data Quality and MDM

MDM serves as a comprehensive tool focused on managing master data at the enterprise level, deviating from traditional maintenance approaches within transaction systems. This shift enables the creation of a consistent and unified view of data and performance throughout the entire enterprise.

In the realm of business intelligence, MDM introduces a range of benefits. It enhances data governance by effectively managing master data entities, providing a centralized mechanism for oversight. Through data profiling, MDM aids in identifying potential data quality issues, shedding light on areas that require attention. Notably, it plays a crucial role in identifying the costs associated with maintaining inaccurate or incomplete data and highlights the potential cost benefits achievable by rectifying these data issues.

Moreover, MDM significantly contributes to improved business insight by offering a reliable tool for addressing and fixing data issues. The efficiency gains are evident through cost reduction, simplification of master data processes, and enhanced control over business processes. Automation is increased, reducing the need for manual work in reconciliation and data fixes. The optimization of services, improvement in analysis, faster analysis capabilities, risk reduction, enhanced regulatory compliance, increased confidence in data accuracy, and improved global capabilities further underscore the multifaceted advantages of integrating MDM into a business intelligence environment.

Data Cleansing Tools

The landscape of data cleansing tools can be broadly divided into two main categories: data error discovery tools and data correction tools. Data error discovery tools primarily focus on identifying inaccurate and inconsistent data, serving as the first line of defense against data quality issues. Data correction tools specialize in rectifying corrupted data, addressing inaccuracies, and ensuring the integrity of the dataset.

Within these categories, a variety of tools are available, each tailored to specific aspects of data cleansing. Notably, many of these tools exhibit dual functionality, excelling in one category while concurrently performing functions in the other. This dual capability underscores the versatility of modern data cleansing tools, allowing organizations to tackle both the identification and correction aspects of data quality management. As a result, these tools play a pivotal role in ensuring the reliability, accuracy, and consistency of data across various organizational systems and processes.

Data Validation

The process of loading data into a target system is a crucial step in the data management lifecycle, but it carries inherent risks, as the imported data may be defective. Data validation becomes a pivotal task, encompassing a comprehensive examination of the imported data to ensure its accuracy, consistency, completeness, and readiness for utilization within the target system to mitigate potential issues post-implementation.

Data validation holds significant importance because it acts as a proactive measure for forestalling serious problems that may arise after the system goes live. This verification process involves a range of checks, including ensuring data accuracy against predefined standards, confirming consistency with existing datasets, validating completeness in terms of required fields, and verifying overall compliance with established business rules. The nature and extent of these validation procedures can vary across different implementations, reflecting the diversity in data structures, formats, and unique business requirements.

By performing rigorous data validation, organizations establish a robust safeguard against potential data-related challenges, allowing for the identification and rectification of discrepancies before the data is actively utilized in the target system. This meticulous approach not only enhances the overall quality of the data but also contributes to a smoother transition into the operational phase of the system, minimizing risks and optimizing the functionality of the implemented data management solution.

Resources for Data Clean-up and Validation

A considerable amount of effort is required to clean and validate data before it is made available to the analytics system. Since this task is frequently neglected or underestimated, insufficient resources are allocated to the clean-up and validation tasks. This has often created problems during the implementation phase as well as during operations. In many cases, failure to address this task adequately has caused serious reliability and operational problems after a rollout because queries based on incorrect data produced inconsistent and unreliable results.

CHAPTER 6

GOVERNANCE, SECURITY, PRIVACY, AND ETHICS

DATA GOVERNANCE

Need for Governance

The significance of data quality in BI is closely intertwined with the need for effective governance. In BI, the integrity and reliability of data are paramount, as decisions are driven by the insights derived from this information. Data quality ensures that the data used for analysis, reporting, and decision-making is accurate, consistent, and trustworthy. Achieving and maintaining data quality requires a structured governance framework.

Data governance involves establishing policies, processes, and controls to ensure data accuracy, integrity, and security throughout its lifecycle. By implementing robust governance practices, organizations can systematically address issues related to data quality, enforce standards, and create a framework for accountability. This not only safeguards the accuracy of BI outputs but also fosters a culture of responsible data management, enabling organizations to derive maximum value from their BI initiatives and instill confidence in the decision-making process.

Data Governance Policies

Establishing data governance policies is a foundational step in ensuring the effective management and utilization of organizational data. Data governance involves developing and implementing policies, procedures, and standards to guide the collection, storage, processing, and sharing of data across an organization. These policies are designed to maintain data quality, integrity, and security, addressing issues such as accuracy, consistency, and compliance with regulatory requirements.

Key components of data governance policies include defining data ownership, outlining data stewardship responsibilities, specifying data quality standards, and establishing protocols for data access and usage. Successful data governance policies are comprehensive, align with the organization's overall business objectives, and involve collaboration across departments to ensure a unified and consistent approach to data management. By laying the groundwork through well-defined governance policies, organizations can foster a data-driven culture, enhance decision-making processes, and build trust in their data assets.

SECURITY

Security is a critical aspect of BI systems, given the sensitive nature of the data involved. Protecting BI assets, such as reports, dashboards, and underlying datasets, is paramount for preventing unauthorized access, data breaches, and potential misuse. Authentication mechanisms, including robust user authentication and access controls, play a vital role in ensuring that only authorized personnel can access specific BI resources. Encryption is another key security measure for safeguarding data during transmission and storage. BI platforms often implement role-based access controls, limiting user privileges based on their roles within the organization, which helps maintain the confidentiality and integrity of sensitive information.

Furthermore, audit trails and monitoring features are crucial for detecting and responding to potential security incidents. BI systems should provide comprehensive logging of user activities, allowing administrators to track who accessed what information and when. Regular security assessments, including vulnerability scanning and penetration testing, contribute to identifying and addressing potential weaknesses in the BI infrastructure.

Security in BI extends beyond technical measures; it involves educating users about best practices, fostering a security-aware culture within the organization, and ensuring compliance with data protection regulations. A holistic approach to security not only protects sensitive business information but also establishes trust in the BI system, encouraging its effective and secure use across the enterprise.

PRIVACY

Privacy is a critical dimension in the BI landscape as organizations navigate the complexities of handling vast amounts of data to extract meaningful insights. BI processes involve collecting, processing, and analyzing diverse datasets, often including personal information. Safeguarding individual privacy is essential, and organizations must adhere to robust privacy measures and compliance standards. This involves implementing stringent data protection policies, ensuring secure data storage and transmission, and obtaining explicit consent when dealing with sensitive information.

An inherent challenge in BI is balancing the need for detailed insights with privacy concerns. Striking this balance requires adopting privacy-by-design principles, where privacy considerations are integrated into the entire BI lifecycle. Anonymizing or pseudonymizing data, implementing access controls, and employing encryption techniques are strategies for protecting individual privacy.

Moreover, organizations need to stay abreast of evolving privacy regulations and adapt their BI practices accordingly to comply with frameworks such as the General Data Protection Regulation (GDPR) or the California Consumer Privacy Act (CCPA). By prioritizing privacy as a fundamental aspect of BI strategy, organizations not only meet regulatory requirements but also build trust with their stakeholders, fostering a responsible and ethical approach to data-driven decision-making.

ETHICS

Ethics play a pivotal role in the realm of BI, shaping responsible practices in data collection, analysis, and decision-making. As organizations harness BI to extract insights from vast datasets, ethical considerations become paramount for ensuring the fair and just treatment of individuals and the responsible use of information. One key ethical concern involves privacy, emphasizing the importance of obtaining informed consent when collecting personal data and ensuring that data is anonymized or de-identified when appropriate. Transparent communication with stakeholders regarding how their data will be used and the potential impact on them is essential in maintaining ethical standards.

Moreover, ethical BI practices involve addressing bias and discrimination in data analysis. BI algorithms and models can inadvertently perpetuate existing biases present in historical data, leading to unfair outcomes. Ethical BI involves constant scrutiny of algorithms to identify and mitigate biases, promoting fairness and equality.

Organizations must prioritize inclusivity and diversity in their BI processes, considering the potential social implications of their analytics. Establishing ethical guidelines and governance frameworks within the BI strategy is crucial for fostering a culture of responsibility, ensuring that organizations not only achieve their analytical goals but also uphold ethical standards in the evolving landscape of data-driven decision-making.

CHAPTER 7

DATA WAREHOUSING

BACKGROUND

Objective

A data warehouse aims to serve as a central repository for storing, managing, and analyzing vast volumes of data from disparate sources within an organization. Unlike transactional databases focused on day-to-day operations, a data warehouse is designed with a strategic perspective, emphasizing the consolidation and integration of data for business intelligence purposes. The primary goal is to provide decision-makers with a unified and consistent view of the organization's data, supporting both historical and current perspectives. By structuring data in a way that facilitates efficient querying and reporting, a data warehouse enables users to extract valuable insights, identify trends, and make informed decisions, contributing to the organization's overall strategic objectives.

Definition

The term *business data warehouse* was coined in the late 1980s by IBM researchers Barry Devlin and Paul Murphy. According to Bill Inmon, better known as the father of data warehousing, "a data warehouse is a subject-oriented, integrated, nonvolatile, and time-variant collection of data in support of management's decisions."

In practical terms, a data warehouse is a large analytical database populated from various source systems that typically run a business. It acts as the corporate centralized repository where consistent, detailed, summarized, current, and historical data is stored. It contains transaction as well as nontransaction data and is designed for querying, reporting, and analysis. The data in a data warehouse can be accessed flexibly and interactively using a variety of front-end, easy-to-use data-access and mining tools.

Evolution of Information Processing Requirements

The task of obtaining meaningful data or information from early computer systems used to be tedious. Consequently, a number of methods, techniques, and tools were developed to solve that problem. They included decentralized processing, extract processing, executive information systems (EIS), query tools, relational databases, and so on. The need for timely and accurate decisions also led to the development of decision support systems, ranging from simple to very sophisticated systems. The data warehouse is a tool in this evolution, which started becoming popular about three decades ago.

Evolution of Data Chaos

Traditional business applications were designed and developed with the objective of helping specific departments or functions such as marketing, human resources, finance, manufacturing, and loan processing. Since such applications were typically developed independently and without coordination, they often collected redundant data over a period of time. Additionally, the data available from these applications, which were often developed on different platforms, was incompatible and inconsistent. Consequently, there was poor data management, enterprise view of data was lacking, and, frequently, a query returned different answers depending on the application that was accessed and analyzed.

What made the situation even worse, especially after 1981, when personal computers were developed, was the explosion in the number of systems as well as the quantity and type of data being collected. The loss of a central data repository coincided with the widespread demand for more timely information.

Limitations of OLTP Systems

Online transaction processing systems (OLTPs) were developed to capture and store data from business operations. Since robustness was their top priority, rather than reporting or user accessibility, they suffered from several serious limitations. Their most obvious shortcomings were the inability to address the business users' need to access stored transaction data and management decision support requirements in a timely manner. OLTPs also did not address history and summarization requirements or support integration needs—the ability to analyze data across different systems and/or platforms.

Evolution of Data Warehousing

The failure of OLTP systems to provide decision support ultimately led to the data warehousing concept in the late 1980s. Its objective, in contrast to OLTP systems, was to extract information instead of capturing and storing data, and hence, it became a strategic tool for decision-makers. In the past three decades, data warehousing has attempted to become the foundation of corporate-wide business reporting and analytics by becoming the enterprise information hub for supporting both tactical and strategic decision-making.

Decentralization to Centralization with a Twist

In a way, the data warehouse concept involved traversing a full circle. After the personal computer was invented, islands of data sprouted in an independent move away from the centralized mainframe concept. The data warehouse, which collected data stored in disparate systems, was a return to the centralized concept. A key difference exists. A data warehouse enables enterprise and local decision support needs to be met while permitting independent data islands to continue flourishing. It provides a central validated data repository that can provide "one version of the truth" while supporting the satellite systems that it feeds.

Architecture

In terms of architecture, a data warehouse typically follows a multitiered structure. An ETL process is employed to extract data from various sources, transform it into a consistent format, and load it into the data warehouse. The data is then organized into a dimensional model or a star schema, which involves structuring the data into fact tables containing metrics and dimension tables providing context. This architecture facilitates efficient data retrieval and analysis. Additionally, data warehouses often incorporate data marts, which are subsets of the larger warehouse focused on specific business areas, further enhancing the agility and relevance of data for end-users. Overall, the architecture of a data warehouse is intricately designed to support the analytical needs of the organization and its decision-makers.

Role of Data Warehouses in BI

Data warehouses play a pivotal role in the realm of BI, serving as the backbone for effective decision-making and strategic analysis within organizations. By acting as a centralized repository, a data warehouse consolidates data from various sources, both internal and external, into a cohesive and standardized format. This integration allows for the creation of a comprehensive and unified view of organizational data, encompassing historical, current, and detailed information.

The structured nature of data warehouses facilitates efficient querying, reporting, and analysis, providing decision-makers with the tools to extract meaningful insights. By enabling users to access and analyze data from diverse sources through user-friendly interfaces, data warehouses empower organizations to make informed decisions, identify trends, and uncover valuable patterns. This strategic use of data, facilitated by data warehouses, enhances the agility and responsiveness of businesses in adapting to dynamic market conditions, ultimately contributing to the success and competitiveness of the organization in the business intelligence landscape.

Benefits

Data warehouses offer a multitude of benefits that extend beyond the broader advantages of business intelligence. First, data warehouses establish a common data model across the enterprise despite drawing data from diverse sources. This standardized representation facilitates seamless reporting and analysis, fostering consistency in data interpretation. Furthermore, ensuring the trustworthiness of the data within a data warehouse is a crucial advantage. Rigorous cleaning and validation processes ensure that reports and analyses run against this data are reliable, instilling confidence in decision-makers.

Another significant benefit lies in the long-term storage capabilities of data warehouses. The extended retention of historical data enables organizations to conduct trending and historical comparisons over extended periods. This proves invaluable for identifying patterns, understanding long-term trends, and making informed decisions based on a comprehensive historical context. Additionally, data retrieval in a data warehouse is optimized for efficiency, in contrast to operational systems that prioritize data writing. This efficiency ensures swift query execution, contributing to a more responsive and agile decision-making process.

Finally, the ability of data warehouses to integrate with other critical applications, such as ERP and CRM systems, underscores their role as central components in the organizational ecosystem. This interoperability enhances the overall functionality and utility of data warehouses, positioning them as indispensable tools for organizations seeking robust data-driven decision-making.

In summary, the identified benefits collectively emphasize the pivotal role of data warehouses in providing a reliable, integrated, and efficient platform for comprehensive data analysis and strategic decision-making.

Shortcomings

Data warehouses, while offering significant advantages, are not without their shortcomings. One notable drawback lies in the temporal misalignment of the data due to the ETL process. This process, often executed on a daily schedule, leads to a lag in data currency between the data warehouse and the OLTP systems feeding it. Consequently, reports generated in these different systems may yield disparate results. This misalignment is typically manageable through user training and awareness of the loading schedule. Another limitation pertains to the handling of data types, where data warehouses excel in structured data but exhibit limitations or even the absence of support for unstructured data.

The implementation and maintenance costs of enterprise data warehouse systems are considerable, rendering them expensive endeavors. The complexity and expenses associated with these systems pose challenges, particularly in a business landscape characterized by rapid changes. The need for agility in adapting to swift business changes can be hindered by the inherent difficulty in implementing quick modifications, from both technical and business perspectives. Despite these shortcomings, organizations can navigate these challenges through strategic planning, user education, and a thorough understanding of the limitations inherent in data warehousing systems.

TYPES OF DATA WAREHOUSES

There are three types of data warehouses:

- enterprise data warehouse
- data mart
- operational data store

Enterprise Data Warehouse

An enterprise data warehouse (EDW) contains data extracted from an organization's different systems, such as ERP and CRM, which run its business. A typical company can have anywhere from five to twenty systems feeding its EDW. Such an EDW contains detailed transaction data as well as summarized data. The data stored in such a data warehouse, which is organized according to subjects such as sales or inventory, can range from a couple of years to more than twenty years. This period is determined by the organization's business requirements. The volume of data stored in an EDW can range in the hundreds of gigabytes or terabytes. Many data warehouses now contain data volumes that are in the petabyte range.

Data Mart

A data mart is a focused subset of a data warehouse that is designed to meet the specific analytical needs of a particular business unit, department, or group within an organization. It serves as a smaller, more specialized repository of data that is extracted, transformed, and loaded from the larger EDW or directly from source systems. Unlike a comprehensive data warehouse that caters to the entire organization, a data mart is tailored to the requirements of a particular user group or business function.

Data marts are typically organized around specific subject areas, such as sales, marketing, finance, or human resources. This thematic organization enables users within a specific domain to access and analyze data relevant to their operations without the complexity of navigating the entire EDW. By providing a more focused and simplified view of the data, data marts enhance the efficiency and responsiveness of analytical processes.

Organizations often choose to implement data marts to improve accessibility, promote user autonomy, and streamline the analytical workflow for specific business units, thereby facilitating quicker and more targeted decision-making.

Operational Data Store

An operational data store (ODS) functions as a dynamic and subject-oriented database that plays a pivotal role in managing structured data extracted directly from operational systems, commonly referred to as OLTP systems. Unlike traditional data warehouses, an ODS primarily holds current or nearly real-time data, providing a valuable resource for meeting the ad hoc querying and day-to-day tactical needs of operational users. Its subject-oriented nature allows it to cater to specific business areas, facilitating a focused and streamlined approach to accessing data within operational environments.

Crucially, an ODS operates independently of the production system database, maintaining autonomy and separation to ensure a dedicated space for operational data. This independence positions the ODS as a staging area in the data integration process, serving as an intermediary step before the data is seamlessly imported into a data warehouse. This dual functionality underscores its importance in the broader context of data management, acting both as a real-time analytics resource and a critical component in the ETL pipeline.

Unlike static data warehouses, an ODS is designed for frequent updates, even in real-time, directly from operational systems. This dynamic characteristic enables it to stay closely aligned with the ever-evolving data landscape within operational settings, ensuring that it remains a responsive and adaptive component in the overall data architecture.

Data Warehouse Applications

Data warehousing has become increasingly pervasive, evolving into a mainstream practice applied across diverse industries and functions. Both small enterprises and large corporations embrace data warehousing as an integral component of their data management strategies. This widespread adoption is driven by the recognition of the transformative impact it can have on various business facets.

The implementation of data warehouses aligns seamlessly with the broad spectrum of applications encompassed by business intelligence. Organizations are leveraging data warehouses for a myriad of purposes, spanning operational and strategic reporting, multidimensional analysis, forecasting, trend analysis, and a range of specialized domains. From enhancing marketing and sales strategies to refining financial operations, customer profiling, fraud analysis, and optimizing logistics, data warehousing has emerged as a versatile tool that empowers businesses to extract valuable insights and drive informed decision-making across a multitude of functions. As a result, the integration of data warehousing has become synonymous with the pursuit of data-driven excellence across the entire business landscape.

DESIGN OBJECTIVE

OLTP systems are designed to handle high volumes of transactional data efficiently, ensuring real-time processing and data integrity for daily business operations. Data warehouse systems, on the other hand, aim to support analytical tasks by consolidating data from various sources and optimizing it for complex queries and reporting.

OLTP Systems

An OLTP relational database is a collection of two-dimensional tables, which are organized into rows and columns. In such a database, the design objective is to optimize table structures by eliminating all instances of data redundancy. This is achieved through normalization techniques, making database tables as small as possible and, when needed, merging selected tables through joins. Therefore, such a system contains a very large number of small tables in which there is minimum data redundancy.

Data Warehouse Systems

In a data warehouse, the design objective is the opposite of that of an OLTP system. The aim is to make more of the data available in fewer tables, with considerable redundancy that makes the database tables very large, which minimizes the need for table joins when a query is executed. The objective is to enable a query to find most of its required data in a single table, reducing the volume of data that must be pulled from other tables. The technique of merging small tables into larger tables with data redundancy, called de-normalization, causes fewer input/output operations, which improves query performance. De-normalization, while suitable for a data warehouse, is not appropriate for a transaction database that emphasizes performance over query processing.

CHARACTERISTICS

Basic Data Warehouse Characteristics

A data warehouse, as described by Bill Inmon, is characterized by four unique data characteristics:

- subject-oriented
- integrated
- time variant
- nonvolatile

Subject-Oriented Characteristic

The data in a data warehouse is organized according to subjects such as customer, vendor, bookings, billings, sales, orders, and products. This contrasts with classical applications that are organized by business functions such as loans, finance, and inventory. In a data warehouse, the major subject areas are physically implemented as a series of related database tables. A data warehouse can contain a few, scores, or even hundreds of subject areas, depending on how widely it has been implemented across the enterprise.

Integrated Characteristic

Data in a data warehouse is always integrated—without any exception. The source data from multiple systems is consolidated in a data warehouse after undergoing various operations such as extraction, transformation, and loading. The data imported from the source systems reflects integration through consistent naming conventions, data attributes, data definitions, measurements, and so on. A data warehouse can contain data integrated from a few or even hundreds of systems, depending on how widely it has been implemented within the enterprise.

Time Variant Characteristic

The data stored within a data warehouse represents a snapshot of information at a particular moment in time, while transaction data is accurate at the moment of access. The data in a data warehouse consists of a lengthy series of snapshots at various points in time, which can cover a very lengthy period of fifteen to twenty years. In contrast, typical transaction databases contain data for only a six to twenty-four month period. The time-variant characteristic enables data to be trended over various periods. It also enables data to be compared over different periods, such as revenue growth year over year or changes in the average selling prices month over month.

Nonvolatile Characteristic

The data stored in a data warehouse remains static, i.e., read-only. Any new data, which is typically introduced periodically, is appended. The data warehouse data is subjected to regular access and analysis. Activities such as insertions and deletions, which occur routinely with operational systems, do not occur in a data warehouse, which is initially populated through a massive data load from the source systems followed by periodic appends. After data has been introduced into a data warehouse, users can only analyze it—not change it. The only time data is changed in a data warehouse is when a data error is discovered and needs to be rectified.

OLTP VERSUS DATA WAREHOUSE DATABASES

OLTP systems are primarily used to run a company's business. They are transaction-based and support business applications such as procurement, inventory, sales, order management, accounting, and human resources. Such systems require fast access, which is usually predefined, to the database where the data is stored.

Alternatively, data warehouses focus on analytics, including multi-dimensional data analysis and the ability to run ad hoc reports. Such systems are flexible and provide the ability to drill-down, slice and dice, and so on. While the operational systems and applications are performance-driven, data warehouses require flexibility rather than speed.

Furthermore, the characteristics of OLTP data and data warehouse data are also quite different. For example, the characteristics that define data warehouse data include high redundancy, flexible structure, large data volumes, analysis and management-oriented, and ad hoc access. This is in contrast to OLTP data, which is defined by detailed data that is transaction-driven, updated continuously, has smaller data volumes, no redundancy, and high availability and reliability.

Characteristics of an OLTP Database

An OLTP database contains detailed transaction data collected from the organization's business operations. Although such a database may contain some derived data calculated from the basic data elements, it primarily comprises basic data elements at the lowest granular level. For example, the primary element can be the sales price, while the derived data can be the item's average sales price over a period of time.

An OLTP transaction database runs the business and is optimized for update functions—not for querying and analysis. Its data is structured and organized so that it favors performance and speed for capturing business transactions (through normalization and an entity-relationship model), reliability, data integrity, and security. The database contains small tables because it has to capture data efficiently, as performance is an overriding factor. An OLTP database collects a large volume of raw transaction data that cannot be analyzed easily. Such a database does not address the decision support requirements of history, summarization, integration, or metadata.

OLTP systems are not used as repositories of historical data, which is required for analyzing trends. Typically, such systems have inconsistent, dynamic (rapidly changing), and duplicate and/or missing entries. Additionally, the data in transaction databases is not in a form that is meaningful to end-users.

Characteristics of a Data Warehouse Database

A data warehouse database contains transaction data that has been restructured and de-normalized for querying and analysis. It contains detailed, granular data, derived data, and aggregated data. The availability of detailed data permits drill-down to be performed if there is a need to dig deeper after the summarized data has been reviewed. For example, a manager can initially analyze the bookings or sales for the region and, subsequently, selectively drill-down into the details of any under-performing region. Another key difference is that the data warehouse data is historical and, therefore, time-dependent. Its data elements need to be associated with time, which is part of the key for every record in the database.

Data warehouse tables are very large, contain redundant data, and need to be refreshed periodically from multiple sources. Data warehouses are optimized for fast query processing, and access is on an ad hoc basis rather than through a predefined method.

Database Differences

OLTPs or operational databases primarily handle detailed transaction data, possibly incorporating some derived data. These databases are optimized for running daily business transactions and structured for speed, performance, and security. Data warehouses go beyond transactions, encompassing derived and summarized data. With the ability to drill-down and perform trend analysis, they support the exploration of data beyond individual points, associating a time element with each data element.

OLTP databases serve daily business operations, offering application-specific data, while data warehouses focus on data retrieval and analysis. The former deals with constantly changing data, whereas the latter integrates historical and descriptive data. OLTP databases are organized for performance, utilizing a normalized data model, whereas data warehouses adopt a multidimensional model with fewer but larger tables.

Queries in OLTP databases are predefined and optimized for speed, while data warehouse queries are more flexible, allowing unplanned analysis with a focus on trends rather than instantaneous data points. The inclusion of the time element in the structure distinguishes data warehouses from operational databases.

Contrasting Design Requirements

The diverse requirements of operational databases and data warehouses necessitate distinct design and operational characteristics. OLTP databases are structured for efficiency, speed, and security, optimizing the processing of daily business transactions. Conversely, data warehouses prioritize analytical queries, trends, and historical data, demanding a more flexible and integrated structure. These divergent needs under-score the necessity for different databases, each tailored to meet the specific demands of its designated function.

Data Storage in Data Warehouses

In data warehouses, the organization of data is a crucial aspect that directly influences their effectiveness in supporting analytical queries. Data is typically stored in a structured format, organized into tables representing different subject areas such as customers, products, or sales. These tables often follow a relational database model, facilitating the establishment of relationships among different data elements.

One distinctive feature of data warehousing is the use of de-nor-malization techniques. Unlike traditional operational databases that prioritize normalized structures to minimize redundancy, data ware-houses often intentionally incorporate redundancy. This de-normali-zation aids in query performance by reducing the need for complex joins and facilitating quicker data retrieval. Additionally, data ware-houses maintain historical snapshots, capturing changes over time and enabling trend analysis, a critical capability for deriving valuable insights from the stored information. Therefore, the storage design in data warehouses emphasizes the balance between structure, historical context, and performance optimization to support the diverse analyti-cal needs of users.

DESIGN

Designing a robust data warehousing system involves selecting archi-tectures and strategies that optimize data retrieval and support com-plex analytical queries. A well-thought-out design ensures efficient data organization and accessibility, laying the foundation for powerful insights and decision-making.

Star Schema

The star schema is a fundamental architecture in data warehousing that simplifies the organization and retrieval of information for analytical purposes. In this schema, data is structured into a central fact table, representing the core metrics or performance indicators, surrounded by dimension tables that provide context and additional details. The fact table serves as the focal point for queries, capturing quantitative data, while dimension tables hold descriptive attributes that categorize and characterize the information in the fact table. This straightforward arrangement facilitates efficient query processing, enabling users to swiftly navigate and analyze data, making the star schema a popular choice for data warehousing systems aiming to streamline complex analytics and reporting tasks.

Star Schema Characteristics

The star schema, a prevalent design in data warehousing, exhibits distinct characteristics that enhance analytical capabilities. It features a central fact table representing quantitative data, surrounded by dimension tables that provide context. This schema follows a de-normalized structure, allowing for data storage redundancy, promoting query efficiency. Each dimension table is linked to the fact table through primary-key and foreign-key relationships, establishing a clear and organized structure. The simplicity and ease of navigation make the star schema well-suited for complex analytics and reporting in data warehousing environments.

Star Schema Benefits

The star schema in data warehousing offers several advantages that contribute to efficient and effective analytical processes. Its simplicity and intuitive design facilitate ease of use, making it accessible for both business users and analysts. The clear distinction between the central fact table and surrounding dimension tables enhances query performance, enabling faster retrieval of information. Additionally, the de-normalized structure of the star schema minimizes the need for complex joins during queries, optimizing database performance. These benefits collectively make the star schema a preferred choice for businesses aiming to streamline their data analysis and reporting activities in a data warehousing environment.

Benefit of De-Normalization

In the realm of data warehousing, the strategy of de-normalization has emerged as a valuable technique for optimizing query performance and enhancing flexibility. In contrast to normalized transaction databases, which prioritize a structured, nonredundant approach, de-normalization introduces redundancy within expansive tables. This deliberate redundancy significantly diminishes the necessity for intricate joins when executing queries, leading to accelerated data retrieval. The advantage of de-normalization becomes particularly evident in data warehousing environments, where analytical processing and ad-hoc reporting demand a versatile and efficient approach.

It is essential to recognize that while de-normalization proves advantageous for data warehousing scenarios, it is not a universally recommended practice, especially for transactional databases. In transactional settings, where swift and efficient transaction processing takes precedence, maintaining a normalized database structure is preferred for upholding data consistency and avoiding complications associated with redundancy. The appropriateness of de-normalization hinges on the specific requirements and objectives of the database, aligning with its intended use and overarching goals.

PROCESS AND COMPONENTS

The process and components of data warehousing form the foundation for managing, storing, and accessing vast amounts of data to support analytics and decision-making. By integrating diverse activities and tools, this structured approach ensures that data is accurately transformed, stored, and made accessible for business insights.

Data Warehousing Process

Data warehousing is an integrated process that encompasses a variety of technologies and processes. The basic process involves extracting, manipulating, and moving data from different source systems into a central database, where it is stored and subsequently analyzed.

Data warehousing encompasses numerous activities, including planning, extraction, transformation, loading, data design and management, database design and implementation, development, implementation, reporting, security, operation, and maintenance.

Data Warehouse Process Components

The data warehouse process encompasses a variety of components categorized into three main groups. First, the acquisition component interfaces directly with source systems, facilitating the import of data into the data warehouse. This stage ensures seamless connectivity and extraction from diverse sources.

Next, the storage component comprises a substantial physical database dedicated to storing the data imported into the data warehouse. This storage infrastructure is crucial for efficiently managing and organizing the vast volume of data collected from various sources.

Access, the third component, incorporates front-end access and query tools designed to retrieve and analyze data stored within the data warehouse. These tools play a pivotal role in enabling users to interact with and derive insights from the comprehensive dataset housed in the data warehouse.

Acquisition Component

Sources

Data fed into a data warehouse can originate from many sources, although it is typically imported from an organization's transaction databases. The sources of different sizes can be mainframe files, relational and nonrelational databases, flat files, and so on. In the vast majority of cases, the source database is an OLTP system containing current transaction data. In some cases, the source is a non-OLTP database, such as a data warehouse or a data mart. Many organizations also use external sources to feed data into their data warehouses, such as financial, economic, and weather data.

Preimport Operations

Most of the data sources, internal and external, cannot meet the data warehouse requirement for imported data to be in a specific format—a layout that supports query processing. The reason for this limitation is that most data sources are formatted for transaction processing—not querying and analysis. Additionally, imported data is often inconsistent, dirty, and in a nonstandard format.

Therefore, before it can be loaded into a data warehouse, source data typically needs to undergo formatting and transformation operations to remove inconsistencies and achieve standardization. For example, gender in three source systems may be coded differently: M/F, male/female, and 1/2. Hence, before data from these three sources can be imported into a data warehouse, at least two must be transformed so that consistent data is fed into the target database from all three sources.

Acquisition Process

The data acquisition process involves identifying and physically acquiring data to be imported into a data warehouse from the source databases. During data acquisition, the data is extracted from the source(s) and transported to the target database. After acquiring the data, but before loading it into the target, various transformations occur, altering its characteristics. These transformations may include restructuring the data, de-normalizing the tables, and adding new fields and keys.

Prior to loading, the data undergoes operations such as consolidation (merging various datasets into a single master dataset), standardization (of data types and fields), scrubbing (cleaning to remove inconsistencies or inaccuracies), and summarization.

A diverse range of commercial tools is accessible to facilitate the extraction, transformation, and loading of source data into a data warehouse. These tools offer the ability to streamline and automate the complex processes involved in preparing and integrating data for efficient analysis within the data warehouse environment.

Storage Component

The storage component serves as the backbone of a data warehouse, providing a centralized repository for organizing and managing vast volumes of data. This infrastructure is crucial for ensuring data is readily available, efficiently structured, and optimized for analysis and reporting.

Source and Target Databases

There are two databases associated with a data warehouse:

- Source database: Database from where data is imported
- Target database: Database into which data is imported and stored

The core component of a data warehouse system is a very large target database. It stores the imported data in an integrated format. In this database, data is structured in a de-normalized format in contrast to the normalized structure of the source OLTP databases. The size of a target database can be huge, ranging into the terabyte range and, in some cases, even in the petabyte range.

Intermediate Database

While conceptually, only two databases are required (source and target) for a data warehouse, a third type of database is also used frequently. This is an intermediate database, an ODS, into which source data is loaded and staged before being sent to its final destination—the data warehouse (target database).

The ODS is often used for regular storage, just like the main data warehouse database, and not just as an intermediate staging database. In such cases, the ODS acts as an important architecture component that stores data in an OLTP format, against which a query can be executed directly. Whenever needed, the data stored in such an ODS can be used for analysis, often in conjunction with the data in the main data warehouse database. A data warehouse system can contain many ODSs.

Access Component

The access component is the interface between users and the data warehouse, enabling seamless retrieval and analysis of stored data. It incorporates tools and technologies that empower users to query, visualize, and derive actionable insights from the data, fostering informed decision-making.

Access Tools

The objective of an access tool in a data warehouse is to provide users with a means to interact with and retrieve information from the data warehouse. This component can include querying, reporting, and decision support tools. Such tools, which can include data mining software, can typically support queries, calculations, what-if analysis, and other advanced functions. Most data warehouse users use standard reports and queries. Only a small percentage of data warehouse users create ad hoc and custom reports, which are usually developed by business analysts, power/super users, and IT personnel.

Complexity of Data Access Tools

The complexity of data access tools varies significantly. They range from low-end tools with simple querying capabilities to high-end tools that can perform sophisticated multidimensional analyses. The simplest tool is MS Excel, while data mining tools are at the other end of the spectrum. Web-based tools are more versatile, easier to use, eliminate the need to install special software on every desktop, and provide access through a simple browser, which helps reduce costs as it requires less powerful and expensive hardware.

Front-end tools can be used by users at different ends of the skills spectrum and the corporate hierarchies, as they are quite versatile and able to cater to the needs of the diverse user base.

ARCHITECTURE

The architecture of a data warehouse serves as the foundational blueprint, outlining the structure and flow of data from sources to storage and ultimately to user access. It integrates various components and processes, ensuring efficient data management, scalability, and seamless interaction across the entire system.

Architecture Foundation

Ideally, data warehouse architecture should be designed within the context of the enterprise information architecture, which is based on the organization's information requirements that support the strategic goals of the enterprise. The foundation of enterprise information architecture is the enterprise data architecture, which is a fully normalized enterprise data model. The enterprise's technical architecture lays out the vision for the infrastructure, platforms, hardware, operating systems, and so on.

The business requirements should be used as the foundation for the architecture and, therefore, be reflected in the architecture and design of the data warehouse. Instead of specific technologies, these business requirements should be used as the basis for the enterprise data model and components. The architecture should be scalable, flexible, and reflect the need for analytical processing rather than transaction processing.

Architecture Drivers

The drivers influencing data warehouse architecture encompass various factors, including the existing infrastructure and systems, corporate strategy, and political considerations. Business and operational plans play a crucial role, as do emerging technologies and the evolving requirements of end-users. These diverse drivers collectively shape the data warehouse architecture, ensuring alignment with the organization's current state, strategic objectives, technological advancements, and the needs of its end-users.

Components

The data warehouse architecture is structured around four main components: the application layer, data, infrastructure (encompassing technology and security), and support (including processes and resources). These components collectively define the framework within which a data warehouse operates, ensuring seamless integration and efficient functioning.

Within the technical architecture of a data warehouse, numerous components contribute to its overall functionality. These include but are not limited to source inputs, ETL, DBMS, storage, middleware, communication, presentation, metadata management, administration, and security. Each of these elements plays a crucial role in the data warehouse's technical landscape, facilitating the flow of data, maintaining its integrity, and ensuring secure and efficient operations.

Architecture Objective

The overarching goal of the data warehouse architecture is to effectively cater to the strategic and operational information needs of the enterprise. Serving as the structural foundation, it acts as the cohesive force binding the three essential components of the data warehouse—data acquisition, data storage, and information delivery. This architectural framework is meticulously designed to ensure seamless coordination between these critical facets, facilitating a streamlined and comprehensive approach to handling the enterprise's data and enabling efficient information dissemination.

Infrastructure Components Supporting the Architecture

There are two basic infrastructure components required to support a data warehouse:

- physical infrastructure
- operational infrastructure

The physical infrastructure consists of various components, including the server and other hardware, operating system, DBMS, networks, network software, information delivery tools, and access hardware. The operational infrastructure includes the elements needed to implement and operate the data warehouse, which includes resources, procedures, support infrastructure, and so on.

Manifestation of Poor Architecture

Many data warehouse implementations fail because the system is built upon a poorly designed architecture. This can manifest in a number of ways, including deficiencies in schema, data access, ETL, network architecture, client/server architecture, and metadata. Creating a data warehouse based on flawed architecture is a very serious mistake because it is the most difficult and costly mistake to rectify once it has been implemented. Hence, it is imperative that a top-notch data warehouse architect be used to design the overall architecture.

Data Warehouse Application Architecture

The data warehouse application architecture comprises three components, or layers, that make up an application. They are:

- presentation (what the user sees—the client-side view)
- functional logic (underlying business rules)
- data (physical data storage layer)

Presentation Layer

This layer represents the user interface or the client-side view of the application. It includes components such as dashboards, reports, visualization tools, and other interfaces through which users interact with the data warehouse system.

Functional Logic Layer

This layer encapsulates the underlying business rules and logic that govern the behavior of the application. It handles data processing, transformation, aggregation, and other operations necessary to fulfill user queries and requirements. This layer ensures that the data warehouse system operates according to the specific needs and objectives of the organization.

Data Layer

This layer constitutes the physical data storage component of the application. It encompasses the databases, data warehouses, data marts, or other storage structures where the organization's data is stored, organized, and managed. The data layer serves as the foundation upon which the entire application architecture is built, providing the necessary infrastructure to store and access data efficiently.

Designing for a Specific Technology

A data warehouse should not be designed for a particular technology. Its architecture must be designed before the technology is selected. Failure to design the architecture first can prevent the requirements from being supported by the selected technology, which cannot be easily modified or discarded due to the extremely high costs associated with scrapping or modifying a deployed infrastructure.

Many choices and options are available, as many technologies support data warehousing. Therefore, rarely should any factor force an organization to implement a specific technology for its data warehousing needs if it is not in sync with its proposed architecture.

CHAPTER 8

DATA LAKES

OVERVIEW

Unlocking Data Lake's Potential

In the rapidly evolving landscape of data management, organizations are increasingly turning to innovative solutions to harness the full potential of their data. One such transformative concept that has gained prominence is the data lake. Unlike traditional data warehousing approaches that involve structuring and organizing data before storage, data lakes provide a more flexible and scalable alternative. At their core, data lakes serve as vast repositories capable of storing enormous volumes of raw, unstructured, or structured data from diverse sources without the need for predefined schemas.

The fundamental premise of a data lake is to break down silos that often hinder data accessibility and usability. By embracing a centralized and scalable repository, organizations aim to create a unified environment where data from various streams—be it social media, IoT devices, customer interactions, or enterprise systems—can coexist harmoniously. This approach allows businesses to collect, store, and analyze data on an unprecedented scale, fostering a holistic understanding of their operations, customers, and market dynamics.

The potential benefits of data lakes are substantial, as are the challenges. The sheer volume and diversity of data, coupled with the need for robust governance and security measures, demand careful planning and execution. As organizations navigate the complexities of implementing and managing data lakes, it becomes crucial to strike a balance between accessibility and control, ensuring that the data lake serves as a strategic asset rather than a chaotic reservoir.

Key Characteristics

Data lakes represent a paradigm shift in the way organizations handle and leverage their data. Several key characteristics distinguish data lakes from traditional data storage models, shaping their appeal and functionality.

First and foremost, data lakes embrace a schema-on-read approach, where data is stored first, and its structure is defined or read later when used, which starkly contrasts the schema-on-write method employed by traditional databases and data warehouses. In a data lake, raw data is ingested without predefined structures, allowing organizations to defer structuring and formatting until the data is actually used. This flexibility accommodates diverse data types, including structured, semi-structured, and unstructured data, fostering a more agile and adaptable environment.

Scalability is another critical characteristic of data lakes. These repositories can efficiently scale horizontally, handling vast amounts of data from various sources. Whether dealing with petabytes of historical records or real-time streaming data, data lakes provide the capacity to manage the ever-expanding volumes of information that organizations encounter in today's data-driven landscape.

Benefits

Data lakes offer numerous benefits that cater to the dynamic nature of modern data. They support a wide array of data sources and formats, including traditional databases, logs, social media feeds, and IoT sensor data. This inclusivity promotes a comprehensive approach to data analysis, enabling organizations to derive valuable insights by correlating diverse datasets.

A key advantage of data lakes is their ability to handle raw, unstructured, and varied data types at scale. Organizations can ingest large volumes of data from various sources without upfront structuring, allowing for agile and adaptive data environments.

Additionally, data lakes facilitate the democratization of data access and analytics by breaking down silos and providing a centralized repository for all data types. This fosters collaboration among different teams and empowers data scientists, analysts, and business users to explore and analyze data comprehensively. Furthermore, the ability to conduct advanced analytics, such as machine learning and AI, on diverse datasets enhances decision-making and drives innovation.

Challenges

Data lakes boast remarkable versatility, yet governance and security issues can easily undermine their potential, leading to their dreaded transformation into data swamps. Striking a balance between accessibility and control is paramount to fully harnessing their capabilities. Efficient metadata management, comprehensive data cataloging, and robust governance frameworks are indispensable for ensuring that data lakes function as invaluable strategic assets.

Maintaining governance represents a primary concern, particularly with regard to data quality. While the schema-on-read approach offers flexibility, it demands meticulous metadata management and documentation to forestall chaos. Without robust governance frameworks, the integrity, security, and compliance of data lakes may be compromised.

Scalability and performance are critical challenges. Managing infrastructure and optimizing query performance become significant tasks as data lakes expand. Organizations must invest in appropriate technologies, such as distributed computing and storage solutions, for scalability and efficiency.

In summary, while data lakes offer unparalleled flexibility and democratize data access, addressing challenges related to governance, quality, and scalability is essential for unlocking their full potential and deriving actionable insights from the wealth of data they store.

ARCHITECTURAL COMPONENTS

The architectural components of a data lake are crucial for ensuring its effectiveness in storing, managing, and analyzing vast amounts of diverse data. These components collectively form the foundation for a scalable, flexible, and well-governed data lake ecosystem.

Storage Layer

At the core of a data lake is the storage layer, which is responsible for accommodating large volumes of raw and unstructured data. Object storage, such as the Hadoop Distributed File System, or cloud-based storage, such as Amazon S3 or Azure Data Lake Storage, is commonly used. This layer enables data to be ingested without the need for predefined schemas, allowing for schema-on-read flexibility.

Data Ingestion

Data lakes support various mechanisms for ingesting data, including batch processing and real-time streaming. Ingestion tools facilitate the efficient loading of diverse datasets from sources such as databases, logs, sensors, and external systems. This component ensures that data is continuously and reliably imported into the lake.

Metadata Management

Metadata is essential for maintaining visibility and control over the data stored in the data lake. Metadata management tools capture information about the data lineage, quality, and usage. This metadata catalog is crucial for understanding the context of the stored data, aiding in data discovery, and ensuring proper governance.

Data Processing and Analytics

Data lakes incorporate processing and analytics engines to derive meaningful insights. Distributed computing frameworks such as Apache Spark and Apache Flink enable scalable and parallel processing of data. Additionally, tools for data transformation, cleansing, and advanced analytics, including machine learning and AI, are integrated into the architecture.

Security and Governance

Robust security and governance mechanisms are imperative for protecting sensitive data and ensuring compliance. Access controls, encryption, and auditing features are implemented to safeguard the data lake. Governance frameworks help define and enforce policies regarding data quality, privacy, and usage.

Query and Exploration Interfaces

User interfaces and query engines provide a means for data exploration and analysis. These interfaces allow data scientists, analysts, and business users to interact with the data lake, run queries, and derive insights. Integration with popular BI tools further facilitates seamless analysis and reporting.

Integration with External Systems

Data lakes often need to integrate with external systems, both for data ingestion and data export. This integration ensures a continuous flow of data between the data lake and other enterprise systems, supporting a cohesive data ecosystem.

A well-designed data lake architecture takes into account these components, balancing flexibility with governance and scalability to meet the evolving needs of data-driven organizations.

DATA LAKES BACKBONE: DATA INGESTION AND INTEGRATION

Data ingestion and integration play pivotal roles in the functionality and effectiveness of data lakes, ensuring a seamless and efficient process of bringing diverse data into the storage environment.

Data Ingestion

Data lakes are designed to accommodate a wide variety of data types, ranging from structured to semistructured and unstructured data. Data ingestion involves the process of collecting and loading this data into the lake. Batch processing and real-time streaming are common methods used for data ingestion.

In batch processing, large volumes of data are collected over a specified period and loaded into the data lake in chunks. This method is suitable for scenarios where data updates are not time-sensitive. Contrastingly, real-time streaming involves the continuous ingestion of data as it is generated, allowing for near-instantaneous availability of information. This is particularly useful for applications that require real-time analytics and insights.

Data ingestion tools are employed to facilitate these processes. These tools are responsible for extracting data from source systems, transforming it into a suitable format, and loading it into the data lake. They often support connectors for various data sources, ensuring compatibility with databases, logs, external systems, and other repositories.

Data Integration

Data lakes serve as central repositories for diverse datasets, and effective data integration is essential for deriving valuable insights from this amalgamation. Integration involves combining data from different sources, harmonizing formats, and ensuring consistency across the lake.

Schema-on-read is a key feature of data lakes, allowing for flexibility in handling diverse data formats without requiring a predefined schema during the ingestion phase. This flexibility empowers users to interpret and structure the data according to their analytical needs when querying the lake.

Moreover, integration with external systems is a common requirement for data lakes. This integration ensures a continuous flow of data between the data lake and other enterprise systems, supporting a cohesive data ecosystem. By connecting with databases, applications, and cloud services, data lakes become integral components of an organization's broader data infrastructure.

In summary, data ingestion and integration form the backbone of data lakes, enabling the seamless flow of diverse data into a centralized storage environment. Efficient tools and processes in these domains are critical for maintaining the agility and accessibility that are hallmarks of a well-functioning data lake.

DATA GOVERNANCE AND SECURITY

Data governance and security are paramount considerations in the management of data lakes, ensuring that the stored information is reliable, compliant, and protected from unauthorized access.

Data Governance

Data governance encompasses the policies, processes, and standards that govern the availability, usability, integrity, and security of data within an organization. In the context of data lakes, effective data governance is crucial for maintaining the quality and trustworthiness of the data.

Metadata management is a key aspect of data governance in data lakes. Metadata provides essential information about the data, including its source, lineage, quality, and usage. A robust metadata management system helps users understand the context and characteristics of the data, facilitating proper utilization and interpretation.

Establishing clear ownership and accountability for the data is another vital component of data governance. Assigning roles and responsibilities ensures that individuals within the organization are responsible for maintaining the quality and compliance of the data they interact with within the data lake.

Data Security

Data security in data lakes is multifaceted and involves measures to safeguard data at various stages, including ingestion, storage, processing, and retrieval. Encryption is commonly employed to protect data both in transit and at rest. This ensures that the data remains unreadable even if unauthorized access occurs without the appropriate decryption keys.

Access control mechanisms are implemented to regulate who can access, modify, or delete data within the data lake. RBAC and fine-grained access policies help enforce these restrictions, limiting access to sensitive information to authorized personnel.

Audit trails and monitoring functionalities contribute to security by providing a record of data access and modifications. This is essential for tracking any unauthorized activities and ensuring compliance with data protection regulations.

Compliance with industry and regulatory standards such as GDPR, Health Insurance Portability and Accountability Act (HIPAA), or specific data protection laws is a critical aspect of data security in data lakes. Implementing policies and practices that align with these standards helps organizations avoid legal repercussions and build trust with users and stakeholders.

In conclusion, robust data governance and security practices are foundational elements for successfully implementing and maintaining data lakes. These measures not only safeguard sensitive information but also contribute to the overall reliability and integrity of the data stored within the data lake.

USE CASES AND APPLICATIONS

Data lakes have diverse applications across industries, offering flexible and scalable solutions for handling vast volumes of data. Some prominent use cases and applications of data lakes include the following:

Advanced Analytics and Business Intelligence

Data lakes serve as a rich source for advanced analytics and business intelligence. Organizations can leverage the diverse and raw data stored in the lake to derive meaningful insights, identify trends, and make data-driven decisions. The flexibility of data lakes allows analysts to perform complex queries, exploratory data analysis (EDA), and develop predictive models.

Data Science and Machine Learning

Data lakes are instrumental in supporting data science initiatives and machine learning applications. The abundance of varied data types enables data scientists to build and train sophisticated machine-learning models. By accessing raw data in its native form, data scientists can experiment with different feature engineering techniques and enhance the accuracy of predictive models.

Real-Time Data Processing

Data lakes can be integrated with stream processing frameworks for applications requiring real-time data processing. This allows organizations to ingest and process data in near real time, enabling quick decision-making based on the most current information. Use cases include fraud detection, monitoring, and IoT applications where real-time insights are crucial.

Enhancing Customer Experience

Data lakes support the creation of comprehensive customer profiles by aggregating data from various touchpoints, including interactions, transactions, and feedback. This unified view enables organizations to personalize customer experiences, target marketing campaigns more effectively, and enhance customer satisfaction.

Healthcare Analytics

In the healthcare sector, data lakes play a vital role in aggregating diverse healthcare data, such as electronic health records, imaging data, and genomic data. This consolidated data facilitates advanced analytics and predictive modeling for disease diagnosis, treatment optimization, and healthcare management.

Risk Management and Compliance

Financial institutions leverage data lakes for risk management and compliance purposes. By consolidating data related to transactions, market conditions, and regulatory requirements, organizations can analyze risk exposure, detect anomalies, and ensure compliance with financial regulations.

Media and Entertainment

In the media and entertainment industry, data lakes are used to manage and analyze vast amounts of multimedia content, including videos, images, and user-generated content. This facilitates content recommendation engines, audience segmentation, and content optimization.

Supply Chain Optimization

Data lakes help optimize supply chain operations by consolidating data from various sources, including suppliers, logistics, and inventory. Predictive analytics on this data can improve demand forecasting, enhance inventory management, and optimize logistics for more efficient supply chain operations.

These diverse use cases highlight the versatility of data lakes in addressing complex data challenges across different industries, empowering organizations to extract actionable insights and drive innovation.

DATA LAKES AND DATA WAREHOUSING: COMPARATIVE ANALYSIS

Data lakes and traditional data warehousing are two different approaches to storing and managing large volumes of data. There are several key differences between them, several of which are described in the following subsections.

Data Structure and Schema

- Data lakes can store structured, semistructured, and unstructured data. They allow for the storage of raw, unprocessed data without a predefined schema. This flexibility makes them suitable for handling diverse data types and formats.
- Data warehouses typically store structured data with a predefined schema. The schema is designed before loading data into the warehouse, making it well-suited for traditional relational databases.

Data Storage

- Data lakes store data in its raw form, allowing for the storage of large amounts of unprocessed data. This raw data can be subsequently transformed and processed as needed.
- Data warehouses store processed and structured data, often optimized for query performance. The data in a warehouse is usually cleaned, transformed, and loaded before being stored.

Data Processing

- Data lakes often involve on-demand data processing. Users can apply various processing engines and tools to analyze and transform the data when needed.
- Data warehouses are optimized for query performance and often involve batch processing, where data is loaded, transformed, and stored before being made available for analysis.

Schema Evolution

- Data lakes are more accommodating of schema evolution. New data can be added without strict adherence to a predefined schema, making them more agile and adaptable to changing data requirements.
- Data warehouses typically have a rigid schema, and any changes to the schema may require significant effort and planning.

Use Cases

- Data lakes are well-suited for scenarios where the data is diverse, raw, and needs to be explored for new insights. It is commonly used in big data analytics, machine learning, and scenarios where the data structure is not well-defined in advance.
- Data warehouses are ideal for scenarios where the data is well-structured, and the focus is on reporting business intelligence and decision support. Commonly used for structured data from transactional systems.

Costs

- Data lakes are generally more cost-effective for storing large volumes of raw data. Storage costs are typically lower, but processing costs can vary based on the tools and services used.
- Data warehouses may have higher upfront costs, but they can provide optimized query performance for analytical workloads. Costs are often associated with storage and query processing.

Scalability

- Data lakes are highly scalable, as they can accommodate diverse and large data volumes. Maintaining performance as the scale increases may require careful consideration of storage and processing technologies.

▪ Data warehouses' scalability may be limited, and scaling up often involves investing in more powerful hardware or scaling out by adding more nodes to a distributed system.

In practice, organizations may use a combination of data lakes and data warehouses to address different aspects of their data storage and processing needs. This hybrid approach is sometimes referred to as a "lakehouse" architecture, aiming to combine the strengths of both paradigms.

STATUS OF DATA LAKES IN DATA ANALYSIS

Data lakes continue to play a significant role in the field of data analysis, and their popularity has been growing. The following sections describe some trends and considerations based on the status of data lakes in the industry.

Integration with Data Warehouses

Organizations often use a combination of data lakes and data warehouses to create a comprehensive data architecture. This integration, exemplified by the lakehouse architecture where data lakes and warehouses work together, provides both flexibility and optimized query performance.

Improved Tooling and Ecosystem

The tools and ecosystems around data lakes have continued to evolve, making it easier for organizations to manage, analyze, and derive insights from the data stored in data lakes. Many cloud providers offer services and tools specifically designed for data lake management and analytics.

Advancements in Metadata Management

Metadata management has become a crucial aspect of data lakes. Efficient metadata management helps users discover, understand, and trust the data stored in the lake. Various metadata management tools and practices have emerged to address these needs.

Schema-on-Read and Schema Evolution

The schema-on-read approach, where the data schema is applied at the time of analysis rather than at the time of ingestion, continues to be a key feature of data lakes. This flexibility allows easier adaptation to changing business requirements and evolving data structures.

Data Governance and Security

Data governance and security in data lakes have become increasingly important. Organizations are implementing policies and technologies to ensure proper access controls, encryption, and auditing to protect sensitive data stored in the lake.

Machine Learning and Advanced Analytics

Data lakes provide an environment conducive to machine learning and advanced analytics. The ability to store diverse and raw data allows data scientists to explore and experiment with different types of data for building and training machine learning models.

Serverless and Managed Services

Many organizations are leveraging serverless and managed services provided by cloud platforms to build and operate their data lakes. This helps in reducing the operational burden and allows teams to focus more on analytics and less on infrastructure management.

Real-Time Data Processing

The demand for real-time analytics has led to advancements in real-time data processing capabilities within data lakes. Organizations are exploring technologies that enable the processing of streaming data directly within the data lake environment.

Cost Optimization

Cost optimization strategies for data lakes have become a focus for organizations. This includes optimizing storage costs, selecting appropriate data storage formats, and managing the costs associated with data processing and analytics.

It is important to note that the field of data management and analytics is dynamic, and trends may continue to evolve. Organizations should stay informed about the latest developments, tools, and best practices to make informed decisions about their data architecture and analysis strategies.

FUTURE TRENDS IN DATA LAKE TECHNOLOGY

There are several emerging trends in the data lake technology space. It should be kept in mind that the field is dynamic, and new trends will continue to emerge. The following sections explore some potential future trends in data lake technology.

Convergence

The integration of data lakes and data warehouses into unified frameworks, such as the lakehouse architecture, is likely to continue. This approach aims to combine the strengths of both technologies, allowing organizations to handle raw data, unstructured and structured, as well as processed data in a cohesive manner.

Enhanced Metadata Management

Improved metadata management is crucial for making data lakes more discoverable, understandable, and governable. Future trends may include advancements in automated metadata generation, lineage tracking, and data quality monitoring to enhance the overall management of data assets.

Advanced Data Governance and Security

With an increased focus on data privacy and security regulations, data lakes are expected to incorporate more robust governance and security features. This includes fine-grained access controls, encryption, and auditing capabilities to ensure compliance with data protection standards.

Augmented Data Management and Analytics

The integration of AI and machine learning into data lake platforms is likely to increase. Automated data profiling, anomaly detection, and recommendation systems can assist data engineers and analysts in managing and analyzing data more efficiently.

Serverless and Managed Services Adoption

The adoption of serverless and managed services for data lakes is expected to increase. Cloud providers are likely to offer more specialized services that simplify the management, scaling, and optimization of data lakes without requiring extensive manual intervention.

Data Mesh Architecture

The concept of a data mesh, introduced by Zhamak Dehghani, a prominent figure in the field of software engineering and data architecture, emphasizes decentralizing data ownership and infrastructure to improve scalability and agility. This trend may influence the design and implementation of future data lake architectures.

Integration of Real-Time Data Processing

The demand for real-time analytics is likely to drive the integration of real-time data processing capabilities directly within data lakes. Technologies enabling efficient streaming data processing within lake environments may become more prevalent.

Data Observability and Explainability

As data lakes grow in complexity, there may be an increased focus on data observability and explainability. Tools and practices that provide insights into data quality, data lineage, and the reasoning behind analytical outcomes will be essential for building trust in data lakes.

Sustainability and Green Computing

With a growing awareness of environmental sustainability, there might be an increased emphasis on optimizing the environmental impact of data lake operations. This could involve designing more energy-efficient storage and processing solutions.

Multicloud and Hybrid Deployments

Organizations are likely to explore multicloud and hybrid deployment models for data lakes to avoid vendor lock-in, enhance resilience, and leverage the strengths of different cloud providers.

It should be kept in mind that these trends are speculative, and the actual developments in data lake technology will depend on factors such as technological advancements, industry needs, and evolving best practices. It is recommended that users stay updated with the latest industry news and insights to understand how data lake technology will evolve in the coming years.

CHAPTER 9

EXTRACTION, TRANSFORMATION, AND LOADING (ETL)

ETL PROCESS

The ETL process is a systematic approach for gathering data from diverse sources, reshaping it to meet specific requirements, and loading it into a target database for efficient analysis and reporting. In the extraction phase, data is collected from various sources and transferred to a staging area. The transformation phase involves cleaning and structuring the data to ensure consistency and compliance with business rules. Finally, in the loading phase, the transformed data is loaded into the target database, making it accessible for business intelligence and analytics, facilitating informed decision-making based on accurate and organized information.

Crucial ETL Role in Data Management and Analytics

The ETL process plays a crucial role in the realm of data management and analytics, serving several important purposes. First, ETL ensures data integration by extracting information from diverse and often disparate sources, such as databases, spreadsheets, and external systems. This integration is essential for creating a unified and comprehensive view of an organization's data landscape.

Second, ETL enables data quality and consistency. During the transformation phase, the data is cleaned, validated, and standardized to adhere to predefined business rules and standards. This ensures that the data in the target database is accurate, reliable, and suitable for analysis. Without ETL, inconsistencies and errors in the source data can compromise the integrity of the analytical results.

Finally, ETL facilitates efficient data storage and retrieval. By loading transformed data into a centralized database or data warehouse, organizations can optimize data access for reporting and business intelligence purposes. This streamlined structure enhances the speed and effectiveness of data analysis, enabling organizations to derive valuable insights and make informed decisions. In summary, the ETL process is integral to creating a solid foundation for data-driven decision-making by ensuring data integration, quality, and accessibility.

ETL Components

The ETL process includes three main steps:

1. Extraction (E), which involves pulling data from the source system(s).
2. Transformation (T), which involves subjecting the data to a number of operations before it can be imported.
3. Loading (L), which involves physically placing extracted and transformed data in the target database.

Extraction

In this step, data is extracted from the source systems. The objective is to convert the data, which may be in different formats (such as VSAM, ISAM, relational, and flat files), into a single format that is ready for transformation processing. The extracted data is parsed to check whether it conforms to a pattern or a specific structure. The techniques for performing data extraction vary and are influenced by many factors, such as the type and structure of the source data, availability of tools, extraction frequency, and exception handling.

Transformation

Source data is subjected to a number of operations that prepare it for import into the target database. To perform this task, integration and transformation programs are used. As needed, these programs apply business rules or functions to the extracted data to reformat, recalculate, modify the structure and data elements, and add time elements. They are also used to perform calculations and a variety of other tasks, such as summarization and de-normalization.

In a few cases, very little or no manipulation is needed. In many cases, a range of operations may be required on some or all of the data. Some of the operations include filtering, joining, translating values, encoding, sorting, aggregating, calculating a newly derived value, and pivoting (transposing).

Loading

The loading process involves physically moving extracted and transformed data into the target database. Initially, a large volume of data is loaded. Subsequently, an extraction procedure periodically loads fresh data based on business rules and a predetermined frequency.

The loading process and volume can vary according to business requirements. For example, some functional areas may require data to be added daily, while some may require real-time or near-real-time data loading. The requirements can also vary depending on the period for which the data, detailed or aggregates, needs to be made available, which, consequently, influences the ETL process and frequency.

The amount of data to be loaded influences the time required for the extraction and loading process. Depending on the data volume, the loading time can vary from a few minutes to many hours. The loading time can also impact the analysis. For example, if the loading takes four hours, then data will not be available for any prior four-hour period. Therefore, it will not be possible to run reports during that four-hour period. Most data loading is performed after normal working hours, usually at night, to avoid performance impact issues.

ETL Operations

The ETL process encompasses a series of essential operations to prepare source data for integration into analytics storage systems. These operations include mapping, cleaning of dirty data, restructuring, reformatting, recalculation, selecting/filtering, summarization, validation, and reconciliation. Each operation serves a distinct purpose in ensuring data accuracy, consistency, and suitability for analytical purposes. The iterative nature of these processes allows for the transformation of raw source data into a standardized format that aligns with predefined business rules and facilitates effective analysis.

In addition to the fundamental operations, ETL tasks may extend to more specialized functions. These include merge processing for handling data from multiple sources, purge processing to filter out unwanted data, staging for temporary storage before importing into the analytics storage system, and backflushing to feed clean and validated data back to the source systems. These nuanced tasks cater to specific requirements and considerations, highlighting the adaptability of the ETL process to diverse data integration scenarios. Together, these operations and tasks form a comprehensive framework for managing and optimizing the flow of data from source systems to the analytics storage systems.

ETL Process Duration

The duration of the ETL process can vary significantly and is influenced by several factors, including the volume of data, complexity of transformations, hardware capabilities, and efficiency of the ETL tools employed. Small to medium-sized datasets with straightforward transformations may complete the ETL cycle in minutes or hours. Conversely, large-scale datasets with intricate transformations and resource-intensive processing might extend the duration to several hours or even days.

Real-time or near-real-time ETL processes, where data is continuously streamed and processed, often aim for minimal latency, demanding swift and efficient execution. The specific requirements of the business and the urgency of data availability also play a crucial role in determining the acceptable duration for the ETL process. As organizations continually seek to optimize their data processing workflows, advancements in technology and ETL tools contribute to reducing the overall duration of the ETL cycle.

ETL TESTING

ETL testing is performed by the development team. It involves the testing of various processes, including data extraction, transformation, data cleansing, and loading. The essential elements required for testing the extraction, transformation, and loading process are described in the following subsections.

Completeness

This testing involves multiple subtasks, including performing a full load, incremental load, verifying that new records have been added as expected, validating loading (all records, fields, and content of each field), performing volume counts, comparing unique values of key fields between source data and data loaded into the target, validating that no truncation occurs at any step in the process, and so on.

Transformation

This involves validating that data is transformed correctly, based on business rules, either manually or through an automated process. This is done by comparing the range and distribution of values in each field between the source and target data, validating the correct processing of ETL-generated fields such as surrogate keys, and validating parent-to-child relationships in the data.

Data Quality

Data quality testing is a comprehensive evaluation that delves into how the ETL system manages aspects such as data rejection, correction, and notification, ensuring that the integrity of the original data is maintained to the greatest extent possible while applying necessary modifications. This process plays a crucial role in affirming that the ETL application accurately identifies and appropriately deals with invalid data, adhering to predefined business rules and criteria. Modifications, such as data cleansing and transformation, are performed in a controlled and documented manner to meet predefined quality standards and ensure the resulting data remains accurate, reliable, and suitable for its intended use.

Performance

This involves identifying any potential weaknesses in the ETL design, such as reading a file multiple times or creating unnecessary intermediate files. Tasks performed include comparing ETL loading times to loads performed with a smaller amount of data for anticipating scalability issues, comparing the ETL processing times component by component to point out any areas of weakness, monitoring the timing of the rejection process, determining how large volumes of rejected data are handled, performing simple and multiple join queries to validate query performance on large database volumes, and so on.

Scalability

Scalability testing examines the ETL system's capacity to easily expand its capabilities in response to escalating load volumes and heightened demands for data retrieval through queries. This assessment ensures that the system maintains optimal performance and efficiency as it accommodates the growth in data processing requirements over time.

Testing is absolutely essential because failure, at a later stage, will be far more expensive and disruptive to the business.

ETL CHALLENGES AND ISSUES

The ETL process is critical for preparing data for analysis, but it is not without its challenges. Organizations often face issues which can impact the efficiency and reliability of analytics workflows.

Challenges

The ETL process encounters a multitude of challenges that are pivotal to address for project success and smooth business operations. These challenges encompass various dimensions, including the complexity of integrating diverse environments, multiple sources with different architectures, and incompatible data formats. Issues such as poor data quality, suboptimal data model design, and complex transformation and cleansing rules contribute to the intricacies of ETL implementation.

Complicating matters further are challenges related to conflicting business definitions and rules, historical data conversion issues, and the impact of organizational changes over time. The absence of established procedures for resolving inconsistencies, coupled with the use of outdated or incompatible tools and technologies, can hinder the efficiency of the ETL process. Inattention to data validation, the time-consuming nature of the process, and the need for constant ETL changes due to evolving requirements during development pose additional hurdles.

Moreover, challenges are also posed by issues related to the testing process, including flaws in the testing methodology and inadequate tools. Inferior developer skills and infrastructure-related issues further compound the challenges faced during the ETL task. Recognizing and addressing these varied challenges is imperative for ensuring the reliability and efficiency of the ETL process in handling diverse data integration scenarios.

Underestimation

The ETL task is the most challenging and labor-intensive component of a data migration project and is often underestimated, leading to cost overruns and project delays. This underestimation arises for various common reasons, including incorrect assumptions about the initial data quality, complexities emerging in the design phase, and unforeseen intricacies of business logic. Furthermore, inaccuracies in estimating the programming effort needed, unrealistic expectations regarding the capabilities of ETL tools, and the unexpectedly high complexity involved in extracting and loading data from diverse sources all contribute to the challenges faced in this pivotal task.

In addition to these factors, the ETL task is frequently underestimated due to larger-than-expected data volumes, necessitating additional validation efforts and posing unanticipated challenges. The absence of SMEs to provide guidance further compounds the difficulties encountered in navigating the intricacies of the ETL process. Recognizing and addressing these common underestimation factors is crucial for better aligning project expectations with the complexities inherent in the ETL task, ultimately promoting more accurate planning and successful project execution.

TOOLS

Tools for ETL

ETL tasks involve the utilization of a diverse array of tools, each serving specific functions within the data integration process. Certain tools, such as file transfer programs, are relatively straightforward. Other tools, especially those designed for data transformation, can be considerably complex. These sophisticated tools play a crucial role as they automate data extraction from multiple sources, facilitate the mapping of sources to the target database, execute transformations and manipulations on the data, and ultimately load the processed data into the ultimate destination.

The technologies employed in the ETL process encompass a range of formats and protocols, including ASCII, XML, HTML, DB Connect, IDoc, BAPI, and SOAP. These technologies contribute to the efficiency and versatility of ETL tools, allowing seamless data integration across diverse sources and facilitating the transformation of raw data into a structured and usable format. The combination of various tools and technologies underscores the complexity and sophistication inherent in ETL tasks, which are crucial for effective data management and analysis.

Tasks Performed by ETL Tools

ETL tools serve three primary functions: reading data from diverse sources such as relational database tables or flat files, manipulating data based on specific rules (including filtering, modification, or enhancement), and writing the resultant data to a target database. These core operations are essential for extracting, transforming, and loading data into a structured and usable format. Throughout and after these primary ETL processes, there are numerous intermediate and post-loading steps, including building reference data, validation, cleaning, integrity checking, building aggregates, staging, archiving, and purging.

In addition to the primary functions, ETL tools perform specific tasks such as converting data to a unified format, deriving new data through mathematical formulas, filtering out unwanted data, integrating data from different databases and platforms, summarizing data by combining tables, and selecting and loading data based on triggers. These tasks showcase the versatility and comprehensiveness of ETL tools in handling diverse data transformation requirements within the data integration process.

ETL Tool Categories

The functionality of available ETL tools spans a broad spectrum, with costs ranging from minimum to hundreds of thousands of dollars. At the lower end, simple data migration tools focus on basic extraction and loading functions. In contrast, more versatile tools are highly sophisticated, offering a multitude of capabilities, including complex transformations and handling diverse input formats and sources.

These tools generally fall into three main categories: data transformation engines, code generators, and data capture through replication. Each category represents distinct functionalities, contributing to the varied landscape of ETL tools and their suitability for different data integration needs.

ETL Tool Selection Criteria

The chosen ETL tool must align with the specific environment, prioritizing support for fundamental functions such as transformation and cleansing. Selection criteria should be based on the desired and necessary ETL features for a particular implementation. Business considerations such as cost, reliability, scalability, vendor reputation, and resource availability further influence the tool selection. In instances where third-party tools are impractical due to cost or complexity, especially in highly intricate data transformation scenarios, in-house custom programs for the ETL process may be a more viable alternative.

CHAPTER 10

DATA DESIGN

DATA MODELING FOR BUSINESS DECISION-MAKING

Basics of Data Modeling

Data modeling is the process of creating a visual representation or abstraction of an organization's data and its relationships. It involves defining data entities, their attributes, and the associations between them. The primary goal is to provide a clear and structured overview of how data is organized and flows within an organization.

Data models serve as a blueprint for database design and application development, helping stakeholders, including database administrators, developers, and business analysts, understand the structure and semantics of the data.

Data Modeling in Business Decision-Making

Data modeling plays a crucial role in enhancing business decision-making by providing a systematic and organized approach to managing and analyzing data. A well-designed data model ensures that the data is accurately represented, making it easier for decision-makers to comprehend and leverage information effectively. It facilitates the identification of relationships between different data elements, helping businesses uncover patterns, trends, and insights crucial for strategic decision-making.

Moreover, a robust data model supports data integrity and consistency, ensuring that the information used for decision-making is reliable and trustworthy. Overall, data modeling acts as a foundational step in establishing a data-driven culture within organizations, fostering informed decision-making processes across various business functions.

ENTITIES AND ATTRIBUTES

Entities and attributes are foundational concepts in data modeling, representing the core elements of a database system. Entities define real-world objects or concepts, while attributes describe the characteristics or properties of these entities, enabling structured data organization and meaningful analysis.

Significance of Entities in Data Modeling

Understanding entities as business objects is a fundamental aspect of data modeling, wherein entities represent the core building blocks of an organization's data structure. In the context of data modeling, an entity encapsulates a distinct business concept or object, such as customers, products, or orders, and is characterized by a set of attributes that describe its properties. Viewing entities as business objects enables a more intuitive and business-aligned approach to data representation, ensuring that the data model reflects the real-world entities and relationships within an organization. This perspective helps bridge the gap between technical data structures and the operational aspects of the business, facilitating clearer communication between stakeholders and contributing to the development of comprehensive and effective data models that align with the organization's objectives and processes.

Identifying and Defining Entity Attributes

Identifying and defining attributes for entities is a pivotal step in data modeling, involving the characterization of specific properties or features associated with each business object. Attributes provide detailed information about entities, offering a granular understanding of their characteristics. For instance, in a customer entity, attributes may include name, address, and contact details.

This process of attribute definition not only aids in the accurate representation of data but also contributes to the overall clarity and specificity of the data model. By meticulously identifying and defining attributes, data modelers ensure that the resulting structure effectively captures the essential details of each entity, laying the foundation for precise database design and facilitating meaningful data analysis for informed business decision-making.

RELATIONSHIPS

Relationships in data modeling illustrate the connections between entities, highlighting how they interact and depend on one another. These relationships are essential for creating a coherent database structure, enabling seamless data retrieval and meaningful insights.

Role of Entity Relationships in Data Modeling

Explaining relationships between entities is a crucial aspect of data modeling, highlighting how different business objects or entities are interconnected. In data modeling, relationships define the associations and dependencies between entities, providing a deeper understanding of how data elements interact within an organizational context. Relationships are categorized into types such as one-to-one, one-to-many, or many-to-many, each conveying specific linkages between entities.

By elucidating these relationships, data modelers not only establish the structural integrity of the data but also lay the groundwork for comprehensive database designs. This process ensures that stakeholders can discern how various entities collaborate, fostering clarity and coherence in the representation of organizational data and facilitating the development of effective and insightful data analyses.

Relationship Types

Types of relationships in data modeling are fundamental for capturing diverse associations within an organization's data ecosystem. These relationships include:

- *One-to-one relationship:* Each record in one entity is uniquely associated with a single record in another entity, creating a direct and singular correspondence.
- *One-to-many relationship:* One record in a particular entity can be linked to multiple records in another entity, allowing for a more flexible and expansive association.
- *Many-to-many relationship:* Multiple records in one entity can be related to multiple records in another entity, fostering a versatile and interconnected data structure.

Understanding these relationship types is essential for effective data modeling and insightful data analysis, providing a systematic framework for capturing the diverse and intricate associations within an organization's data ecosystem.

NORMALIZATION

Role of Normalization in Data Modeling

Normalization in data modeling is a fundamental process aimed at organizing and structuring relational databases to minimize data redundancy and dependency. The primary objective is to achieve systematic and efficient data organization that enhances data integrity and reduces anomalies during data manipulation. Normalization involves breaking down large tables into smaller, interrelated tables by adhering to a set of rules known as normal forms.

These normal forms, ranging from first normal form (1NF) to higher forms like third normal form (3NF) and Boyce-Codd normal form (BCNF), guide the elimination of redundant data and ensure that each piece of information is stored in only one place within the database. By applying normalization, data modelers create a more streamlined and maintainable database structure, promoting consistency and accuracy in data storage and retrieval operations.

Normalization for Data Integrity

Normalization is of paramount importance for ensuring data integrity in a relational database. By systematically organizing and structuring data through normalization, redundancies are minimized, and dependency issues are addressed, resulting in a more reliable and consistent database. This process eliminates data anomalies such as insertion, update, and deletion anomalies, which can arise when information is redundantly stored across tables.

Normalization, by adhering to specific normal forms, ensures that each piece of data is stored in a logical and singular location within the database. This not only enhances the accuracy and reliability of the stored information but also facilitates efficient data retrieval and maintenance. In essence, normalization acts as a safeguard against inconsistencies and inaccuracies, contributing significantly to the overall data integrity and effectiveness of database operations.

PRIMARY KEYS AND FOREIGN KEYS

Primary keys and foreign keys are fundamental components of database design that establish and maintain relationships between tables. They ensure data integrity by uniquely identifying records and linking related information across different tables.

Primary Keys

Defining primary keys is a critical aspect of data modeling because it ensures the unique identification of records within a relational database. A *primary key* is a specific attribute or combination of attributes that uniquely identifies each record in a table. This designation not only provides a structured and efficient means of organizing data but also serves as a foundation for establishing relationships between tables.

The uniqueness of a primary key is crucial for preventing duplicate entries and maintaining data integrity. Typically, primary keys are assigned to columns that inherently hold distinctive values, such as an employee ID or product code. By defining primary keys, data modelers establish a clear and unambiguous method for identifying and accessing individual records, laying the groundwork for robust relational database structures.

Foreign Keys

Foreign keys play a pivotal role in linking tables within a relational database, contributing to the establishment of relationships and ensuring data integrity. A *foreign key* is a field in one table that corresponds to the primary key in another table, creating a connection between the two. This linkage enables the representation of relationships, such as one-to-many or many-to-many, between entities.

Foreign keys act as references, enforcing referential integrity by ensuring that values in the foreign key column correspond to existing values in the primary key column of the referenced table. This not only facilitates the normalization process but also enables the creation of relationships that reflect real-world connections between different data entities. Utilizing foreign keys in data modeling enhances the coherence and efficiency of relational databases, allowing for structured and interrelated data that supports comprehensive and accurate information retrieval.

DATA TYPES

Data types define the nature of the values that can be stored in a database, ensuring consistency and accuracy in data storage and retrieval. By specifying data types, databases can optimize storage, enforce rules, and maintain data integrity across different fields.

Data Types and Their Uses

In data modeling, various data types are employed to categorize and represent different kinds of information within a database. Text data types, such as VARCHAR or CHAR, are used for storing alphanumeric characters and textual information. Numeric data types, including INTEGER or DECIMAL, are employed for numerical values, allowing for precision in mathematical operations. Date data types, such as DATE or TIMESTAMP, are utilized for storing temporal information, ensuring accuracy in recording and querying dates and times.

Each data type serves a specific purpose, contributing to the efficiency and accuracy of data storage and retrieval. Understanding and appropriately selecting data types in the data modeling process is crucial for maintaining data integrity and optimizing database performance, ensuring that the representation of diverse information aligns with the requirements of the system and the nature of the data being stored.

Choosing Data Types

Selecting appropriate data types for different attributes is a critical decision in data modeling because it directly influences the efficiency, storage, and accuracy of a relational database. The choice of data types should align with the nature of the information each attribute represents. For instance, character data types such as VARCHAR may be suitable for storing names or descriptions, while numeric data types such as INTEGER are more appropriate for numerical values.

Date and time data types such as TIMESTAMP ensure the precise storage and retrieval of temporal information. By matching data types to the inherent characteristics of each attribute, data modelers optimize resource usage, enhance data integrity, and streamline the database structure. This thoughtful selection process contributes to a more robust and well-organized database schema, aligning with the specific requirements and characteristics of the data being managed.

MODELING TOOLS

Role of Data Modeling Tools

Data modeling tools are essential software applications designed to facilitate the creation, visualization, and management of data models within a database environment. These tools provide a user-friendly interface for data modelers and database administrators to define entities, attributes, relationships, and other components of a data model. They often support various notations, such as entity-relationship diagrams (ERDs) or unified modeling language (UML), allowing users to visually represent complex data structures.

Data modeling tools also assist in enforcing normalization rules, defining primary and foreign keys, and generating SQL scripts for database implementation. Additionally, they often include collaboration features, version control, and documentation capabilities, ensuring a systematic and collaborative approach to data modeling across diverse teams. These tools play a crucial role in enhancing efficiency, accuracy, and collaboration in the process of designing and managing databases.

Enhancing Database Design

Data modeling tools play a crucial role in visualizing and designing databases by providing a comprehensive and intuitive platform for data modelers and database administrators. These tools enable users to create visual representations of complex data structures, such as ERD or UML diagrams, which offer a clear and accessible overview of the relationships between entities, attributes, and tables. With interactive interfaces, users can easily define entities, establish relationships, and set constraints, fostering a visual understanding of the database schema.

Moreover, data modeling tools often support reverse engineering, allowing users to generate visual models from existing databases. The visualization capabilities aid in identifying potential issues, optimizing database designs, and ensuring that the structure aligns with business requirements. Overall, these tools streamline the design process, enhance collaboration among stakeholders, and contribute to the creation of well-organized and efficient database architectures.

CARDINALITY

Understanding Cardinality in Data Modeling

Cardinality in relationships within data modeling refers to the numerical association between records in connected tables. It defines the number of instances in one entity that can be linked to instances in another entity.

There are three primary types of cardinality: one-to-one, one-to-many, and many-to-many. In a one-to-one relationship, each record in one table corresponds to exactly one record in another table, and vice versa. In a one-to-many relationship, each record in one table can be associated with multiple records in another table, but each record in the second table is linked to only one record in the first table.

Many-to-many relationships allow multiple records in both tables to be associated with each other. Cardinality is crucial for accurately reflecting the real-world connections between data entities, guiding the implementation of foreign keys, and influencing the overall database structure to maintain data integrity and support efficient querying and analysis.

Impact of Cardinality in Relational Databases

Cardinality significantly influences data retrieval and reporting within a relational database, shaping the way information is extracted and presented. The cardinality of relationships between tables dictates the number of records that can be linked, directly impacting query results. In a one-to-one relationship, retrieval is straightforward, focusing on singular associations between records. In a one-to-many relationship, data retrieval may involve aggregation or filtering to manage multiple related records effectively. Many-to-many relationships often necessitate complex queries and the use of intermediary tables to consolidate information.

Understanding cardinality is paramount for optimizing data retrieval processes, as it guides the selection of appropriate join operations, filtering conditions, and aggregation methods. Precise consideration of cardinality in data modeling ensures that reporting mechanisms align with the intricacies of the relationships, facilitating accurate, efficient, and meaningful data extraction for analysis and decision-making.

DE-NORMALIZATION

Objective

De-normalization is a database optimization technique that involves intentionally introducing redundancy into a relational database by merging tables or incorporating redundant data. It is considered when there is a need to improve query performance, especially in scenarios where complex joins or aggregations cause a bottleneck. De-normalization can be beneficial in read-heavy applications where the data retrieval speed is prioritized over minimizing the storage space and update anomalies.

By reducing the number of joins required in queries, de-normalization can increase the speed of data retrieval, making it particularly useful in data warehousing and reporting systems. It comes with trade-offs, such as increased storage requirements and potential data update complexities. Therefore, de-normalization is a strategic choice based on specific performance needs and careful consideration of the application's use case and workload characteristics.

Balancing Normalization and Performance

Balancing normalization and performance is a crucial consideration in database design, requiring careful evaluation of trade-offs to meet specific application requirements. Normalization, with its focus on minimizing data redundancy and maintaining data integrity, is essential for ensuring a well-organized and structured database. Over-normalization can lead to complex joins and queries, impacting performance, especially in read-intensive scenarios. Striking the right balance involves selectively de-normalizing certain parts of the database to optimize query performance while maintaining a normalized structure for essential data integrity.

This process requires a thorough understanding of the application's workload, the types of queries it will encounter, and the overall system requirements. It is a nuanced decision-making process that aims to achieve an optimal trade-off between normalized designs for data integrity and de-normalized structures for improved query performance, ensuring that the database meets both functional and performance criteria.

These topics provide a foundational understanding of data modeling concepts and their relevance to business operations. Tailoring explanations to real-world examples within a specific business context can enhance comprehension for business users.

MULTIDIMENSIONAL DATA MODELING

Multi-dimensional data modeling is a core concept in data warehousing that organizes data into dimensions and facts to facilitate analytical processing. This approach enables businesses to analyze data across various perspectives, making it easier to identify trends, patterns, and insights.

Concept

Multidimensional data modeling revolutionizes the representation of information by extending beyond traditional two-dimensional tables. Unlike conventional structures, multidimensional models introduce additional dimensions, each representing a unique attribute or characteristic of the data. This multidimensional approach provides a richer framework for organizing and exploring data, enabling users to simultaneously analyze relationships and patterns from multiple perspectives.

By transcending the confines of two-dimensional structures, multidimensional models offer a nuanced understanding of data relationships.

Each dimension serves as an axis along which data is categorized, allowing for a layered examination of the dataset. This comprehensive organization facilitates the exploration of complex patterns, trends, and dependencies that may be overlooked in simpler models. In essence, multidimensional modeling empowers users to navigate through a multidimensional space of data, providing a flexible and insightful framework that aligns with the intricate nature of real-world business scenarios.

Benefits

Multidimensional data modeling enhances the depth and effectiveness of data analysis. It provides a comprehensive representation by organizing data across multiple dimensions, allowing users to explore relationships, patterns, and trends from various perspectives simultaneously, fostering a richer understanding. These models support complex analytical queries, facilitating quicker and more intuitive decision-making. Additionally, they offer improved scalability and flexibility, accommodating dynamic business data and evolving analytical needs.

This multidimensional perspective empowers users to uncover hidden insights and dependencies that may remain obscured in traditional two-dimensional structures. Users can traverse a multidimensional space by organizing data across multiple dimensions and simultaneously exploring various aspects of the dataset. Examining data from different angles enhances the granularity of analysis and fosters a more holistic and nuanced comprehension of the underlying data, propelling more informed decision-making in complex business scenarios.

Practical Applications

Multidimensional data modeling has revolutionized data analysis across various business sectors. In retail, it enables detailed sales performance analysis by integrating dimensions like geography, time, and product categories, aiding in trend identification and inventory optimization.

In finance, multidimensional data modeling supports portfolio analysis by concurrently examining factors such as asset classes, risk levels, and market trends, facilitating more informed investment decisions. This approach to financial analysis enhances understanding of investment performance and risk by dissecting complex datasets that include dimensions like financial instruments and market conditions.

Healthcare utilizes multidimensional modeling to improve patient outcomes through dimensions like treatment effectiveness, patient demographics, and time, providing a comprehensive understanding of healthcare data. These applications showcase how multidimensional data modeling empowers businesses in diverse sectors to gain insights, driving strategic decisions and operational efficiency.

This modeling approach is particularly relevant in areas such as business intelligence and performance reporting. In business intelligence, it offers a comprehensive view of organizational metrics and KPIs. In performance reporting, multi-dimensional models offer granular insights across dimensions like regions, products, and customer segments. This not only streamlines reporting but also enables decision-makers to derive actionable insights, fostering informed decision-making across critical business domains.

Challenges

Implementing multidimensional data models presents challenges that organizations must navigate for successful deployment. One significant hurdle is the heightened complexity inherent in these models, which intensifies as dimensions multiply. This complexity escalates the intricacy of relationships and dependencies, demanding meticulous design and maintenance efforts to ensure clarity and effectiveness.

Managing data redundancy is another concern, as the inclusion of multiple dimensions may inadvertently result in duplications, impacting storage efficiency and potentially compromising data integrity. Additionally, the necessity for specialized tools and expertise poses challenges, requiring users and IT teams to possess a proficient understanding of multidimensional databases and modeling techniques.

Despite these challenges, organizations can mitigate them through careful planning, effective data governance, and continuous training initiatives. By striking a balance between complexity and usability, organizations can ensure that the benefits of multidimensional data models outweigh the complexities associated with their implementation. Successfully navigating these considerations requires implementing comprehensive data governance practices and investing in the necessary tools and skills to maximize the benefits of multidimensional data modeling while minimizing associated challenges.

Integration with BI and Analytics Tools

Multidimensional data modeling seamlessly integrates with BI and analytics tools, augmenting their capabilities and expanding the depth of analysis. BI platforms leverage multidimensional models to enable users to explore data from various dimensions, providing a more comprehensive and interactive experience. This integration allows for the creation of dynamic dashboards and reports that incorporate multidimensional insights, fostering a holistic understanding of business data.

Analytics tools, equipped with multidimensional data models, facilitate intricate and nuanced analysis by allowing users to drill-down into specific dimensions, uncovering detailed patterns and trends. As a result, organizations can extract more meaningful and actionable insights from their data, enhancing the overall effectiveness of BI and analytics initiatives and empowering users to make informed decisions in complex business environments.

Popular BI platforms actively support and enhance the usability of multidimensional data models, providing robust compatibility for advanced analysis. These platforms, such as Microsoft Power BI, Tableau, and IBM Cognos, are designed to seamlessly integrate with multidimensional structures, allowing users to explore data from various dimensions effortlessly. Features such as drag-and-drop interfaces and intuitive visualization tools make multidimensional analysis accessible to a broader audience, even those without extensive technical expertise.

This compatibility ensures that business users can interact with multidimensional models directly within familiar BI environments, fostering a user-friendly experience and democratizing the analytical capabilities embedded in these models. This support in BI platforms significantly contributes to the accessibility and usability of multidimensional analysis, empowering organizations to derive actionable insights and make informed decisions based on a more comprehensive understanding of their data.

ONLINE ANALYTICAL PROCESSING (OLAP)

Online Analytical Processing (OLAP) is a powerful technology designed for swift and multidimensional analysis of large datasets. By enabling users to explore data across various dimensions, OLAP supports complex queries and facilitates in-depth decision-making processes.

Concept

OLAP represents a powerful approach to data analysis that goes beyond the capabilities of traditional relational databases. OLAP focuses on multidimensional data modeling, allowing users to interactively analyze and explore data from various dimensions. The multidimensional nature of OLAP enables users to view data from different perspectives, facilitating a deeper understanding of trends, patterns, and relationships within the dataset.

OLAP cubes, the core structures in OLAP systems, organize data into dimensions (such as time, geography, or product) and measures, enabling users to perform complex analyses with ease. The ability to slice and dice data, drill-down into detail, and pivot across dimensions empowers decision-makers to gain actionable insights. OLAP plays a crucial role in business intelligence and reporting, providing a flexible and intuitive framework for conducting sophisticated data analysis and supporting informed decision-making processes.

OLAP Data Characteristics

The characteristics of OLAP data encompass its multidimensional nature, serving as an analytical platform equipped with a user-friendly interface. Engineered for rapid query response times, these systems prioritize speed while offering versatility in data navigation and analysis. They facilitate collaborative usage through shared and secure access, ensuring both confidentiality and integrity of data. Moreover, OLAP systems specialize in presenting summarized data, providing aggregated views tailored for higher-level analysis.

In comparison to data warehouses, OLAP systems store less data, emphasizing the provision of preaggregated data for analytical purposes. Additionally, OLAP systems typically support a client/server architecture, allowing users to interact with the system through client applications while data processing occurs on the server side.

Benefits

OLAP allows quick, efficient, and interactive data access, enabling users to explore information without needing in-depth technical knowledge. The data is organized in dimensions as perceived by business users, enabling them to query and analyze it from different perspectives. Unlike data warehouses based on relational database technology, OLAP systems can conduct "what if" analysis, simulating the impact of decisions.

The key benefits of OLAP include supporting multidimensional analysis, providing valuable insights to executives, managers, and analysts, identifying business trends, fostering innovation, and facilitating drill-down/across actions. OLAP also performs complex calculations and trend analysis, manipulates data with numerous inter-relationships, and allows direct interaction with the data.

OLAP insulates users from the SQL language and the relational model, improves query performance for rapid analysis of large data volumes, offers high scalability, and supports a diverse array of tools. OLAP can present data in multiple formats, automate the maintenance of indexes and summaries, reduce the demand for reports from IT, and find applications in diverse areas such as forecasting, profitability analysis, customer analysis, budgeting, and marketing analysis.

OLAP versus OLTP

OLAP and online transaction processing (OLTP) are two distinct types of database systems designed for different purposes, and they exhibit key differences in structure, usage, and functionality.

Purpose

- OLAP: OLAP databases are optimized for complex queries and data analysis. They are designed to handle read-heavy workloads where users need to perform in-depth analysis, reporting, and decision-making based on historical data.

- OLTP: OLTP databases are designed for transactional processing. They excel in managing day-to-day operations and support a high volume of short, fast transactions, such as inserting, updating, and deleting records. OLTP systems are optimized for write-heavy workloads.

Data Structure

- OLAP: OLAP databases typically use a multidimensional data model, organizing data into cubes. These cubes consist of dimensions (categories by which the data is analyzed, such as time geography) and measures (quantitative data points).

- OLTP: OLTP databases use a relational data model with normalized tables. They focus on maintaining data integrity and efficiency in transaction processing. Relationships between tables are often normalized to reduce redundancy.

Operations

- OLAP: OLAP operations involve complex queries, aggregations, and data mining. Users perform operations such as slicing, dicing, drill-down, and pivoting to gain insights from historical data.

- OLTP: OLTP operations involve routine transactions such as insert, update, and delete. These systems prioritize maintaining the consistency and accuracy of real-time data for daily business operations.

Concurrency

- OLAP: OLAP systems are optimized for read-intensive operations, and concurrency is generally less of a concern. Analytical queries often run independently of each other.

- OLTP: Concurrency is a critical consideration in OLTP systems where multiple users may simultaneously execute transactions. These systems must ensure data consistency and enable concurrent access.

Data Storage

- OLAP: OLAP databases often use de-normalized or partially de-normalized data for faster query performance. Aggregations and pre-calculated measures commonly enhance analytical processing speed.

- OLTP: OLTP databases usually employ normalized data structures to minimize redundancy and maintain data integrity. This helps in efficient transaction processing.

In summary, OLAP and OLTP serve different purposes in the database landscape, with OLAP focused on analytical processing and OLTP on transactional processing. Each type's design, structure, and optimization align with the specific requirements of their intended use cases.

DATA DESIGN FOR BUSINESS

Data design for business focuses on structuring data to align with organizational goals and decision-making needs. By creating models and frameworks tailored to business processes, it ensures data is accessible, relevant, and actionable for driving strategic outcomes.

Role of Data Design in Business Operations

In the dynamic landscape of modern business operations, the concept of data design stands as a linchpin, orchestrating the systematic structuring and organization of information to catalyze informed decision-making. In essence, data design involves crafting the architecture and relationships within databases to ensure that data is stored and strategically positioned to drive efficiency, productivity, and strategic insights.

Imagine it as the blueprint guiding the flow of information within an organization, where well-designed data structures are akin to a well-oiled machine, seamlessly facilitating processes from sales forecasting and customer interactions to inventory management.

In a world where data is a strategic asset, data design emerges as the backbone, streamlining information access, analysis, and utilization. Its relevance extends beyond IT departments, resonating with every facet of the business, ensuring that data becomes a static repository and a dynamic force propelling organizations toward success in an increasingly data-driven era.

Strategic Importance of Data Structures

Well-designed data structures serve as the bedrock upon which organizational efficiency, effective decision-making, and overall business success are built. These structures are the invisible architects that determine how data flows and interacts within an organization. By organizing information systematically, they streamline processes, reduce redundancies, and enable swift access to critical data. In the realm of decision-making, well-designed data structures empower leaders with reliable, real-time insights, facilitating strategic and informed choices.

Whether optimizing supply chain logistics, personalizing customer experiences, or predicting market trends, the efficiency and coherence of data structures underpin the agility and competitiveness of a business. As the heartbeat of information management, these structures are instrumental in turning raw data into actionable intelligence, propelling businesses toward sustainable growth and success in an increasingly data-centric business landscape.

USER-CENTRIC DATA DESIGN

User-centric data design prioritizes the needs and experiences of end-users by ensuring data systems are intuitive, accessible, and aligned with user workflows. This approach enhances usability and empowers users to derive actionable insights effectively.

Needs of Business Users

The significance of designing data systems with a focus on the needs and perspectives of business users cannot be overstated. In a landscape where data is a key driver of decision-making, aligning data systems with the user experience ensures that information becomes an accessible and valuable asset rather than an inscrutable resource. Business users are not just consumers but also active contributors to the data ecosystem, and tailoring data systems to their needs enhances their ability to extract meaningful insights.

Benefits of User-Centric Data Design

User-centric data design offers numerous benefits that enhance the overall user experience and drive organizational success. Prioritizing intuitive navigation and empowering users to generate customized reports fosters a collaborative approach to data exploration. This emphasis on the user experience cultivates a data-driven culture, enabling business users to leverage data proficiently for strategic decision-making, thereby propelling the entire organization toward greater efficiency and success.

At its core, user-centric data design serves as the cornerstone of a more intuitive and productive user experience. Data systems are tailored to ensure seamless interaction and are crafted with a deep understanding of user workflows, preferences, and objectives. Intuitive interfaces and simplified navigation facilitate effortless access, analysis, and interpretation of data, reducing the learning curve and promoting fluid interaction.

Moreover, user-centric design incorporates tailored features such as customizable dashboards and interactive visualizations, empowering users to explore data in alignment with their specific needs. By abstracting complexities and presenting information comprehensibly, this approach encourages users to derive insights more efficiently. Ultimately, user-centric data design transforms data from a technical hurdle into a valuable tool, contributing to a maximally productive user experience.

VERSATILITY AND IMPACT OF EFFECTIVE DATA DESIGN

Effective data design ensures adaptability across various business needs while maximizing the usability and relevance of data systems. Its versatility enables organizations to streamline decision-making processes, driving impactful outcomes in dynamic and competitive environments.

Effectiveness of Data Design

Effective data design serves as a catalyst for positive transformations across diverse business processes. In supply chain management, streamlined and well-designed databases ensure accurate tracking of inventory levels, optimizing the entire supply chain for improved logistics and reduced costs. In CRM, organized and accessible customer data enables businesses to personalize interactions, anticipate needs, and enhance overall customer satisfaction. Financial decision-making benefits from data design through precise and real-time insights into revenue, expenses, and profitability.

Moreover, marketing strategies become more targeted and efficient as data design facilitates the analysis of customer behavior and the effectiveness of campaigns. These real-world examples highlight how thoughtful data design underpins operational excellence, strategic decision-making, and the ability to adapt to dynamic market conditions, ultimately fostering success across a spectrum of business domains.

Applications of Effective Data Design

Effective data design has an impact on diverse business applications, notably on streamlined reporting, improved CRM, and enhanced data-driven decision-making. Streamlined reporting becomes a reality as well-designed data structures enable the efficient extraction and presentation of relevant information. In CRM, organized and accessible customer data empowers businesses to build meaningful relationships by personalizing interactions, anticipating needs, and tailoring services.

Additionally, data design plays a pivotal role in data-driven decision-making, ensuring that leaders have access to accurate, real-time insights for strategic planning and informed choices. In essence, these applications underscore the versatile influence of data design, which transforms raw information into actionable intelligence that propels businesses toward increased efficiency, customer satisfaction, and overall success.

BEST PRACTICES FOR EFFECTIVE DATA DESIGN

Adopting best practices for effective data design ensures that data systems are reliable, scalable, and aligned with business goals. These practices help organizations optimize their data structures for improved performance, usability, and long-term adaptability.

Fostering Collaborative Data Design

Effective data design is a collaborative effort, and business users play a crucial role in ensuring that data systems meet their needs and contribute to overall usability. The clear articulation of business objectives and collaboration with IT and data experts are foundational steps, fostering a shared understanding of functional requirements and technical considerations. Understanding data sources their quality and advocating for user-friendly interfaces are pivotal to enhancing the user experience. Additionally, business users can contribute to data governance by adhering to standards and security protocols, promoting the reliability of the information.

Actively participating in user testing and feedback loops ensures that the design aligns with user preferences and needs. Continuous learning about data design advancements, documenting use cases, and advocating for scalability and flexibility are essential practices. Facilitating cross-functional communication further supports a holistic understanding of data needs, fostering a collaborative data culture within the organization. These practical guidelines empower business users to contribute effectively to the success of data design initiatives, creating systems that are not only functional but also adaptable to evolving business requirements.

Key Considerations

Considerations such as data accuracy, consistency, and standardized naming conventions are paramount in the realm of effective data design, influencing the reliability and usability of the entire data system. Data accuracy ensures that the information within the system reflects the real-world scenario it represents, preventing misleading insights and misguided decision-making. Consistency is vital for maintaining uniformity across datasets, reducing discrepancies, and enhancing the overall integrity of the data.

Standardized naming conventions play a crucial role in promoting clarity and understanding, facilitating seamless collaboration among users, and maintaining a coherent structure that is easy to navigate. When these considerations are prioritized, businesses can rely on their data systems as trustworthy sources of information, ensuring that the insights derived are accurate, consistent, and comprehensible, laying a robust foundation for informed decision-making and strategic planning.

TRENDS IN USER-FOCUSED DATA DESIGN

Emerging trends and advancements in data design are reshaping user involvement, making data solutions more accessible, intuitive, and sophisticated. These developments signal a shift toward addressing the specific needs and expectations of business users, ushering in a new era of user-centricity in data utilization.

Self-Service Analytics

One notable trend is the rise of self-service analytics platforms, empowering business users to independently explore and analyze data without extensive technical expertise. These platforms feature intuitive interfaces and user-friendly tools, prioritizing ease of use and enabling users to generate reports, visualize data, and derive insights on demand. By reducing dependence on technical experts, self-service analytics foster agility in business operations and promote a more responsive approach to data-driven decision-making.

Augmented Analytics

Complementing self-service analytics is the integration of augmented analytics, leveraging machine learning and AI algorithms to automate data preparation, uncover hidden patterns, and suggest actionable insights. Collaborating with business users, these intelligent algorithms streamline the analytics process, expediting analysis and increasing the depth and accuracy of insights. Augmented analytics not only enhances the sophistication of analysis but also empowers users to make informed decisions with greater confidence.

Evolution of Tools

Furthermore, advancements in data design include the evolution of tools with multidimensional analysis capabilities, providing users with a holistic understanding of business information. These tools enable simultaneous exploration of data from various perspectives, facilitating navigation through complex datasets and visualization across multiple dimensions. By democratizing the data landscape and fostering a collaborative environment, multidimensional analysis empowers business users to actively contribute to the design and analysis of data, driving more informed and strategic decision-making processes within organizations.

CHAPTER 11

R, SQL, AND PYTHON

R FOR BUSINESS USERS

Overview

In the dynamic landscape of modern business, the application of R stands as a beacon of innovation and efficiency in data analytics. R, originally conceived as a statistical computing language, has evolved into a versatile programming tool that empowers businesses to unlock the full potential of their data. As organizations grapple with an ever-expanding volume of information, R emerges as a crucial ally, offering a comprehensive suite of capabilities for data analysis, statistical modeling, and visualization.

This introductory exploration into the application of R in business seeks to unravel the multifaceted ways in which this programming language has become an indispensable asset, driving informed decision-making, fostering strategic insights, and ushering in a new era of data-driven excellence across diverse industry sectors.

Evolution

The historical context of R is rooted in the realm of statistical computing and data analysis. Developed by Ross Ihaka and Robert Gentleman at the University of Auckland, New Zealand, R emerged as an open-source alternative to proprietary statistical software in the mid-1990s. The language was built upon the S programming language, aiming to provide a free and accessible tool for statisticians and data scientists.

Over the years, R has evolved into a robust and versatile programming language, garnering a dedicated global community of users and developers. Its historical journey reflects a commitment to democratizing statistical analysis, making advanced data analytics accessible to a broader audience, and establishing R as a foundational tool in the modern data science landscape.

Key Features

R boasts a rich set of key features that solidify its standing as a powerhouse in statistical computing and data analysis. One of its prominent features is its extensive library of packages, contributed by a thriving community of developers, which significantly expands its functionality. This allows users to seamlessly integrate additional tools and techniques into their analyses. R's robust statistical capabilities, encompassing a wide range of tests and models, make it a preferred choice for researchers and analysts working with complex datasets. Its open-source nature fosters collaboration and innovation, enabling users to customize and extend the language to meet specific needs.

Moreover, R's exceptional data visualization tools, including the popular ggplot2 package, empower users to create compelling and insightful graphics for effective communication of findings. The interactive and dynamic nature of R, coupled with its adaptability to diverse data types, positions it as a versatile language, catering to the evolving demands of data scientists and analysts across various industries.

Business Applications of R

In the dynamic business landscape, the applications of R extend far beyond its origins as a statistical computing language. R has become a pivotal tool for businesses seeking to harness the power of data for strategic decision-making. The versatile nature of R finds expression in various domains, encompassing data analysis, statistical modeling, and visualization.

Data Analysis

Data analysis stands as a cornerstone of R's applications in the business realm, making it an indispensable tool for organizations aiming to extract actionable insights from their data reservoirs. R's robust and extensive set of statistical and analytical functions facilitates a comprehensive exploration of datasets, enabling business analysts to uncover patterns, trends, and outliers. With its versatile data manipulation capabilities, R allows professionals to clean, transform, and preprocess data efficiently, ensuring a solid foundation for meaningful analysis.

Business users leverage R to conduct EDA, hypothesis testing, and regression analysis, among other techniques. This proficiency in data analysis equips organizations with the means to derive valuable information, enabling evidence-based decision-making, strategic planning, and a competitive edge in today's data-driven business landscape. From market research to performance evaluation, R empowers businesses to navigate and thrive in an increasingly complex and information-rich environment.

Statistical Modeling

One of the paramount applications of R in business lies in its robust capabilities for statistical modeling. R provides a sophisticated and flexible environment for building and deploying statistical models, making it an invaluable asset for businesses seeking predictive insights. From linear and logistic regression to more advanced techniques such as machine learning algorithms, R accommodates a diverse array of modeling approaches. This capability is instrumental in various business scenarios, including sales forecasting, risk analysis, and customer behavior prediction.

The rich ecosystem of R packages, such as caret and randomForest, facilitates the implementation of complex modeling methodologies, empowering business analysts to develop accurate and nuanced models tailored to specific organizational needs. Through the application of statistical modeling in R, businesses can derive actionable insights, enhance decision-making processes, and gain a competitive edge in an increasingly data-centric landscape.

Visualization

R's ability to visualize data is the cornerstone of its applications within the business domain. Through its dedicated packages, such as ggplot2, R empowers business users to create compelling and informative visual representations of complex datasets. This extends beyond mere aesthetic appeal, serving as a potent tool for conveying intricate insights to diverse stakeholders. R facilitates the generation of a wide array of visualizations, from basic charts to intricate graphs, allowing businesses to explore trends, patterns, and outliers in their data.

Visualization in R is not limited to static images; it also supports interactivity and dynamic graphics, providing a deeper level of engagement with the data. This proficiency is paramount in areas such as market analysis, performance tracking, and decision support, where conveying complex information in an accessible manner is critical. Whether through interactive dashboards or publication-quality graphics, R's visualization capabilities empower businesses to transform raw data into meaningful narratives, enhancing comprehension and facilitating strategic decision-making processes.

Advantages and Limitations of R

Advantages

The advantages of R in the realm of data analytics and statistical computing are manifold, which has established it as a preferred tool for business applications. First and foremost, R's open-source nature fosters a collaborative environment, enabling a global community of users to contribute, share, and enhance its functionality continuously. Its extensive package ecosystem provides a vast repository of tools for diverse analytical tasks, allowing users to access specialized functions easily. R's versatility is evident in its applicability to various statistical methods and machine learning algorithms, making it adaptable to the evolving needs of data scientists and analysts.

Furthermore, R excels in data visualization, offering powerful and customizable tools such as ggplot2, enabling the creation of insightful graphics. With a strong emphasis on statistical rigor, reproducibility, and adaptability, R emerges as a comprehensive and flexible solution for businesses seeking to derive meaningful insights from their data, contributing significantly to evidence-based decision-making processes.

Limitations

While R is a formidable tool in data analytics, it is not without its limitations. One notable challenge is its steep learning curve, particularly for users new to programming or statistical languages. Its intricate syntax and diverse functions can be intimidating, potentially hindering widespread adoption, especially in less technically inclined business environments. Additionally, the memory management of R can be resource-intensive, leading to performance issues when dealing with exceptionally large datasets.

Despite the presence of a vast and active community, the support and documentation for certain packages may vary, posing challenges in troubleshooting and problem-solving. Another limitation lies in the execution speed, as R can be relatively slower than languages optimized for performance. While efforts are continuously being made to address these limitations, businesses considering the adoption of R should be mindful of these challenges and weigh them against the language's numerous strengths in statistical modeling, data analysis, and visualization.

Case Study: Predictive Maintenance

In a manufacturing setting, a company seeks to optimize its maintenance processes to reduce downtime and enhance overall operational efficiency. Leveraging the power of R, the data science team embarked on a predictive maintenance project. Historical data on equipment failures, maintenance schedules, and sensor readings were collected and processed using R's data manipulation capabilities. The team employed time-series analysis techniques and statistical modeling in R to identify patterns leading to equipment failures. Through the creation of predictive models, the company could anticipate when a machine was likely to fail, enabling proactive maintenance interventions.

The flexibility of R allowed the team to experiment with various machine learning algorithms, such as random forests and gradient boosting, to refine the predictive accuracy. The results were visualized using R's ggplot2 package, providing intuitive visual representations of maintenance predictions and historical failure patterns. As a result of implementing predictive maintenance strategies guided by R, the company experienced a substantial reduction in unplanned downtime, leading to increased productivity, cost savings, and improved overall equipment reliability.

This case study showcases the effectiveness of R in transforming raw data into actionable insights, thereby optimizing operational processes and delivering tangible business value.

SQL FOR BUSINESS USERS

SQL for business users empowers non-technical professionals to interact with and extract valuable insights from databases using simple, structured queries. By bridging the gap between data and decision-making, SQL enhances accessibility and enables informed, data-driven business strategies.

Overview

The role of structured query language (SQL) in business is fundamental to effective data management, accessibility, and decision-making.

SQL serves as the standard language for interacting with relational databases, providing businesses with a powerful tool to retrieve, manipulate, and analyze structured data. Its role is crucial in managing vast datasets, ensuring data integrity, and facilitating seamless communication between various applications and databases.

In the realm of business intelligence, SQL is a linchpin that enables professionals to craft complex queries for insightful reporting and analysis. It empowers organizations to extract specific information from databases swiftly, supporting diverse functions such as CRM, financial reporting, and inventory management. The scalability and efficiency of SQL make it indispensable for businesses of all sizes, as it helps foster data-driven decision-making and contributes to the overall success and competitiveness of modern enterprises.

Fundamental Concepts

At its core, SQL is built upon fundamental concepts that form the backbone of relational RDBMs. The language revolves around the concept of tables, which represent the structured storage of data. Each table comprises rows and columns, where rows contain individual records, and columns define the attributes or characteristics of those records. The fundamental operations in SQL include querying data using SELECT statements, inserting new data with INSERT, updating existing records using UPDATE, and deleting data with DELETE.

Primary keys uniquely identify each record in a table, while foreign keys establish relationships between tables, both crucial for maintaining data integrity. The SQL data definition language (DDL) encompasses statements such as CREATE, ALTER, and DROP, allowing the definition and modification of database structures. These fundamental concepts empower users to interact with databases seamlessly, retrieve information efficiently, and maintain the integrity of the data housed within relational databases.

Database Management Systems

Database management systems (DBMSs) play a pivotal role in the effective implementation of SQL within business operations. A DBMS serves as an infrastructure that organizes, stores and manages vast volumes of data in a structured manner, enabling businesses to leverage the full potential of SQL. The synergy between SQL and DBMS allows seamless interaction with relational databases, facilitating data retrieval, manipulation, and maintenance. DBMS ensures data integrity and security, managing concurrent access by multiple users and providing mechanisms for backup and recovery.

Business operations, ranging from CRM to inventory tracking, heavily rely on the efficiency of DMSs in conjunction with SQL queries. The robustness of this combination not only enhances data-driven decision-making but also supports the scalability and reliability essential for businesses to thrive in an increasingly data-centric landscape.

Business Applications of SQL

SQL serves as a vital tool in BI, enabling efficient data retrieval, manipulation, and analysis to support decision-making processes. From generating reports to monitoring performance metrics, SQL enhances operational efficiency and strategic planning across industries.

Data Retrieval

A common use case in business for data retrieval involves extracting information from a customer database to analyze purchasing patterns. Consider a retail company aiming to understand customer behavior and preferences for strategic decision-making. Using SQL, the business can execute queries to retrieve relevant data from its customer database. For instance, a SELECT statement might be crafted to obtain details such as customer IDs, purchase history, product preferences, and demographic information.

The SQL query could further involve JOIN operations to combine data from multiple tables, allowing the company to correlate customer information with product categories or sales promotions. The retrieved data can then be analyzed to identify trends, popular products, or seasonal variations in customer buying behavior. This valuable insight can enable inventory management, marketing strategies, and personalized customer engagement initiatives, illustrating how data retrieval through SQL contributes directly to informed decision-making and business optimization.

Data Modification

A common use case in business for data modification using SQL revolves around inventory management and product updates. Consider a retail company that regularly receives new stock, discontinues certain products, or adjusts pricing. In such scenarios, SQL's UPDATE and DELETE statements become vital tools. For instance, the business may need to update the price of a specific product category or modify the stock levels after a new shipment arrives. SQL queries can be designed to efficiently update these records in the database.

Additionally, if a particular product is discontinued, the DELETE statement can be applied to remove relevant records from the inventory database. By leveraging SQL for data modification, businesses ensure that their databases accurately reflect real-time information and support accurate inventory levels, pricing updates, and effective product management, ultimately contributing to streamlined operations and improved decision-making processes.

Data Definition

A common use case in business for data definition using SQL involves creating and modifying database structures to accommodate evolving business needs. Consider a scenario where a financial institution introduces a new banking product, such as a specialized savings account. The data definition language of SQL is used to capture the specific details and attributes associated with this product. Using statements such as CREATE TABLE, the business can define a new table to store information about specialized savings accounts. The DDL statements allow the specification of attributes such as account type, interest rates, and eligibility criteria.

In addition, ALTER TABLE statements can be employed to modify existing tables, perhaps to add new fields or adjust data types. By leveraging SQL's data definition capabilities, businesses can seamlessly adapt their database structures to incorporate new business offerings, regulatory requirements, or other changes, ensuring that the database remains aligned with the evolving needs of the organization.

Advanced SQL Applications in BI

Advanced SQL applications in BI empower organizations to perform complex data analyses, optimize query performance, and generate actionable insights. These applications extend beyond basic data retrieval, enabling tasks like predictive analytics, data warehousing, and advanced reporting for strategic decision-making.

Reporting and Analysis

The importance of SQL in BI cannot be overstated, particularly in regard to reporting and analysis. SQL serves as the backbone for querying and extracting relevant information from databases, enabling BI professionals to retrieve, filter, and aggregate data for analytical purposes. Its declarative nature allows users to articulate complex queries that efficiently sift through large datasets to extract meaningful insights. The role of SQL in BI reporting is particularly crucial for creating customized and dynamic reports that cater to specific business requirements.

With the ability to perform calculations, group data, and join tables, SQL empowers BI analysts to transform raw data into comprehensible reports, dashboards, and visualizations. The speed and precision with which SQL operates are essential for the real-time and ad-hoc analysis demands of business intelligence, providing decision-makers with the timely and accurate information they need to make informed choices and steer the organization toward its strategic objectives.

Data Warehousing

The importance of SQL in BI for data warehousing lies in its capacity to efficiently manage and manipulate vast datasets within the context of a centralized and optimized data storage system. SQL plays a pivotal role in designing, querying, and maintaining data warehouses, where large volumes of structured and unstructured data are consolidated for analytical purposes. Through SQL's DDL capabilities, BI professionals can create and modify the schema of data warehouse tables, ensuring alignment with reporting needs.

Furthermore, SQL's data manipulation language (DML) facilitates the extraction and transformation of data within a warehouse, enabling complex queries and aggregations necessary for comprehensive BI analysis. The structured nature of SQL queries in data warehousing allows seamless integration with reporting and analysis tools, streamlining the extraction of meaningful insights from the warehouse's rich repository. In essence, SQL is indispensable in the realm of BI for data warehousing, providing the foundation for effective data storage, retrieval, and analysis critical to informed decision-making.

Best Practices

SQL best practices ensure efficient, accurate, and maintainable database interactions, supporting robust data management and analytics. By adhering to these practices, organizations can enhance query performance, reduce errors, and streamline data processes to meet business objectives effectively.

Writing Efficient Queries

The best practices and optimization in SQL, especially concerning the crafting of efficient queries, are pivotal for ensuring optimal database performance. One key practice involves indexing, where strategically placing indexes on columns used in WHERE clauses or JOIN conditions significantly accelerates query execution. Properly structuring queries, avoiding the use of unnecessary SELECT * statements, and retrieving only the required columns contribute to minimizing data transfer and improving query efficiency. Parameterizing queries instead of using hardcoded values enhances query plan reuse and, subsequently, performance.

Regularly analyzing and optimizing the database schema, ensuring appropriate data types and normalization, further aids in improving query speed. Monitoring query execution plans, identifying and resolving performance bottlenecks, and leveraging the EXPLAIN statement are also essential practices. Finally, employing appropriate caching mechanisms and considering the utilization of stored procedures contribute to enhancing the overall efficiency of SQL queries, aligning them with best practices for optimal database performance.

Security Considerations

Best practices and optimization in SQL, particularly concerning security considerations, are paramount for safeguarding sensitive data and preventing unauthorized access. Employing parameterized queries or prepared statements helps defend against SQL injection attacks by ensuring that user input is properly sanitized. Implementing the principle of least privilege, wherein users are granted only the necessary permissions, enhances the security posture of the database. Regularly updating and patching the DBMS, as well as monitoring security advisories, guards against vulnerabilities. Encrypting sensitive data at rest and in transit further fortifies data protection.

Additionally, auditing and logging activities, such as failed login attempts and critical transactions, contribute to maintaining a secure environment. Leveraging strong authentication mechanisms, employing firewalls, and restricting network access to the database server are essential components of a comprehensive security strategy. Staying informed about emerging security threats and adopting industry-standard encryption protocols are ongoing practices that contribute to robust security measures in SQL environments.

PYTHON FOR BUSINESS USERS

Python has become a powerful tool for business users, offering versatility in data analysis, automation, and visualization. Its simplicity and extensive libraries make it an ideal choice for solving complex business challenges and driving data-driven decisions.

Overview

In the contemporary landscape of business, Python has emerged as a powerful and versatile programming language, reshaping the way organizations approach data analysis, automation, and software development. Renowned for its readability, simplicity, and extensive ecosystem of libraries, Python has transcended its origins as a general-purpose language to become a strategic asset for businesses seeking efficiency and innovation. From data analytics and machine learning to Web development and automation, Python's adaptability and scalability make it a favored tool for addressing diverse business needs.

Evolution

The evolution of Python has been a compelling journey marked by continuous refinement and community-driven innovation. Conceived in the late 1980s by Dutch programmer Guido van Rossum, Python was officially released as Python 0.9.0 in 1991. The language's design philosophy, emphasizing readability and simplicity, has remained a guiding principle throughout its evolution. Over the years, Python has undergone significant updates and enhancements, with each version introducing new features, libraries, and optimizations.

The release of Python 2.0 in 2000 and the subsequent transition to Python 3 in 2008 marked a pivotal phase, addressing language inconsistencies and improving functionality. The popularity of Python surged in the 2010s, fueled by its robust community support, diverse applications in data science, machine learning, and Web development, and its adoption by major technology companies. The language's evolution has not only solidified its status as one of the most versatile and accessible programming languages but also positioned Python as a driving force behind technological innovation in the realms of business, academia, and open-source development.

Role in Business Analytics

Python plays a central and transformative role in the field of business analytics, offering a comprehensive suite of tools and libraries that empower organizations to derive actionable insights from their data. Renowned for its simplicity and readability, Python serves as a versatile language for data manipulation, statistical analysis, and machine learning. Libraries such as NumPy, pandas, and scikit-learn provide robust functionalities for data cleaning, exploration, and predictive modeling. Python's integration with popular business intelligence tools, coupled with its ability to handle big data through frameworks such as Apache Spark, makes it a go-to choice for businesses dealing with diverse and large datasets.

Additionally, Python's visualization libraries, including Matplotlib and Seaborn, facilitate the creation of compelling graphs and charts for effective data communication. As businesses increasingly rely on data-driven decision-making, Python's role in business analytics has become instrumental, enabling professionals to uncover patterns, trends, and correlations that drive strategic insights and enhance overall operational efficiency.

Business Applications of Python

Python has emerged as a powerful tool for business applications, offering versatility and efficiency in data analysis, automation, and decision-making. Its simplicity and rich ecosystem of libraries make it an ideal choice for solving complex business challenges across various industries.

Automation and Scripting

Python has emerged as a linchpin in business automation and scripting, offering a robust and user-friendly environment for streamlining workflows and enhancing operational efficiency. Its clean syntax and extensive standard library make it an ideal choice for automating repetitive tasks, ranging from data processing and file manipulation to system administration and deployment scripting. The versatility of Python allows businesses to create custom scripts that seamlessly integrate with existing systems and software, facilitating seamless communication and task orchestration.

Additionally, the compatibility of Python with various platforms ensures that automation scripts can be deployed across diverse environments. From automating routine administrative functions to scripting complex business processes, Python's role in automation and scripting empowers organizations to reduce manual effort, minimize errors, and foster a more agile and responsive operational framework. As businesses increasingly prioritize efficiency and productivity, Python's accessibility and adaptability position it as a key tool in the automation toolbox.

Machine Learning and Predictive Analytics

Python has become a cornerstone in business applications of machine learning and predictive analytics, revolutionizing the way organizations harness data for strategic decision-making. The language's rich ecosystem of libraries, which includes TensorFlow, PyTorch, and scikit-learn, empowers businesses to develop sophisticated machine learning models and predictive analytics solutions. Python's readability and versatility expedite the entire machine learning pipeline, from data preprocessing and feature engineering to model training and evaluation. Its integration with Jupyter Notebooks facilitates interactive and collaborative exploration of data, fostering a dynamic environment for experimentation.

Businesses leverage Python's capabilities to predict customer behavior, optimize supply chain logistics, and make informed financial forecasts. As a result, Python stands as a key enabler, democratizing the application of advanced analytics and machine learning across diverse industries and paving the way for data-driven insights that drive innovation and competitive advantage.

Web Development and Integration

Python has emerged as a powerhouse in the realm of Web development and integration, playing a pivotal role in shaping dynamic and scalable digital solutions for businesses. Through frameworks such as Django, Flask, and Pyramid, Python offers a streamlined and efficient approach to building Web applications. Its simplicity, readability, and extensive libraries facilitate rapid development, allowing businesses to create robust and feature-rich Web sites. The versatility of Python extends beyond Web development; it serves as an excellent tool for integrating diverse systems and technologies.

With libraries such as Requests for HTTP requests and RESTful API interactions, businesses can seamlessly connect their applications, databases, and third-party services. The compatibility of the language with major Web servers and cloud platforms enhances deployment flexibility. Whether crafting interactive Web sites, developing APIs, or orchestrating complex integrations, Python's role in Web development and integration empowers businesses to create scalable, agile, and interconnected digital ecosystems that cater to evolving user needs and industry standards.

Integrating Python with Other Business Tools

Integrating Python with other business tools enhances its utility, enabling seamless data exchange, automation, and advanced analytics. This integration empowers businesses to create cohesive workflows by connecting Python with platforms like Excel, databases, and cloud-based applications.

Connecting to Databases

Integrating Python with databases is a crucial aspect of leveraging its capabilities for data-driven applications. Python's versatility and extensive support for database connectivity make it an ideal choice for businesses aiming to manage and manipulate their data seamlessly. Libraries such as SQLAlchemy provide a powerful and database-agnostic toolkit, facilitating the creation of robust, efficient, and maintainable database-driven applications. Python's standard library includes modules such as sqlite3 for SQLite databases and psycopg2 for PostgreSQL, offering native support for widely used database systems.

Furthermore, popular object-relational mapping (ORM) frameworks such as Django ORM and SQLAlchemy ORM simplify database interactions by abstracting SQL queries into Python code. Whether connecting to traditional relational databases or modern NoSQL databases, Python's integration capabilities enable businesses to handle data effectively, ensuring smooth and flexible interaction between their applications and the underlying data storage systems.

API Integration

Python's versatility shines when it comes to seamless API integration, making it an invaluable tool for businesses aiming to connect and communicate with various Web services and third-party applications. Python's requests library provides a straightforward and powerful interface for sending HTTP requests and handling responses, forming the backbone of API interactions. Additionally, frameworks such as Flask and Django enable the creation of robust Web services, allowing businesses to expose their APIs for external consumption or integrate with external APIs effortlessly. With the popularity of RESTful APIs, Python's simplicity in handling JSON data further streamlines the integration process.

Libraries such as requests-oauthlib facilitate secure authentication and authorization processes, which are crucial for API integration. Whether retrieving data from social media platforms, integrating payment gateways, or automating interactions with cloud services, Python's extensive ecosystem empowers businesses to achieve seamless API integration, fostering interoperability and expanding the functionality of their applications.

Python Challenges

While Python is a powerful tool for business applications, it comes with challenges such as managing dependencies, ensuring scalability, and addressing performance issues. Overcoming these hurdles is crucial to fully leverage Python's potential in dynamic business environments.

Learning Curve

A notable challenge associated with Python lies in its learning curve, particularly for individuals new to programming or transitioning from languages with different syntax structures. While Python is celebrated for its readability and simplicity, grasping fundamental programming concepts can still pose a hurdle for beginners. The use of indentation for code blocks, which is unique to Python, may initially be unfamiliar and may require adjustment for those accustomed to braces or other delimiters.

Additionally, Python's dynamic typing and lack of explicit variable declarations can lead to unexpected behavior for those accustomed to statically typed languages. It is important to note that the learning curve diminishes quickly with practice, and many resources, including extensive documentation, tutorials, and an active community, are available to support newcomers as they navigate the initial challenges and discover the language's strengths.

Maintenance and Support

A challenge associated with Python in the context of maintenance and support involves version compatibility and the transition from Python 2 to Python 3. The decision to sunset Python 2 in favor of Python 3, while necessary for language improvements, has created a period of coexistence where legacy codebases may require updates for continued support. This transition has posed challenges for businesses, especially those with extensive existing projects running on Python 2, as they navigate the process of migrating and ensuring compatibility with the latest versions.

Additionally, the diverse landscape of third-party libraries and packages may not be immediately updated, potentially causing compatibility issues and necessitating diligent maintenance efforts. While the community actively works to mitigate these challenges, managing the transition and ensuring the longevity of Python applications can be a noteworthy consideration for businesses relying on the language for their software solutions.

CHAPTER 12

REPORTING IN BI

Reporting in business intelligence involves presenting data-driven insights to support decision-making. The key topics or aspects related to reporting in BI are described in this chapter.

DATA VISUALIZATION

Data visualization is a crucial aspect of BI reporting. It involves presenting data in visual formats such as charts, graphs, and dashboards to make complex information more understandable. Effective data visualization enhances the communication of trends, patterns, and outliers in the data.

Types of Data Visualization

Data visualization encompasses a diverse range of techniques, including charts, graphs, and maps, each serving a unique purpose in conveying information. Charts, such as bar charts or pie charts, are effective for showcasing proportions and trends, while line charts or scatter plots are ideal for illustrating relationships and patterns. Alternatively, maps provide geographical insights. Understanding the distinct strengths of each visualization type empowers analysts to select the most appropriate method based on the nature of the data and the insights they aim to communicate.

Choosing a Visualization

Selecting the appropriate visualization for different data types is a critical aspect of effective data presentation. Categorical, numerical, and temporal data may require distinct visualization methods to represent their characteristics accurately. For categorical data, bar charts or pie charts are often suitable, while numerical data might be best presented through histograms or box plots. Temporal trends, however, can be effectively communicated using line charts. By aligning the visualization method with the inherent nature of the data, analysts enhance the clarity and impact of their insights.

Best Practices

Following best practices in data visualization is essential for creating impactful and accurate representations of information. Clarity, simplicity, and relevance are key principles, emphasizing the importance of avoiding unnecessary complexity and embellishments that could obscure the message. Proper labeling, color usage, and consistent formatting contribute to a clear and user-friendly visual presentation. Additionally, adhering to principles of data integrity ensures that visualizations accurately reflect the underlying data, fostering trust among stakeholders who rely on these insights for decision-making.

Data Visualization Tools

A myriad of tools is available to facilitate data visualization, each offering unique features and capabilities. Tableau, renowned for its user-friendly interface, empowers users to create interactive and visually appealing dashboards. Power BI, integrated with Microsoft's ecosystem, excels in transforming raw data into compelling visual narratives. D3.js, a JavaScript library, provides extensive flexibility for custom visualizations. Selecting the most suitable tool depends on factors such as user expertise and data complexity. These tools enable organizations to leverage effective and tailored data visualization based on the desired level of interactivity.

Storytelling

Data storytelling involves weaving a narrative around data insights to make them more compelling and accessible to a broader audience. Beyond the visual representation of data, storytelling techniques focus on constructing a narrative that engages and informs. This involves identifying key insights, structuring a coherent storyline, and aligning the narrative with the audience's level of understanding. Effective data storytelling goes beyond presenting numbers; it contextualizes data, providing a meaningful framework for decision-makers to interpret and act upon the insights gleaned from the visualizations.

KEY PERFORMANCE INDICATORS (KPIs)

KPIs are measurable values that demonstrate how effectively a company is achieving its key business objectives. Reporting in BI often involves tracking and presenting KPIs to provide a snapshot of performance. This helps stakeholders monitor progress toward goals and make informed decisions.

Strategic Selection of KPIs

The process of identifying and defining KPIs is fundamental to effective performance management. Organizations must carefully select KPIs that align with their strategic objectives, reflecting the critical aspects of performance that directly contribute to overall success. This involves a thorough understanding of the business context, collaboration among stakeholders, and a focus on measurable outcomes. Whether it is customer satisfaction, revenue growth, or operational efficiency, well-defined KPIs serve as compass points, guiding organizations toward their desired goals and allowing for meaningful assessment and improvement.

Performance Analysis through KPIs

Once KPIs are identified, measuring and quantifying performance through appropriate metrics is essential for meaningful analysis. Organizations employ specific metrics aligned with each KPI to provide quantitative insights into performance levels. Whether using financial metrics such as revenue growth, customer-centric metrics like net promoter score (NPS), or operational metrics such as efficiency ratios, accurate measurement ensures that organizations gain a precise understanding of their current performance status. Effective KPI measurement requires consistent data collection, standardized metrics, and a robust analytics infrastructure to derive actionable insights from the accumulated data.

Setting KPI Targets and Benchmarks

Establishing realistic targets and benchmarks for KPIs is a crucial step in performance management. Targets provide a clear direction for improvement and act as motivators for teams to strive for excellence. Benchmarks, derived from industry standards or historical performance, offer valuable context for evaluating an organization's standing relative to peers or past achievements. Striking the right balance between challenging yet achievable targets is essential to drive continuous improvement. Effective goal-setting aligns with the organization's overarching strategy, ensuring that KPIs serve as meaningful indicators of progress and success.

Monitoring and Analyzing KPI Trends

Continuous monitoring and analysis of KPI trends provide organizations with the agility to respond promptly to changing circumstances. Regularly tracking KPIs allows for the identification of emerging patterns, potential issues, or areas requiring intervention. This proactive approach facilitates data-driven decision-making, enabling organizations to adapt strategies in real-time. Analyzing KPI trends involves employing statistical methods, data visualization techniques, and trend analysis to extract actionable insights. By remaining vigilant about evolving KPI trends, organizations can optimize their operations, enhance their performance, and promptly address challenges.

Aligning KPIs with Business Objectives

The ultimate effectiveness of KPIs lies in their alignment with broader business objectives. KPIs should not exist in isolation but rather serve as integral components of the organization's strategic framework. Ensuring a direct connection between KPIs and business objectives establishes a clear line of sight, allowing stakeholders at all levels to understand how their efforts contribute to the overarching goals of the organization. This alignment fosters a sense of purpose, engagement, and collective responsibility, creating a performance management ecosystem where every KPI serves a strategic purpose in driving the organization toward success.

AD HOC REPORTING

Ad hoc reporting allows users to create custom reports on the fly without relying on predefined templates. It empowers users to explore data, ask specific questions, and generate reports tailored to their unique needs. Ad hoc reporting enhances flexibility and supports more dynamic decision-making.

Role of Ad Hoc Reporting

Ad hoc reporting refers to the ability to generate on-the-fly, customized reports in response to specific and unplanned information needs. The primary purpose of ad hoc reporting is to empower users with the flexibility to explore and analyze data without relying on predefined reports. It caters to the dynamic and evolving nature of business inquiries, allowing users to quickly access, manipulate, and visualize data as per their immediate requirements. Ad hoc reporting plays a crucial role in democratizing data access within organizations, enabling users at various levels to make informed decisions based on real-time insights.

Creating Ad Hoc Reports in BI Tools

The process of creating ad hoc reports with business intelligence tools involves a user-friendly interface that enables nontechnical users to generate reports without extensive IT support. Users typically interact with drag-and-drop functionalities, select relevant data elements, apply filters, and arrange visualizations in a way that suits their analysis. BI tools provide a range of prebuilt templates and data connectors, facilitating a seamless experience for users to extract meaningful information from the underlying data sources. The emphasis is on simplicity and user empowerment, allowing individuals to be self-sufficient in generating reports tailored to their unique analytical needs.

Customizing Ad Hoc Reports

An essential feature of ad hoc reporting is the ability to customize reports in real-time as users interact with the data. This customization extends to modifying visualizations, adjusting data filters, and selecting different dimensions or metrics on the fly. The goal is to provide users with immediate control over how the data is presented, ensuring that the reporting output aligns precisely with their current analysis goals. This real-time customization capability distinguishes ad hoc reporting from traditional reporting methods, offering a dynamic and interactive experience for users seeking agile and responsive data exploration.

Ad Hoc Query Builders and Filters

Ad hoc query builders are integral components of BI tools that empower users to construct queries without the need for complex coding or SQL expertise. These builders facilitate the creation of customized queries to retrieve specific data subsets for inclusion in ad hoc reports. Additionally, the use of filters allows users to refine data based on criteria such as time frames, geographical regions, or product categories. The combination of query builders and filters ensures that users have granular control over the data they include in their reports, enhancing the precision and relevance of the insights derived through ad hoc reporting.

Best Practices

Ad hoc reporting, when employed effectively, can significantly enhance data-driven decision-making within organizations. The best practices in ad hoc reporting involve fostering a user-friendly BI environment, providing adequate training and support, and encouraging a culture of data exploration. It is crucial to establish data governance policies to ensure data accuracy and consistency across ad hoc reports.

Moreover, organizations should regularly assess the performance and usability of their ad hoc reporting tools, seeking feedback from users to continually improve the reporting experience. Clear communication of available features, data sources, and reporting capabilities contributes to maximizing the benefits of ad hoc reporting while maintaining data integrity and reliability.

SCHEDULED REPORTING

Scheduled reporting involves the automated generation and delivery of reports at predefined intervals. This ensures that stakeholders receive timely and consistent information without manual intervention. Scheduled reports are often used for regular updates, performance reviews, and compliance reporting.

Automated Report Scheduling

Automated report scheduling is a critical functionality in BI systems that streamlines the process of report generation and distribution. This feature allows users to set predefined schedules for report creation, ensuring that up-to-date insights are delivered to stakeholders without manual intervention. Automated scheduling enhances efficiency by eliminating the need for users to initiate report generation manually, enabling timely and consistent delivery of information to decision-makers. This feature is particularly beneficial for recurring reports, such as monthly performance summaries or weekly sales dashboards, contributing to a more streamlined and automated reporting workflow.

Frequency for Scheduled Reports

Selecting the appropriate frequency for scheduled reports is a key decision that depends on the nature of the information and the specific needs of the stakeholders. The frequency could range from daily updates for operational metrics to monthly or quarterly summaries for strategic planning. Understanding the cadence of business activities and the urgency of decision-making guides the determination of report frequency. Striking a balance between providing timely insights and avoiding information overload is crucial. Careful consideration of the reporting frequency ensures that stakeholders receive the right level of detail at the right intervals, aligning with the organization's operational and strategic objectives.

Managing and Customizing Reports

Efficient management and customization of scheduled reports are essential for tailoring the reporting experience to the diverse needs of stakeholders. BI tools often provide user-friendly interfaces for managing scheduled tasks, allowing users to modify, pause, or delete scheduled reports as business requirements evolve. Customization options may include choosing specific recipients, adjusting report formats, and incorporating personalized annotations. By offering flexibility in managing and customizing scheduled reports, organizations can adapt their reporting practices to changing circumstances, ensuring that each stakeholder receives information in a format that best suits their decision-making processes.

Integrating Scheduled Reports

The integration of scheduled reports with other systems enhances the overall impact and accessibility of BI insights. BI platforms often support integration with email systems, collaboration tools, or ERP systems. This integration ensures that scheduled reports seamlessly reach users within their preferred communication channels, fostering a connected and collaborative environment. By linking scheduled reports with broader business systems, organizations can enable stakeholders to access relevant insights within the context of their daily workflows, further enhancing the value and utility of BI-generated information.

Data Accuracy

Data accuracy is paramount in the context of scheduled reports, as stakeholders rely on these reports for informed decision-making. Ensuring the integrity and accuracy of data involves implementing robust data governance practices, validating data sources, and performing regular quality checks. Organizations should establish protocols for data validation and reconciliation to detect and address discrepancies before scheduled reports are generated and distributed. By prioritizing data accuracy, organizations instill confidence in the insights derived from scheduled reports, strengthening the impact of BI on strategic and operational decision-making.

DRILL-DOWN AND DRILL-UP CAPABILITIES

Drill-down and drill-up functionalities enable users to navigate through different levels of data granularity. Users can start with summarized data and then drill-down to more detailed information or drill-up to view higher-level aggregates. These capabilities enhance the ability to explore data hierarchies and understand trends at various levels.

Drill-Down and Drill-Up in BI

Drill-down and drill-up are essential features in BI that empower users to navigate through data hierarchies for deeper insights. Drill-down involves moving from a higher-level summary of data to a more detailed view, revealing additional layers of information. Conversely, drill-up allows users to summarize detailed data back into higher-level overviews. These capabilities are instrumental in exploring data relationships, identifying patterns, and understanding the nuances within datasets. The flexibility of drill-down and drill-up enhances the user's ability to interact with data dynamically, contributing to a more comprehensive understanding of business metrics.

Drill-Down Hierarchies

The successful implementation of drill-down hierarchies is crucial for delivering a seamless and intuitive user experience in BI applications. Drill-down hierarchies define the structured layers of data that users can navigate through, providing a logical and organized framework. This involves establishing relationships between different levels of data, such as moving from yearly to monthly or from region to individual stores. BI tools often offer intuitive interfaces for defining and configuring drill-down hierarchies, allowing organizations to tailor the data exploration experience to their specific reporting needs.

Data Exploration Through Drill-Down

Drill-down capabilities significantly enhance data exploration by allowing users to delve into specific subsets of information. This feature enables users to investigate trends, anomalies, or outliers within the data, providing a more detailed and nuanced understanding of underlying patterns. By facilitating a granular exploration of data, drill-down empowers users to answer specific questions, validate assumptions, and discover valuable insights that might be concealed in higher-level summaries. The iterative nature of drill-down supports a dynamic and interactive data exploration process, fostering a more insightful and informed decision-making environment.

Drill-Up for Summarizing Data Levels

Drill-up functionality is equally important for summarizing data levels and maintaining a comprehensive perspective. After exploring detailed data, users can employ drill-up to aggregate information back to higher-level overviews. This is particularly valuable for presenting concise summaries in reports and dashboards or when transitioning from a focus on specific elements to a broader context. Implementing effective drill-up mechanisms ensures that users can seamlessly navigate between different levels of granularity, balancing detailed exploration with the need for summarized insights.

User Interaction and Experience

The success of drill-down and drill-up functionality hinges on the user interaction and experience provided by BI tools. Intuitive interfaces, responsive design, and clear visual cues contribute to a positive user experience, allowing users to navigate effortlessly between data levels. Providing contextual information and tooltips enhances user understanding during drill-down, while smooth transitions and clear navigation paths contribute to a seamless exploration process. User-friendly BI applications ensure that both novice and experienced users can leverage drill-down and drill-up features effectively, promoting widespread adoption and maximizing the value derived from interactive data exploration.

INTERACTIVE REPORTING

Interactive reporting allows users to engage with data dynamically. It includes features such as interactive filters, sorting, and user-driven exploration of datasets. Users can manipulate the data in real-time, fostering a more immersive and personalized reporting experience. Interactive reporting empowers users to gain deeper insights by interactively analyzing data based on their preferences.

Interactive Features of BI Tools

Interactive features are integral components of modern BI tools, providing users with dynamic and engaging experiences when exploring and analyzing data. These features encompass a range of functionalities, such as drill-down, filtering, and real-time updates, fostering a user-centric approach to data exploration. By incorporating interactive elements, BI tools empower users to tailor their analytical journeys, facilitating a deeper understanding of the underlying data and revealing actionable insights.

User Interaction with Reports

Enabling user interaction with reports is a key objective in BI design, promoting engagement and customization. BI tools offer a variety of interactive elements, including clickable charts, expandable data points, and personalized dashboards, allowing users to interact with the information presented. This interactivity not only enhances user satisfaction but also enables a more dynamic exploration of data, fostering a collaborative and iterative approach to decision-making.

Filtering and Sorting

The capability to filter and sort data in interactive reports is fundamental for users to focus on specific information relevant to their analysis. BI tools provide intuitive interfaces for users to apply filters, refine data based on criteria, and sort information for clearer insights. These features empower users to navigate through large datasets efficiently, ensuring that the presented data aligns with their analytical objectives.

Real-Time Data Interaction

Real-time data interaction is a sophisticated feature of BI tools that allows users to engage with data as it updates in real-time. This capability is particularly valuable for monitoring live metrics, responding to changing conditions promptly, and making data-driven decisions in dynamic environments. BI tools that support real-time data interaction contribute to a proactive decision-making culture where users can stay informed and responsive to evolving scenarios.

Balancing Complexity and Simplicity

Achieving a delicate balance between complexity and simplicity is crucial in designing effective interactive reports. BI tools need to provide advanced functionalities for users with in-depth analytical needs while ensuring that the interface remains user-friendly and accessible to a broader audience. The challenge lies in offering sophisticated features without overwhelming users, promoting ease of use and accessibility in interactive reporting interfaces.

MOBILE REPORTING

With the increasing prevalence of mobile devices, BI reporting must cater to mobile users. Mobile reporting ensures that stakeholders can access reports on smartphones or tablets, providing flexibility in how and where they consume information. Responsive design, mobile-friendly dashboards, and optimized visualizations contribute to a seamless reporting experience on various devices.

Empowering Decisions with Mobile Reporting

Mobile reporting has become increasingly vital in the realm of business intelligence as professionals demand on-the-go access to critical insights. The importance of mobile reporting lies in empowering decision-makers to access relevant data anytime and anywhere, facilitating timely and informed decision-making. Mobile reporting ensures that KPIs, dashboards, and analytics are readily available on mobile devices, enhancing the agility and responsiveness of organizations in a fast-paced business landscape.

Responsive Design for Mobile BI

Responsive design is a pivotal aspect of mobile BI, ensuring that reporting interfaces adapt seamlessly to various screen sizes and device types. In the context of BI tools, responsive design optimizes the user experience on mobile devices by adjusting layouts, content, and interactions dynamically. This approach enhances accessibility and usability, allowing users to navigate reports effortlessly, regardless of the device they are using. A well-implemented responsive design is fundamental for delivering a consistent and effective mobile BI experience.

Mobile BI Tools and Platforms

Mobile BI tools and platforms play a central role in delivering BI content to mobile users. These tools are specifically designed to address the unique requirements of mobile reporting, offering functionalities such as touch-optimized interfaces, interactive dashboards, and intuitive navigation. Leading BI platforms provide dedicated mobile applications or Web-based solutions that enable users to consume, interact with, and share BI insights directly from their mobile devices.

Offline Access and Mobile BI

Offline access is a critical feature of mobile BI, ensuring that users can access and interact with reports even in environments with limited or no Internet connectivity. This capability is essential for mobile professionals who may need to review BI content while traveling or in areas with unreliable network coverage. Mobile BI tools that support offline access empower users to remain productive and make data-driven decisions regardless of their immediate connectivity status.

Security in Mobile Reporting

Security considerations are paramount in the implementation of mobile reporting to safeguard sensitive business information. Mobile BI tools need to adhere to robust security measures, including data encryption, secure authentication, and authorization protocols. Additionally, features such as remote wipe capabilities and multifactor authentication contribute to securing BI content on mobile devices. Organizations must prioritize the protection of data during transit and on mobile devices to ensure the confidentiality and integrity of BI insights accessed through mobile reporting solutions.

DASHBOARDING

Consolidating multiple visualizations and KPIs into a unified interface, represented by a dashboard, provides an at-a-glance view of business metrics and performance.

Design Principles

Effective dashboards are built upon sound design principles that prioritize clarity, simplicity, and relevance. Designing an impactful dashboard involves thoughtful consideration of the visual hierarchy, color schemes, and data representation to convey insights in a concise and user-friendly manner. A cohesive design aligns with the overall goals of the organization and ensures that users can quickly grasp key information without unnecessary complexity.

Crafting Actionable Dashboards

Actionable dashboards go beyond presenting data; they empower users to make informed decisions and take specific actions. To create actionable dashboards, it is crucial to align data visualizations with KPIs and strategic objectives. Incorporating interactive elements, such as filters and drill-down capabilities, enhances user engagement and allows stakeholders to explore data in a way that directly supports decision-making processes.

Integrating Data Sources in Dashboards

Modern organizations often draw data from diverse sources, and effective dashboards integrate information seamlessly for a comprehensive view. The integration of multiple data sources in dashboards requires robust data connectivity, transformation, and consolidation. Whether pulling data from internal databases, cloud services, or third-party applications, a well-designed dashboard should harmonize disparate datasets to provide a unified and coherent narrative.

Real-Time Dashboard Updates

The demand for real-time insights has made real-time dashboard updates a critical feature. Dashboards that reflect the most current data enable users to respond promptly to changing conditions and emerging trends. Implementing real-time updates requires efficient data processing and connectivity to ensure that the information presented on the dashboard is accurate and up-to-the-minute.

Enhancing Dashboard Usability

User customization and personalization enhance the usability and relevance of dashboards. Allowing users to customize dashboards based on their preferences and roles ensures that the displayed information aligns with their specific needs. Personalization features might include the ability to rearrange widgets, set default views, or choose specific metrics for monitoring. This adaptability promotes user adoption and ensures that dashboards cater to the unique needs of different stakeholders.

Design Basics

Designing interactive and informative dashboards involves mastering the fundamentals of data visualization, layout, and interactivity. The basics encompass selecting suitable chart types, organizing content logically, and providing intuitive navigation options. An effective dashboard strikes a balance between being visually appealing and delivering meaningful insights, fostering a user-friendly experience.

Best Practices

An optimal dashboard layout and user experience are foundational to delivering value to end-users. Best practices in this realm involve organizing content in a logical flow, using consistent visual elements for clarity, and prioritizing the most relevant information. The thoughtful placement of key metrics, effective use of white space, and adherence to accessibility principles contribute to an enhanced user experience and ensure that dashboards convey insights efficiently.

REPORTING TOOLS

Reporting tools play a critical role in transforming raw data into actionable insights, enabling businesses to make informed decisions. These tools streamline the process of data visualization, analysis, and presentation, ensuring stakeholders have access to clear and concise information.

Tool Ecosystem

Reporting tools encompass a broad spectrum of applications, ranging from specialized data visualization platforms such as Tableau and Power BI to comprehensive BI suites such as Looker and Qlik. Understanding the diverse landscape of reporting tools is crucial for organizations to select the most suitable solution based on their specific needs and requirements.

User-Friendly Interfaces

Many modern reporting tools prioritize user-friendly interfaces, enabling individuals with varying levels of technical expertise to create, customize, and interpret reports. Intuitive dashboards, drag-and-drop functionalities, and interactive features contribute to a seamless user experience, empowering users to derive insights without extensive training.

Connectivity and Integration

The ability of reporting tools to connect seamlessly with various data sources, databases, and external applications is a critical factor. Tools that offer robust integration capabilities ensure that users can access and analyze data from multiple platforms, fostering a comprehensive and unified approach to reporting.

Scalability

Scalability is essential as organizations grow and data volumes increase. Reporting tools should efficiently handle large datasets and maintain optimal performance even as the complexity of reports and analyses expands. Scalability ensures that reporting tools can meet the evolving needs of an organization over time.

Collaboration

Effective reporting often involves collaboration among team members. Reporting tools with collaborative features, such as shared dashboards, real-time collaboration, and the ability to annotate and comment on reports, enhance teamwork and decision-making processes within an organization.

Security

Security is a paramount concern when dealing with sensitive business data. Reporting tools should adhere to robust security standards, offering features such as RBACs, data encryption, and compliance with data protection regulations. Ensuring data security and compliance is vital for maintaining the integrity and confidentiality of reports.

Tool Features

Organizations often have specific requirements for reporting tools, such as advanced analytics capabilities, predictive modeling, or support for specific data formats. Identifying and prioritizing these key features ensures that the selected reporting tool aligns with the organization's unique goals and facilitates more accurate and insightful reporting.

These key points provide a foundation for evaluating and selecting reporting tools that align with an organization's goals and reporting requirements.

EXCEL

Role in Data Analysis

Excel, a venerable spreadsheet software from Microsoft, has long been a cornerstone in the realm of business intelligence and data analysis. Widely embraced for its user-friendly interface and versatile functionalities, Excel serves as a powerful tool that empowers businesses to organize, analyze, and derive insights from vast datasets. Its ubiquity in the business world makes it a go-to platform for professionals across diverse industries, enabling them to make informed decisions, perform complex calculations, and visualize data trends. From financial modeling to data visualization and reporting, Excel's adaptability has solidified its position as an indispensable asset in the toolkit of analysts, managers, and decision-makers, bridging the gap between raw data and actionable insights.

Features

Excel, a powerhouse in the realm of spreadsheet software, boasts a rich array of features that make it a versatile tool for data manipulation and analysis. At its core, it utilizes a user-friendly grid of cells neatly arranged in numbered rows and letter-named columns, providing an intuitive structure for organizing and processing data. This grid becomes the canvas for a myriad of data manipulations, ranging from fundamental arithmetic operations to more advanced statistical, engineering, and financial calculations.

One of Excel's standout features lies in its extensive library of prebuilt functions that offer a diverse set of tools that cater to various analytical needs. By unraveling complex statistical patterns, tackling intricate engineering problems, or delving into financial computations, Excel's functions provide a robust foundation for users to address a wide spectrum of challenges.

Beyond its computational prowess, Excel shines in data visualization. Users can seamlessly translate raw data into meaningful insights through dynamic representations such as line graphs, histograms, and charts. While its three-dimensional graphical display is somewhat limited, it still offers insight into spatial relationships within datasets.

In essence, Excel stands as more than just a spreadsheet tool; it is a comprehensive platform that empowers users not only to organize and manipulate data efficiently but also to present findings visually, transforming numbers into narratives that drive informed decision-making.

Analysis Functions

Excel serves as a cornerstone in the realm of data analysis, providing a versatile platform equipped with a myriad of tools. Its features extend beyond simple data organization, showcasing robust capabilities essential for professionals seeking meaningful insights, performing complex calculations, and making informed decisions.

Excel boasts a rich array of features that significantly enhance data manipulation and analysis. Key functionalities such as sorting and filtering enable users to arrange data and focus on specific criteria, while conditional formatting enhances visual interpretation. Moreover, Excel supports diverse chart types, providing dynamic visual representations that aid in conveying complex information.

Pivot tables stand out as a prominent feature in Excel, empowering users to reorganize and summarize selected data for customized reports. Additionally, Excel tables offer a convenient way to organize data, streamlining the analysis process for quick insights. These combined features make Excel an indispensable tool for professionals navigating the complexities of data analysis.

Beyond these fundamental features, Excel provides advanced capabilities such as what-if analysis, allowing users to simulate the impact of altering values on formulas in the worksheet. The Solver tool, part of Excel's command suite, assists users in finding optimal values for formulas while considering constraints on other formula cells. Additionally, the Analysis ToolPak, an Excel add-in program, extends the software's capabilities by providing specialized tools for financial, statistical, and engineering data analysis. Collectively, these features make Excel a versatile and powerful tool for a wide range of data-related tasks.

CHAPTER 13

CLOUD COMPUTING

OVERVIEW

Cloud computing has revolutionized the way businesses store, process, and access data by offering scalable, on-demand resources. This technology empowers organizations to enhance efficiency, reduce costs, and improve flexibility in managing their IT infrastructure.

Understanding Cloud Computing

The cloud is just a metaphor for the Internet. Cloud computing is often referred to simply as "the cloud." It involves the delivery of on-demand computing resources, which include everything from applications to data centers, over the Internet on a pay-per-use basis. In cloud computing, users store and access data and programs on the Internet instead of on their computer's hard drive.

Cloud computing allows consumers and businesses to use applications, such as Yahoo Mail or Gmail, without any software installation. Users can access their email or personal files using any computer that is connected to the Internet. In this case, the server and email management software are all in the cloud (Internet) and are managed by the cloud service provider (Yahoo or Google). This technology allows for much more efficient computing by centralizing data storage, processing, and bandwidth.

Computing Resources

Cloud computing provides a set of shared computing resources that includes applications, computing, storage, networking, development, and deployment platforms, as well as business processes. It helps transform traditional siloed computing assets into shared pools of resources, whose underlying foundation is the Internet. Cloud computing is sold as a service, managed by a third-party provider, and delivered over a network.

Sharing of Resources

The cloud focuses on maximizing the effectiveness of shared resources. Cloud resources are usually shared by multiple users and dynamically reallocated per demand. This approach can work for allocating resources to users. For example, a cloud computer facility that serves European users during European business hours may reallocate the same resources to serve North American users during North America's business hours. Therefore, overall server requirements will be lower compared to having dedicated servers for Europe and America, leading to lower power consumption, rack space, monitoring, and so on.

Enabling Technologies

Cloud computing is the result of the evolution and adoption of existing technologies and paradigms. It has been spurred by the availability of high-capacity networks, low-cost computers, and storage devices, widespread adoption of hardware virtualization, service-oriented architecture, utility computing, and the ability to scale up or scale down as computing needs increase or decrease.

The main technology that enables cloud computing is virtualization. Virtualization software separates a physical computing device into one or more "virtual" devices, each of which can be easily used and managed to perform computing tasks. With operating system–level virtualization essentially creating a scalable system of multiple independent computing devices, idle computing resources can be allocated and used more efficiently.

Virtualization provides the agility required to speed up IT operations and reduce costs by increasing infrastructure utilization. The process through which a user can provision resources on-demand is automated. By minimizing user involvement, automation speeds up the process, reduces labor costs, and reduces the possibility of human errors.

Shared Characteristics

Cloud computing shares characteristics with the client-server model, which broadly refers to any distributed application distinguishing between service providers (servers) and service requestors (clients). It also exhibits similarities to grid computing, a form of distributed and parallel computing where a cluster of networked, loosely coupled computers collaborates to perform very large tasks.

Additionally, cloud computing draws parallels with mainframe computers, powerful machines utilized for critical applications, especially bulk data processing such as ERP and financial transaction processing. Moreover, it resembles utility computing, involving the packaging of computing resources such as computation and storage as a metered service, akin to a traditional public utility such as electricity.

Characteristics of Cloud Computing

The National Institute of Standards and Technology's definition of cloud computing identifies "five essential characteristics." They are as follows.

On-Demand Self-Service

The consumer can unilaterally provision computing capabilities such as server time and network storage as needed, automatically, without requiring human interaction with each service provider.

Broad Network Access

Capabilities are available over the network and accessed through standard mechanisms that promote use via heterogeneous thin or thick client platforms (such as mobile phones, tablets, laptops, and workstations).

Resource Pooling

The computing resources of providers are pooled to serve multiple consumers using a multitenant model, with different physical and virtual resources dynamically assigned and reassigned according to consumer demand.

Rapid Elasticity

Capabilities can be elastically provisioned and released, in some cases automatically, to scale rapidly as demand increases. The capabilities available for provisioning often appear unlimited and can be appropriated in any quantity at any time.

Measured Service

Cloud systems automatically control and optimize resource use by leveraging a metering capability at some level of abstraction appropriate for the type of service (such as storage, processing, bandwidth, or active user accounts). Resource usage can be monitored, controlled, and reported, providing transparency for both the provider and consumer of the utilized service.

Benefits

Economies of scale in cloud computing enable the sharing of resources, akin to a utility delivering electricity across the electric grid. While individuals can produce electricity using generators, they lack the efficiency and cost-effectiveness of the utility's superior infrastructure for production, distribution, and service sharing. Organizations benefit from reduced implementation costs, as they do not need to invest upfront in dedicated hardware and software. Instead, they can utilize a shared cloud infrastructure and pay only for specific usage, following a pay-as-you-go model. Cloud computing enhances agility, enabling enterprises to swiftly deploy applications and improve the ability to re-provision infrastructure resources. It facilitates meeting unpredictable demand by allowing IT to rapidly adjust resources to fluctuating and unpredictable business needs.

Cloud computing ensures device and location independence, allowing users to access systems through Web browsers or various devices such as tablets or smartphones. Maintenance becomes more straightforward for cloud applications than for those installed on numerous desktops. Multitenancy is supported, allowing the sharing of resources and costs across a broad user pool. Performance is closely monitored, allowing for quick addition of CPUs, memory, or storage without a lengthy procurement or provisioning process. Productivity improves as users can simultaneously work on the same data or application. Due to the reliability benefits of multiple redundant sites, well-designed cloud computing is suitable for business continuity and disaster recovery.

Scalability and elasticity are inherent in cloud systems because they can respond easily to elastic or temporary demand. Security can be enhanced through the centralization of data and increased security-focused resources, although concerns exist about controlling sensitive data, particularly in multitenant systems shared by unrelated users. Cloud computing transforms storage by enabling the use of new database architectures, specifically NoSQL databases, designed to leverage the cloud computing environment.

CLOUD SERVICE MODELS

Cloud computing providers offer their services according to three fundamental models:

1. Infrastructure as a Service (IaaS): Examples include virtual machines, servers, storage, load balancers

2. Platform as a Service (PaaS): Examples include CRM, email, virtual desktops, games

3. Software as a Service (SaaS): Examples include Web browsers, mobile apps, thin client

Infrastructure as a Service

IaaS is a foundational category of cloud computing service that offers virtualized computing resources over the Internet. In the IaaS model, users gain access to and have control over crucial computing infrastructure elements, including virtual machines, storage, and networking components, on a pay-as-you-go basis.

This cloud computing approach eliminates the need for organizations to invest in and maintain physical hardware, providing a scalable and flexible computing environment. Users can dynamically adjust their infrastructure resources, allowing for efficient scaling based on varying computing demands.

The benefits of IaaS include cost-effectiveness, as organizations only pay for the resources they consume, scalability, which accommodates changing workloads, and the elimination of the operational overhead associated with hardware management. IaaS empowers businesses to focus on innovation and application development rather than the complexities of maintaining and owning underlying infrastructure, making it a versatile and accessible solution for diverse IT services in the cloud.

Platform as a Service

PaaS is a cloud computing service model that provides a comprehensive platform for developers to build, deploy, and manage applications without the complexities of managing the underlying infrastructure. In PaaS, the cloud provider furnishes a preconfigured platform that includes development tools, runtime environments, and other essential services, allowing developers to focus solely on coding and application logic.

PaaS abstracts the intricacies of infrastructure management, such as server provisioning and configuration, enabling developers to streamline the development lifecycle. This approach enhances collaboration among development teams, accelerates time-to-market, and facilitates continuous integration and deployment.

The benefits of PaaS include increased development productivity, reduced operational overhead, seamless scalability, and the ability to leverage built-in services such as databases, messaging, and storage. PaaS empowers organizations to create and deploy applications more efficiently, fostering innovation and agility in the rapidly evolving landscape of software development.

Software as a Service

SaaS is a cloud computing model that delivers software applications over the Internet on a subscription basis. In SaaS, users can access and use software applications without the need for installation, maintenance, or management of the underlying infrastructure. The software is hosted and maintained by a third-party provider, who ensures updates, security patches, and system availability. This approach eliminates the burden of software ownership and allows organizations to pay for the services they use, typically on a monthly or annual basis.

SaaS provides flexibility and accessibility, enabling users to access applications from any device with an Internet connection. The benefits of SaaS include cost-effectiveness, rapid deployment, scalability, automatic updates, and the ability to access software applications from anywhere, promoting collaboration and enhancing user experience. SaaS has become a prevalent model for delivering a wide range of business applications, from productivity tools to ERP systems.

Cloud Clients

Users access cloud computing using networked client devices, such as desktop computers, laptops, tablets, and smartphones. Some of these devices, called cloud clients, rely on cloud computing for all or a majority of their applications, which essentially makes them useless without it. Examples include thin clients and the browser-based Chromebook.

Many cloud applications do not require specific software from the client; instead, they use a Web browser to interact with the cloud application. With Ajax and HTML5, these Web user interfaces can achieve a similar, or even better, look and feel to native applications.

DEPLOYMENT MODELS

Cloud deployment models define how cloud services are structured and delivered, tailored to meet the diverse needs of organizations. These models—public, private, and hybrid clouds—offer varying levels of control, scalability, and security to align with specific business objectives.

Private Cloud

A private cloud deployment model involves the exclusive use of computing resources, such as servers and storage, by a single organization. These resources can be physically located on-premises within the organization's data center or hosted by a third-party provider. Private clouds offer enhanced security and control, making them suitable for industries with strict regulatory requirements or organizations handling sensitive data.

With a private cloud, businesses can customize the infrastructure to meet their specific needs, ensuring optimal performance and scalability. While private clouds provide advantages in terms of data governance and customization, they may entail higher initial costs and require ongoing maintenance.

Public Cloud

Public cloud deployment involves the use of computing resources provided by third-party service providers over the Internet. These resources are shared among multiple users, making it a cost-effective option with pay-as-you-go pricing. Public clouds offer scalability, flexibility, and accessibility, allowing businesses to quickly adapt to changing demands. Major cloud services providers, such as Amazon AWS, Microsoft Azure, and the Google Cloud Platform (GCP), offer a wide range of services, including computing power, storage, and applications.

Public clouds are suitable for startups, small to medium-sized enterprises, and large corporations seeking cost-effective solutions without the need for significant upfront investments in infrastructure.

Hybrid Cloud

Hybrid cloud deployment combines elements of both private and public clouds, allowing data and applications to be shared between them. This model provides greater flexibility, enabling organizations to leverage the benefits of both private and public clouds based on their specific requirements.

Hybrid clouds are particularly useful for businesses with dynamic workloads or fluctuating resource needs. Organizations can use the private cloud for sensitive or critical workloads that require enhanced security while utilizing the public cloud for scalable and less sensitive applications. This approach offers a balance between the control of private clouds and the cost-effectiveness and scalability of public clouds. Managing data and applications across different environments requires careful planning and integration to ensure seamless operation.

Essential Cloud Capabilities

Core cloud capabilities remain crucial in any deployment model, providing essential features for an effective cloud environment. Elasticity and self-service provisioning enable users to dynamically scale resources based on actual needs, ensuring efficient resource utilization and cost optimization. Billing and metering of service usage are inherent, with public clouds charging customers for consumed resources and private clouds implementing potential charge-back systems under IT management.

Workload management plays a central role in cloud environments, fostering a federated and distributed setting where resources collaborate seamlessly. Workloads are strategically designed to align tasks with appropriate cloud services, optimizing overall efficiency. Additionally, management services are imperative for a well-operated cloud platform. Security and governance services are paramount for safeguarding applications and data, especially considering the dynamic nature of data movement across cloud environments. Data management holds significance, emphasizing the need for robust strategies to handle data flows within and between cloud environments.

MISCELLANEOUS

Challenges

Several key issues surround the widespread adoption and implementation of cloud computing. One notable concern is the challenge of ensuring robust security measures in the cloud environment. As organizations migrate sensitive data and critical applications to the cloud, they must address potential vulnerabilities and protect against unauthorized access. Another issue revolves around compliance and regulatory requirements, particularly for industries with strict guidelines governing data handling and storage. Ensuring that cloud operations align with these regulations is essential for legal and ethical considerations.

Additionally, the complexity of managing multicloud or hybrid cloud environments poses a significant challenge, requiring careful orchestration and integration of diverse services. Data privacy concerns also persist, especially as cloud providers may host data in various geographical locations, raising questions about jurisdictional control and data sovereignty.

Furthermore, issues related to downtime and service reliability remain critical, emphasizing the need for robust contingency plans and service level agreements (SLAs) to mitigate potential disruptions and ensure business continuity. Addressing these key cloud issues is vital for organizations to fully capitalize on the benefits of cloud computing while effectively navigating the associated challenges.

Myths About Cloud Computing

Cloud computing has been surrounded by various myths that sometimes create misconceptions about its capabilities and implications. One common myth is that the cloud is inherently insecure. In reality, cloud providers invest significantly in security measures and often have more resources than individual organizations to safeguard data.

Another myth suggests that migrating to the cloud is a one-size-fits-all solution. The reality is that each organization's needs and requirements are unique, and a thoughtful, tailored approach is necessary for successful cloud adoption. Additionally, there is a misconception that the cloud is always cost-effective; while it can provide cost savings, it requires proper management to avoid unexpected expenses.

Another prevalent myth is that once data is in the cloud, it is entirely the responsibility of the service provider; however, shared responsibility exists, and organizations must actively manage and secure their data. Dispelling these myths is essential for fostering a more accurate understanding of cloud computing and enabling organizations to make informed decisions about their technology infrastructure.

Managing Operational Risks

Operational risk in cloud computing encompasses various areas that organizations must carefully navigate to ensure the reliability and security of their cloud-based operations. One significant area of concern is service availability and downtime. Reliance on third-party cloud providers introduces the risk of service disruptions, which can impact business continuity and productivity. To mitigate this risk, organizations can implement measures such as redundancy and failover systems across multiple cloud providers or regions. Additionally, negotiating SLAs with cloud providers that include uptime guarantees and compensation for downtime can provide assurances against service disruptions.

Data breaches and unauthorized access constitute another operational risk, as sensitive information stored in the cloud may become susceptible to cyber threats. Cloud service outages, although rare, can still occur and disrupt critical business functions. Additionally, compliance and legal issues arise as organizations must ensure that their cloud activities align with industry regulations and legal frameworks.

The dynamic nature of cloud environments introduces challenges in data management and portability, making it crucial for organizations to have a clear understanding of where their data resides and how it can be seamlessly transferred between different cloud platforms. Effective risk management in cloud computing involves thorough planning, robust security measures, and a proactive approach to address these operational concerns.

Big Data Meets the Cloud

Big data intersects seamlessly with cloud computing, as the processing demands of large datasets find an ideal match in the scalable infrastructure provided by the cloud. This convergence is driven by the necessity for clusters of servers to handle the vast, high-speed, and diverse data formats inherent in big data applications. Clouds, already deployed on server pools, can dynamically scale resources up or down as needed, offering a cost-effective solution for supporting big data technologies and advanced applications that contribute significant business value.

Six compelling reasons underscore the compatibility of big data and the cloud. The first is the growing imperative to expedite enterprise time-to-insight through data analytics. Additionally, the cloud effectively addresses the need for agility in adapting to swiftly changing business demands and the influx of data sources. The transition from pilot to production applications, marked by unpredictable infrastructure scaling demands, is facilitated by cloud flexibility. Cloud solutions are less capital-intensive than in-house alternatives, making them financially advantageous. Robust security measures safeguard vital customer and corporate data in the cloud environment. Finally, the right cloud partner has the potential to deliver end-to-end solutions, enhancing the seamless integration of big data processes.

CHAPTER 14

DATA VISUALIZATION

D ata visualization transforms raw data into graphical representations, making complex information easier to understand and analyze. By leveraging charts, graphs, and other visual tools, organizations can uncover trends, patterns, and insights that drive informed decision-making.

OVERVIEW

Techniques, Goals, and Challenges

Data visualization is the technique of presenting data in a pictorial or graphical format to communicate information clearly and efficiently to users. The human brain processes visual information faster than textual data, making charts and graphs more effective than sifting through spreadsheets or lengthy reports. As the volume of collected and analyzed data continues to grow, decision-makers at all levels seek data visualization software to visualize analytical results, identify relevance among numerous variables, convey concepts and hypotheses, and even predict future trends.

The primary goal of data visualization is to present information clearly and efficiently through selected information graphics, such as tables and charts. Effective visualization aids users in analyzing and reasoning about data, making complex information more accessible, understandable, and usable. Tables are typically employed when users need to look up specific measures of a variable, while various chart types reveal patterns or relationships in data for one or more variables.

Benefits

A well-crafted data visualization serves as a powerful tool for uncovering trends, gaining insights, exploring data sources, and narrating compelling stories. The key to effective communication lies in achieving a harmonious balance between aesthetic form and functionality. Unfortunately, designers often fall short of striking this equilibrium, producing stunning visualizations that miss the mark in conveying information—their primary purpose.

Visualizations play a pivotal role in making the previously obscure evident to observers. Even when dealing with extensive datasets, patterns can be discerned swiftly and comprehensively. They facilitate the universal transmission of information, simplifying the sharing of ideas across diverse audiences.

The significant business benefits of adept data visualization include improved operational efficiency, rapid response to business changes, identification of new opportunities, heightened productivity, increased return on data assets, financial accountability, and transparency, leveraging technological advancements such as mobile capabilities, and ensuring better regulatory compliance and governance. In essence, beyond their aesthetic appeal, visualizations contribute substantively to strategic decision-making and business success.

Data Visualization and Decision-Making

Data visualization represents a convergence of technological advancements, insights from cognitive research, the evolution of graphical interfaces, widespread adoption of rich Internet application standards, and the growing interest in analytics and data discovery. This intersection has empowered nontechnical SMEs to engage in self-directed data exploration, contributing significantly to the interpretation and dissemination of insights derived from analytics. The implementation of robust chart engines and the expanding repertoire of visualizations in graphics libraries have ushered in a new era of visual analysis, allowing users to move beyond traditional bar and pie charts to express more sophisticated insights about quantitative information.

At the core of successful businesses lies sound decision-making, a process heavily reliant on the availability of data for analysis. As organizations expand and the volume of available data grows, the challenge of analyzing this data intensifies, particularly when presented in static reports or spreadsheets. This challenge necessitates the adoption of business intelligence tools, especially those with visual capabilities, to aid decision-makers in making timely and informed choices.

Data visualization proves invaluable in this context, offering benefits such as facilitating quick analysis of large data volumes, identifying exceptions, exposing problems early on, providing early warning alerts, and presenting trends in a format easily understood by stakeholders. Interactive charts and graphs further enhance the decision-maker's ability to pinpoint areas requiring attention, understand customer behavior, optimize product placement, predict sales volumes, and strategize for revenue growth or expense reduction.

Principles of Effective Data Visualization

Effective data visualization is guided by several key principles that aim to enhance the understanding, clarity, and communication of information. These principles contribute to creating visualizations that are insightful and facilitate decision-making. The following are some fundamental principles of effective data visualization:

Clarity and Simplicity

Clarity and simplicity are paramount in effective data visualization. It is crucial to ensure that the visualization is clear and easily comprehensible to the audience. Complex information should be distilled to its essential components, eliminating unnecessary details that could impede understanding. Avoiding embellishments and distractions is equally important in maintaining a straightforward and easily interpretable visual representation.

Relevance

Relevance is essential in data visualization. It is crucial to display only data that contributes to the intended message while eliminating extraneous details that could confuse or dilute the main point.

Accuracy

Accuracy is critical in data visualization, requiring diligence in representing data without distorting or misinterpreting information. Utilizing appropriate scales, labels, and annotations helps provide context and prevent misinterpretation.

Consistency

Consistency in design elements, such as color coding and labeling, facilitates easy interpretation and ensures uniformity across multiple visualizations for cohesive reporting. Intuitiveness is another key factor; visualizations should be designed to convey the intended message without the need for extensive explanation. Using familiar metaphors and symbols enhances comprehension for a more accessible interpretation of the data.

Interactivity

Engagement and interactivity are pivotal in data visualization. Making visualizations interactive fosters user engagement by enabling users to explore and interact with the data for deeper insights. Features such as hover-over details, clickable elements, or filters enhance the hands-on user experience. This interactive approach marks a significant advancement in presenting information, transcending the static nature of graphics and spreadsheets. Unlike traditional methods, it utilizes computers and mobile devices to offer dynamic engagement, enabling users to delve deeper into charts and graphs for more detailed information. The interactivity extends beyond mere observation, allowing users to actively participate in exploration, instantly modifying displayed data and adjusting processing in real-time. This approach not only enhances the user experience but also empowers individuals to tailor their analysis, providing deeper insights and a more nuanced understanding of the data.

Hierarchy, Emphasis, and Narrative

Ineffective data visualization, hierarchy, and emphasis play crucial roles. A visual hierarchy is used to emphasize essential elements and guide the viewer's attention strategically, employing color, size, or position to highlight key data points. Storytelling is another significant aspect, which involves crafting a narrative within the visualization to guide the viewer through the data. It is essential to ensure that the visualization tells a coherent and compelling story aligned with the communication goal. Context is provided by incorporating relevant labels, captions, and annotations, considering the broader context in which the data exists to enhance understanding.

Accessibility

Accessibility is a key consideration in design, ensuring that visualizations are comprehensible to a diverse audience. This involves using alt text, providing alternative formats, and selecting color palettes that accommodate individuals with visual impairments.

By adhering to these principles, data visualizations can be used to effectively communicate complex information, empower decision-makers, and offer valuable insights.

Generating Best Visuals

Generating the best visuals for displaying data involves considering several key concepts. First, it is crucial to understand the data being visualized, including its size and cardinality, which refers to the uniqueness of the data values in a column. Next, the purpose of the visualization and the specific information that is to be communicated should be clearly determined. Understanding the audience is paramount; designers should be aware of how they process visual information so that the visuals can be tailored effectively. Finally, a visual representation that conveys the information in the best and simplest form should be chosen.

Data visualization, as both an art and a science, encompasses numerous graphical techniques aimed at helping individuals comprehend the narrative within their data. By adhering to these fundamental concepts, visuals can be created that not only effectively communicate information but also resonate with the audience.

Using Data Visualization Effectively

Successfully using data visualization involves several key considerations. First, it is essential to choose the most appropriate type of data visualization for the specific purpose. When presenting data, it should be ensured that it is supplemented with contextual information to provide clarity and enable users to take meaningful action.

To achieve effective data visualization, key best practices include understanding the audience, designing graphics that can stand alone outside the context of the report, and ensuring that the graphics effectively communicate the key messages.

There are notable barriers to successful data visualization, primarily revolving around skills and budget shortages. Overcoming these challenges is crucial for unlocking the full potential of data visualization and leveraging its ability to convey information effectively.

Characteristics of Effective Graphics

In his 1983 book, *The Visual Display of Quantitative Information*, Edward Tufte articulates principles for effective graphical displays, defining them as a means of communicating complex ideas with clarity, precision, and efficiency. The characteristics of effective graphics, according to Tufte, include the ability to show the data clearly, prompt viewers to think about the substance rather than focus on methodology or design, avoid distorting the data's message, and present numerous numbers in a compact space.

Effective graphics also make large datasets coherent, encourage comparisons between different data points, and reveal data at various levels of detail, from a broad overview to a fine structure. Moreover, they should serve a clear purpose, such as description, exploration, tabulation, or decoration, and be closely integrated with the statistical and verbal descriptions of a dataset.

According to Tufte, graphics play a vital role in revealing data, offering precision and insights beyond conventional statistical computations. By embodying these characteristics, effective graphics become powerful tools for communicating intricate ideas with clarity and impact.

Quantitative Messages

Stephen Few, a renowned expert in the field of data visualization and information design, has described eight types of quantitative messages that users might attempt to understand or communicate from a set of data and the associated graphs used to help communicate the message.

Time-Series

A line chart is ideal for visualizing the trend of a single variable over time, such as the unemployment rate across a ten-year span. It succinctly captures fluctuations and patterns, providing a clear overview of the variable's temporal evolution.

Ranking

Categorical subdivisions are ranked in ascending or descending order, such as a ranking of sales performance (the measure) by a salesperson (the category, with each salesperson a categorical subdivision) during a single period. A bar chart may be used to show the comparison across the salespersons.

Part-to-Whole

Categorical subdivisions are measured as a ratio to the whole (i.e., a percentage out of 100%). A pie chart or bar chart can show the comparison of ratios, such as the market share represented by competitors in a market.

Deviation

Categorical subdivisions are compared again as a reference, such as a comparison of actual versus budget expenses for several departments of a business for a given time period. A bar chart shows a comparison of the actual versus the reference amount.

Frequency Distribution

This shows the number of observations of a particular variable for a given interval, such as the number of years in which the stock market return is between intervals such as 0%–10% and 11%–20%. A histogram, a type of bar chart, may be used for this analysis.

Correlation

This involves a comparison between observations represented by two variables (X, Y) to determine whether they tend to move in the same or opposite directions. For example, unemployment (X) and inflation (Y) can be plotted for a sample of months. A scatter plot is typically used for this purpose.

Nominal Comparison

Categorical subdivisions are compared in no particular order, such as sales volume by product code. A bar chart may be used for this comparison.

Geographic or Geospatial

This involves the comparison of a variable across a map or layout, such as the unemployment rate by state or the number of persons on various floors of a building. Common graphics used in such cases include choropleth maps, point maps, and heat maps.

Analysts reviewing a dataset may consider whether some or all of the messages and graphic types mentioned previously are applicable to their task and audience. The process of trial and error to identify meaningful relationships and messages in the data is part of EDA.

COMMON FORMS OF DATA VISUALIZATION

Data visualization comes in various forms, each tailored to highlight specific data insights effectively. From charts and graphs to interactive dashboards, these visual tools simplify complex datasets, making it easier for users to understand trends, patterns, and relationships.

Types of Presentation Media

In business, the four widely used presentation media include dashboards, scorecards, visual analysis tools, and reports. Each type possesses its own unique attributes and aids users in identifying trends, patterns, correlations, anomalies, deviations, and the overall state of the business.

Charts

The most commonly used type of data visualization is the chart, which encompasses popular forms such as line, bar, area, and pie charts. A well-designed chart should enable the analysis of data and the quick extraction of relevant information.

Popular Visualizations

Some of the most popular visualization types include bar charts, line charts, pie charts, tables, and spreadsheets, which are widely employed for their effectiveness in conveying information.

Advanced Visualizations

Advanced data visualizations, such as bullet graphs, sparkline charts, scatter plots, heatmaps, tree maps, and Pareto charts, offer sophisticated ways to represent complex datasets.

Status Indicators

Status indicators are utilized to signify the status of a particular measure or unit of data. This form of data visualization includes many varieties, including gauges, traffic lights, and symbols. Their effectiveness is enhanced when contextual metrics such as targets and thresholds are incorporated, which provide immediate feedback regarding a specific measure—indicating whether it is good or bad, high or low, or above or below the target.

Visual Display Elements

To facilitate a quick assessment of performance on dashboards and scorecards, users employ various visual display elements, including visual icons, charts, tables, alerts, and maps. These elements contribute to a visually intuitive representation of data, enabling users to grasp information swiftly.

TOOLS FOR DATA VISUALIZATION

The increasing rate of data generation in our information-based economy poses challenges for processing, analyzing, and communicating this data through visualization. As a result, the demand for sophisticated data visualization tools continues to increase. The popular data visualization tools can be grouped based on certain criteria. The following is a grouping based on several common characteristics.

Based on Integration and Ecosystem

- Tableau
- Microsoft Power BI
- Google Data Studio
- QlikView/Qlik Sense
- Looker
- IBM Cognos Analytics

Based on Programming Language

- D3.js (JavaScript)
- Plotly (Python)
- Matplotlib (Python)
- Redash (SQL)
- Metabase (SQL)

Cloud-Based Platforms

- Tableau
- Microsoft Power BI
- Google Data Studio
- Looker
- Domo

Open-Source Tools

- D3.js
- Plotly
- Metabase
- Redash

These groupings are just one way to categorize the tools. The selection of a tool often depends on various factors, including user preferences, the type of data being visualized, integration capabilities, collaboration features, and the specific needs of the project or organization.

The popularity of tools may change over time, and new tools may emerge. Additionally, preferences can vary based on user needs and industry requirements.

BEST PRACTICES

Effective data visualization requires adherence to best practices that ensure clarity, accuracy, and relevance. By focusing on simplicity, appropriate chart selection, and audience understanding, visualizations can communicate insights more effectively and drive better decision-making.

Empower Nontechnical Users

Data visualization and visual analysis should be improved for nontechnical users. Nontechnical users, while not experts in accessing data and creating visualizations possess a deep understanding of their data. Their data interaction experience should be enhanced through visualization tools, empowering them with easier and more powerful means of engaging with data.

Tailor Visualization Capabilities

Match visualization capabilities to users' types of activities. Different users, such as executives or those needing operational alerting, require specific visualization capabilities. Tailor technology deployments to align with the distinct purposes of users, ensuring a seamless fit for their activities.

Broaden Visualization Functionality

Increase the interactivity of the data with broader visualization functionality. In addition to static and tabular data, users often require flexible exploration beyond standard bar and line charts. Explore tools offering a wide range of visualization options, including the ability to integrate visualizations that are not part of the BI tool's standard library.

Create Unified Dashboards

Dashboards should be used to establish a single view of the information. They play a crucial role in providing users with a consolidated interface to view necessary information. In particular, large organizations that deal with multiple application interfaces should aim to consolidate these interfaces into a single or a limited number of dashboards.

Prioritize Self-Service Capabilities

Self-service data visualization and discovery capabilities should be made a priority. The prevailing trend in BI and analytics is self-service. Prioritize tools and platforms that empower users to interact with data independently, fostering creativity in the analysis and selection of visualizations to express insights without requiring hands-on IT development.

Address Time Series Analysis

The time series analysis requirements should be addressed with improved visualizations. Analyzing business performance and changing conditions over time is a common need. By enhancing interactivity and broadening visualization options for time series analysis, users can gain deeper insights into temporal trends.

Leverage Geospatial Analysis

Geospatial analysis and geographic information system (GIS) sources should be evaluated for visual analysis. Recognizing the growing relevance of location as a vital dimension for data analysis. Users in diverse fields are finding new insights through geospatial analysis. Assess whether mapping and geospatial analysis functionality could provide valuable insights for strategic and operational decisions.

Strategize Desktop and Mobile Integration

Develop a strategy for integrating desktop and mobile dashboards. With the increasing demand for BI and analytics capabilities on mobile devices, organizations should develop a comprehensive strategy to ensure a seamless transition between desktop and mobile dashboards, preventing chaotic dashboard proliferation.

Explore In-Memory Computing

In-memory computing can be evaluated to support visual analysis, offering an alternative to the constraints of standard disk-based environments and providing enhanced performance for highly interactive and iterative visual analytics. Consideration of this approach is crucial, as in-memory computing solutions excel in scenarios where data can be loaded into memory for analysis rather than requiring constant access to real-time data streams.

Develop Operational Efficiency

Improved operational efficiency should be made the goal of data visualization and analysis. The primary business benefit sought from deploying data visualization and analysis technologies is improved operational efficiency. Organizations should ensure the availability of the right functionality and visualization options for users' dashboard reporting and analytics, addressing operational challenges effectively.

CHAPTER 15

PREDICTIVE ANALYTICS

ADVANCED ANALYTICS IN BI

Advanced analytics stands at the forefront of transformative capabilities within the realm of BI. As organizations strive to gain a competitive edge and glean actionable insights from their data, the integration of advanced analytics becomes paramount. This section provides an overview of advanced analytics in the context of BI, shedding light on the sophisticated techniques and methodologies that go beyond traditional reporting and descriptive analytics.

Evolution Beyond Descriptive Analytics

In the journey of BI evolution, organizations have transitioned from basic descriptive analytics—revealing what has happened in the past—to advanced analytics, which focuses on predicting future outcomes and prescribing optimal actions. This evolution empowers businesses to move beyond historical analysis and proactively shape their strategies.

Landscape of Advanced Analytics

Advanced analytics encompasses a spectrum of methodologies, including predictive modeling, machine learning, and NLP. These techniques enable organizations to extract valuable insights, identify patterns, and make informed decisions. As the volume and complexity of data grow, the role of advanced analytics becomes increasingly pivotal in navigating the intricacies of modern business landscapes.

Predictive Analytics in BI

A prominent subset of advanced analytics is predictive analytics, which leverages statistical algorithms and machine learning models to forecast future trends and outcomes. Predictive analytics within BI empowers decision-makers with the foresight to anticipate market shifts, customer behaviors, and operational challenges. The foundational principles and applications of predictive analytics within a BI framework will be discussed in subsequent sections.

Addressing Business Challenges with Advanced Analytics

The integration of advanced analytics in BI addresses contemporary business challenges, providing solutions to complex problems. Whether by optimizing supply chain operations, enhancing customer experiences, or mitigating risks, advanced analytics serves as a compass for organizations navigating the dynamic landscapes of the modern business world.

Interplay of Data Science and BI

Advanced analytics blurs the lines between traditional BI and data science. While BI focuses on extracting insights from historical and current data, data science, embedded within advanced analytics, dives deeper into predictive and prescriptive modeling.

This introduction sets the stage for a deeper exploration of predictive analytics within the broader context of advanced analytics in BI. By understanding the landscape and significance of advanced analytics, organizations can harness its potential to elevate their decision-making processes and drive sustainable success.

UNLEASHING PREDICTIVE ANALYTICS

Predictive analytics leverages historical data and advanced algorithms to forecast future trends and outcomes. This powerful approach enables businesses to anticipate challenges, seize opportunities, and make data-driven decisions with greater confidence.

Role of Predictive Analytics

Predictive analytics is a subset of BI technologies designed to reveal relationships and patterns within extensive datasets, enabling the anticipation of future behavior and events. Unlike traditional BI tools, predictive analytics uses past data to project future outcomes.

This process involves sophisticated analytic tools, including modeling, machine learning, and data mining, utilizing current and historical data to make informed predictions about future events. By connecting data to actionable insights, predictive analytics helps organizations draw reliable conclusions about both present conditions and future occurrences.

At its core, predictive analytics identifies and leverages relationships between variables to forecast unknown outcomes. The accuracy and usefulness of these predictions hinge on meticulous data analysis and the quality of underlying assumptions.

In the business realm, predictive models leverage historical and transactional data patterns to discern risks and opportunities. These models assess potential outcomes under specific conditions, guiding decision-making processes.

Predictive Analytics: Shaping Organizational Success

In the realm of analytics, the focus extends beyond mere data representation to uncovering and conveying meaningful patterns within various data dimensions, including corporate, product, channel, and customer information. Analytics involves identifying signals both within and across individual datasets, transcending boundaries to reveal insights.

The shift in how organizations collect, generate, and utilize data is reshaping work dynamics, lifestyles, and recreation, consequently influencing customer expectations and corporate strategies. Fundamentally, predictive analytics prioritizes gaining insights over reflecting on past events, becoming a pivotal aspect of organizational success in achieving key strategic objectives and influencing various facets of business operations.

The strategic objectives of predictive analytics are as follows:

1. Compete: Secure the most potent and unique competitive advantage in the market
2. Grow: Increase sales and maintain a competitive edge in customer retention
3. Enforce: Safeguard business integrity by effectively managing and preventing fraud
4. Improve: Elevate core business capabilities, staying competitive in the market
5. Satisfy: Meet the ever-growing expectations of today's consumers

6. **Learn:** Utilize the most advanced analytics techniques available today

7. **Act:** Transform business intelligence and analytics into actionable insights for strategic decision-making

The transformative power of analytics extends beyond traditional retrospective analysis, driving organizations to proactively shape their future by leveraging predictive analytics. This strategic approach not only fosters a competitive edge but also aligns businesses with the evolving landscape of consumer expectations and technological advancements.

Benefits

Businesses leverage predictive analytics as a strategic tool to analyze data comprehensively, enabling realistic predictions about future environmental conditions. This foresight empowers organizations to make informed decisions and take strategic action to maximize identified opportunities. Predictive analytics uses are bound only by available data, modeling techniques, and creativity.

Predictive analytics offers a range of benefits, including understanding customer behavior for actionable insights, enhancing efficiency by replacing guesswork with data-driven decisions, reducing costs through a clear understanding of risk and uncertainty, and adding consistency to business decisions for improved compliance and customer service. Additionally, it contributes to the overall competitiveness of an organization.

This approach opens up opportunities for organizations to proactively enhance customer service, efficiently acquire more profitable customers, increase sales to existing customers, retain profitable customers for longer periods, and manage risk from fraudulent activities. It also facilitates the optimization of physical and human resources, gaining a competitive edge in new opportunities, executing tasks smarter through advanced planning, and identifying data patterns to alert potential situations requiring attention.

Predictive analytics delivers both qualitative and quantitative benefits. On the qualitative side, it creates a comprehensive picture of the targeted customer demographic, offering valuable insights into customer preferences and behaviors. On the quantitative side, it identifies tangible growth in sales, revenue, or customer base and may result in cost savings, improved customer retention, and overall operational enhancements for organizations.

Use Cases

Predictive analytics is a versatile tool applicable across all industries, with varying degrees of maturity in its implementation. Its widespread use is driven by the shared need to effectively manage challenges such as fraud, risk, equipment failure, and customer interactions. The overarching theme connecting these diverse industries is the exponential growth of data and the collective aspiration to transform this data into valuable insights.

In practical terms, predictive analytics has been applied in several areas. One key facet involves prospecting, where businesses leverage predictive models to identify potential customers and successfully convert prospects into actual clients. Cross-selling and segmentation become streamlined as businesses segment customers based on past purchasing behavior, enabling more targeted and effective promotional offers.

Customer retention, a critical aspect for sustained success, benefits from predictive analytics by analyzing the reasons behind customer loss and implementing cost-effective practices to increase retention and reduce attrition. Capacity planning is another area that benefits from predictive analytics, helping organizations allocate shared infrastructure resources efficiently to avoid unnecessary costs associated with unused capacity.

Market-related analyses, such as market basket analysis and market optimization, leverage predictive analytics to determine optimal product combinations, maximize sales, and identify the most effective marketing campaigns for specific audience segments. A/B analysis, involving testing different changes and comparing results against a baseline, becomes a more data-driven process with the insights provided by predictive analytics.

Churn analysis, an essential strategy for CRM, relies on predictive models to identify the customers most likely to churn, enabling proactive measures to retain them. Sales forecasting, assortment planning, and fraud detection further exemplify the diverse applications of predictive analytics across industries.

In healthcare, predictive analytics takes the form of clinical decision support systems, where experts use predictive analysis to identify patients at risk of developing specific health conditions such as diabetes and asthma. Collection analytics optimizes the allocation of collection resources, increasing recovery while reducing costs.

The spectrum of predictive analytics extends even further, encompassing applications such as forecasting equipment failure, predicting loan defaults, credit scoring, and various other scenarios. The adaptability and efficacy of predictive analytics empower organizations to make informed, data-driven decisions, bridging the gap between historical insights and future foresight across a multitude of domains.

Barriers

A host of barriers can prevent organizations from venturing into the domain of predictive analytics or impede their growth. This "analytics bottleneck" arises from factors such as complexity, where developing sophisticated models has traditionally been a slow, iterative, and labor-intensive process. Data quality is another challenge, as most corporate data is full of errors and inconsistencies, requiring clean, scrubbed, and expertly formatted data for predictive models to work effectively.

Processing expense is a notable barrier, as complex analytical queries and scoring processes can clog networks and negatively impact database performance, especially on desktop computers. Expertise is a critical factor, with qualified business analysts who can create sophisticated models being difficult to find, expensive to pay, and difficult to retain.

Interoperability adds another layer of complexity, as the process of creating and deploying predictive models traditionally involves accessing or moving data and models among multiple machines, operating platforms, and applications, requiring interoperable software. Cost is a significant hindrance, as the expense of most predictive analytic software and the hardware to run it on has been beyond the reach of most midsize organizations.

PREDICTIVE ANALYTICS PROCESS

The predictive analytics process is a series of iterative steps, each crucial to deriving meaningful insights and making informed decisions. The steps involved are described below.

Business Understanding

Business understanding involves engaging with stakeholders to comprehend the broader business context and delineate the specific objectives of the predictive analysis. This step is crucial for aligning the analysis with organizational goals and ensuring that the outcomes generated are relevant and actionable.

Data Understanding

In data understanding, analysts delve into the available datasets, exploring their structure, content, and potential biases. By identifying data sources and understanding their quality, analysts can make informed decisions about which variables to include in the analysis and how to address any data-related challenges.

Data Preparation

In the data preparation stage, feature engineering is a pivotal step aimed at optimizing predictive modeling. Beyond cleaning data and handling missing values, this process involves crafting new variables or adjusting existing ones to better capture nuanced patterns within the dataset. For instance, in a sales dataset, feature engineering might entail creating a new variable that calculates the average purchase frequency per customer over a specific time period, offering deeper insights into customer behavior and enhancing the predictive capabilities of the model.

Modeling

During the modeling phase, analysts select and build predictive models based on the prepared data. This involves choosing appropriate algorithms, training the models using historical data, and fine-tuning parameters to optimize predictive accuracy and generalizability.

Evaluation

Evaluation is a critical step for assessing the performance of the predictive models. Analysts employ various metrics, such as accuracy, precision, and recall, to measure how well the models predict outcomes and whether they align with the defined objectives. This iterative process may involve refining models or adjusting parameters to improve performance.

Deployment

Deployment involves implementing the validated predictive models into operational systems for real-world application. This ensures that the insights derived from the models can be seamlessly integrated into decision-making processes, enabling organizations to leverage predictive analytics for informed and strategic decision-making.

While the process is cyclical and allows revisiting steps as needed, the core focus remains on the data and analytical components. As a general guideline, the distribution of time across each step is as follows:

- business understanding: 5%–15%
- data understanding: 5%–10%
- data preparation: 50%–60%
- modeling: 5%–15%
- evaluation: 5–10%
- deployment: 10–15%

This breakdown provides a flexible framework, allowing organizations to allocate resources based on the unique requirements of each predictive analytics project.

PREDICTIVE ANALYTICS TECHNIQUES

Predictive analytics leverages four core techniques to turn data into valuable, actionable information:

- decision analysis and optimization
- transaction profiling
- predictive search
- predictive modeling

Decision Analysis and Optimization

Decision analysis refers to the broad quantitative field that deals with modeling, analyzing, and optimizing decisions made by individuals, groups, and organizations. Some applications include optimizing supply chain management, tracking KPIs, uncovering hidden sales opportunities, and determining operating cost deviations.

While predictive models analyze multiple aspects of individual behavior to forecast future behavior, decision analysis analyzes multiple aspects of a given decision to identify the most effective action for reaching a desired result.

Optimization capabilities include the use of a proprietary mathematical modeling and programming language, an easy-to-use development and visualization environment, and a state-of-the-art set of optimization algorithms.

Transaction Profiling

Transaction profiling is a technique used to extract meaningful information and reduce the complexity of transaction data used in modeling.

Many solutions operate using transactional or other data that change over time. In its raw form, this data is very difficult to use in predictive models for many reasons. First, an isolated transaction contains very little information about the behavior of the individual who generated the transaction. In addition, transaction patterns change rapidly over time. Finally, this type of data can often be highly complex.

A set of proprietary techniques are used to overcome these issues. They transform raw data into a mathematical representation that reveals latent information, which makes the data more usable by predictive models. This profiling technology accumulates data across multiple transactions of many types to create and update profiles of transaction patterns. These profiles enable neural network models to efficiently and effectively make accurate assessments of, for example, fraud risk and credit risk within real-time transaction streams.

Predictive Search

A predictive search uses a predictive search algorithm based on popular searches to predict a user's search query as it is typed, providing a drop-down list of suggestions that change as the user adds more characters to the search input.

Machine intelligence is increasingly coupled with human insight to engage consumers. The types of target scenarios include:

- personalization based on location
- personalization based on customer behaviors or their absence
- personalization based on social media relationships
- personalization with regard to cross-selling sales

Predictive Modeling

Predictive modeling involves mathematically representing underlying relationships in historical data to explain the data and make predictions or forecasts about future events. These models analyze current and historical data on individuals, generating metrics such as scores that rank-order individuals based on likely future performance. This performance may include the likelihood of making timely credit payments or responding to specific service offers, as well as detecting potential fraudulent transactions (risk detection).

Operationalized in mission-critical transaction systems, predictive models play a pivotal role in driving decisions and actions in near real-time. During live transactions, they perform calculations to evaluate the risk or opportunity associated with a customer or transaction, guiding decision-making processes.

Various analytic methodologies underlie solutions in predictive modeling, including applications of both linear and nonlinear mathematical programming algorithms, such as optimizing objectives within a set of constraints. Advanced "neural" systems, such as neural networks or deep learning, leverage large datasets to learn complex patterns and predict the probability of individuals exhibiting specific behaviors of business interest. Additionally, statistical techniques are employed for analysis and pattern detection within extensive datasets.

Common procedures used for modeling and evaluation during the prediction analysis phase include decision trees, regression (count, linear, and logistic), cluster analysis, time series analysis, association analysis, AB analysis, and scoring. These procedures contribute to the effectiveness and accuracy of predictive models in various business contexts.

Descriptive Models

Descriptive models quantify data relationships in a way often used to classify customers or prospects into groups. Unlike predictive models that focus on predicting single customer behavior (such as credit risk), descriptive models identify many different relationships between customers or products.

Descriptive models do not rank-order customers by their likelihood of taking a particular action according to how predictive models do. Instead, descriptive models can be used, for example, to categorize customers by their product preferences and life stages. Descriptive modeling tools can be utilized to develop further models that can simulate a large number of individualized agents and make predictions.

Decision Models

Decision models describe the relationships among all the elements of a decision—the known data (including the results of predictive models), the decision, and the forecast results of the decision—to predict the results of decisions involving many variables. These models can be used in optimization, maximizing certain outcomes while minimizing others. Decision models are generally used to develop decision logic or a set of business rules that will produce the desired action for every customer or circumstance.

PREDICTIVE MODEL DEVELOPMENT PROCESS

Regardless of methodology, most processes for developing predictive models involve the steps described in the following sections.

Project Definition

In this crucial initial step, the focus is on clearly defining the business objectives and desired outcomes that the predictive model aims to achieve. It involves understanding the organizational goals, KPIs, and specific challenges that the predictive model seeks to address. The translation of these broader objectives into specific predictive analytic objectives and tasks ensures alignment with the overarching business strategy.

Exploration

The exploration phase involves a comprehensive analysis of the source data to determine the most suitable data and model-building approach. This step requires scoping the effort by identifying the relevant variables, understanding the data distributions, and assessing potential challenges or biases in the data. The exploration phase sets the foundation for making informed decisions in subsequent steps and helps in defining the appropriate methodologies for model development.

Data Preparation

Data preparation is a critical step in which the selected data is processed and transformed to create a suitable foundation for building predictive models. This includes tasks such as handling missing values, addressing outliers, scaling variables, and ensuring data quality. The goal is to refine the data into a format that enhances the effectiveness of the predictive models and contributes to their accuracy and reliability.

Model Building

Model building involves the creation, testing, and validation of predictive models. During this step, various algorithms and techniques are applied to the prepared data to develop models that can effectively predict outcomes. Testing and validation ensure that the models perform well on both training and unseen data and that they align with project metrics and goals. Iterative refinement may be necessary to enhance model performance.

Deployment

The deployment phase begins once the predictive models have been successfully built and validated. This step involves applying the results of the models to real-world business decisions or processes. Depending on the scope and requirements, deployment can range from sharing insights with business users to embedding models into applications for automated decision-making. Effective deployment ensures that the predictive models contribute directly to organizational decision-making and operational efficiency.

Model Management

Model management is an ongoing process that aims to optimize the performance and usability of predictive models. It involves monitoring model accuracy, controlling access to models, promoting the reuse of successful models, standardizing toolsets and methodologies, and minimizing redundant activities. Continuous evaluation and improvement are central to model management, ensuring that predictive models remain effective and aligned with evolving business needs.

In summary, these expanded explanations provide a more detailed understanding of each step in the predictive modeling process, emphasizing their significance in creating accurate and impactful predictive models.

ANALYTICAL TECHNIQUES

The approaches and techniques used to conduct predictive analytics can be broadly grouped into regression techniques and machine learning techniques.

Regression

Predictive analytics relies heavily on regression models, with the primary emphasis on creating a mathematical equation that represents the interactions among various variables. This approach provides a robust foundation for understanding and predicting outcomes based on the relationships uncovered in the data. The versatility of predictive analytics becomes apparent when considering the diverse array of models applicable in different situations.

These models encompass well-known techniques such as linear regression, discrete choice models, logistic regression, multinomial logistic regression, probit regression, time series models, survival or duration analysis, classification and regression trees, and multivariate adaptive regression splines. Each of these models offers a distinct set of tools and methodologies for analyzing data, enabling predictive analytics to address a wide range of scenarios and provide valuable insights.

Machine Learning

Initially developed within the realm of AI, machine learning was designed to equip computers with the ability to learn autonomously. This field has evolved significantly and now encompasses a range of advanced statistical methods, particularly in regression and classification. Machine learning applications have expanded across diverse fields, playing pivotal roles in medical diagnostics, credit card fraud detection, face and speech recognition, and stock market analysis.

In some scenarios, the focus of predictive analytics is on directly predicting the dependent variable without delving into the underlying relationships between variables. Conversely, certain situations involve complex dependencies with unknown mathematical forms. For these intricate cases, machine learning techniques come into play, mirroring human cognition by learning from training examples to make predictions about future events.

Commonly utilized methods in predictive analytics that fall under the umbrella of machine learning include neural networks, multilayer perceptron (MLP), radial basis functions, support vector machines, Naïve Bayes, k-nearest neighbors, and geospatial predictive modeling. Each of these methods has unique capabilities for learning patterns, making predictions, and extracting insights from data, contributing to the diverse applications of machine learning in predictive analytics.

PREDICTIVE ANALYTIC TOOLS

Predictive analytics tools empower organizations to harness the power of data through advanced algorithms and machine learning techniques. These tools enable accurate forecasting and insightful decision-making, transforming raw data into actionable predictions.

Evolution

Historically, the utilization of predictive analytics tools and the interpretation of their results were confined to individuals with advanced skills, often limited to IT specialists. A transformative shift has occurred with the evolution of modern predictive analytics tools. In response to increasing integration into decision-making processes and operational workflows, there is a notable trend toward positioning business users as the primary consumers of predictive analytics information.

The demand from business users is for tools that empower them to navigate and utilize predictive analytics independently. In response, vendors are developing new software that simplifies mathematical complexities, incorporates user-friendly graphic interfaces, and includes shortcuts. These enhancements aim to streamline the process, such as recognizing available data and suggesting appropriate predictive models.

Current Status

Contemporary predictive analytics tools have reached a level of sophistication that allows any data-savvy information worker to analyze the data and extract meaningful insights effectively. These tools present findings through easily interpretable charts, graphs, and scores, clearly indicating the likelihood of various outcomes.

A multitude of tools are available for executing predictive analytics, catering to a range of user sophistication levels. Some tools are designed for minimal user complexity, while others target expert practitioners. The distinguishing factors among these tools often lie in the degree of customization and the handling of extensive datasets.

Types of Tools

Predictive analytics, as a dynamic field, relies on a diverse toolkit to unveil patterns, trends, and insights from data. This toolkit encompasses both open-source and commercial tools, offering organizations a versatile array of options for predictive modeling and analysis.

Open-Source Predictive Analytic Tools

The following are some of the leading tools in this category:

- scikit-learn: A robust machine learning library for Python, scikit-learn offers a wide array of tools for predictive data analysis
- KNIME: An open-source platform that allows the creation of data science workflows, KNIME supports various predictive modeling tasks
- OpenNN: Focused on neural network processing, OpenNN is an open-source tool for implementing predictive analytics in the domain of AI

- Orange: A visual programming tool for data visualization and analysis, Orange includes components for predictive modeling
- R: A powerful statistical computing language that provides an extensive set of tools for predictive analytics through various packages
- RapidMiner: Offers an integrated environment for data science, which facilitates predictive modeling and advanced analytics
- Weka: A collection of machine learning algorithms for data mining tasks, which is written in Java and provides a comprehensive suite for predictive analytics

Commercial Predictive Analytic Tools

The following are some of the leading tools in this category:

- IBM SPSS Statistics and IBM SPSS Modeler: IBM's SPSS suite includes statistical analysis tools and a modeler for predictive analytics
- Mathematica: Beyond mathematical computation, Mathematica includes tools for predictive analytics and machine learning
- MATLAB: A commercial platform widely used in academia and industry, it offers a range of tools for predictive modeling and data analysis
- Minitab: Focused on statistical analysis and quality improvement, Minitab includes features for predictive analytics
- Oracle Data Mining (ODM): Integrated with the Oracle Database, ODM provides data mining and predictive analytics capabilities
- SAS and SAS Enterprise Miner: SAS is a comprehensive analytics platform, and SAS Enterprise Miner is specifically designed for predictive modeling and data mining
- TIBCO: TIBCO provides commercial solutions for analytics and data science, including predictive modeling capabilities

These predictive analytic tools, spanning open source and commercial domains, empower organizations to extract valuable insights and make informed decisions based on predictive modeling and data analysis. The selection of a tool often depends on factors such as user preferences, integration capabilities, collaboration features, and the specific needs of the project or organization.

CHAPTER 16

BI AND DATA ANALYSIS

Business intelligence and data analysis are closely related concepts that often work together to help organizations make informed decisions based on data. While they share common goals, they have distinct roles and functions within the realm of data-driven decision-making. This section provides an overview of their relationship and interplay.

BI AND DATA ANALYSIS RELATIONSHIP

Definition

Business Intelligence

BI encompasses a suite of technologies, tools, and processes designed to facilitate the collection, analysis, and presentation of business information. In essence, BI acts as the backbone for organizations seeking to convert raw data into meaningful insights. This transformative process enables strategic decision-making by providing stakeholders with a comprehensive understanding of their operational landscape.

Through BI, businesses gain the capability to identify trends, patterns, and KPIs, fostering a data-driven culture. The ultimate goal of BI is to empower decision-makers at all levels, from executives to frontline employees, with the information needed to make informed and impactful choices that drive the organization's success.

Data Analysis

Data analysis, a fundamental aspect of business intelligence, represents a comprehensive approach to examining data. This broader term encapsulates a myriad of techniques and methods employed to inspect, clean, transform, and model data with the overarching aim of discovering valuable information. The process of data analysis goes beyond mere examination; it involves drawing meaningful conclusions and insights from datasets, ultimately supporting effective decision-making within an organization.

Data analysts utilize statistical methods, machine learning algorithms, and visualization tools to reveal patterns, correlations, and trends hidden within the data. By leveraging data analysis, organizations can unlock the full potential of their information assets, gain a competitive advantage, and enhance their ability to adapt to the dynamic demands of the business environment.

Scope

The scope of BI and data analysis spans a broad spectrum, encompassing the collection, integration, and interpretation of data to drive informed decision-making. These practices empower organizations to uncover trends, predict outcomes, and optimize strategies across various business domains.

Business Intelligence

BI has a comprehensive scope, concentrating on delivering insights across various temporal dimensions. The primary focus of BI spans historical, current, and predictive perspectives of business operations. This entails meticulously examining past performance, an in-depth analysis of present conditions, and anticipating future trends.

Within this framework, BI commonly employs the creation of dynamic dashboards, detailed reports, and informative scorecards. These visual representations serve as essential tools for stakeholders, aiding in the interpretation of complex datasets. By leveraging BI, organizations can facilitate a holistic understanding of their performance metrics and operational trends, empowering decision-makers to devise informed strategies and navigate the intricacies of their business landscape.

Data Analysis

The scope of data analysis is notably expansive, encompassing various methodologies and techniques for obtaining insights from diverse datasets. It extends beyond traditional boundaries to include EDA, statistical analysis, and machine learning.

EDA involves the initial examination of data to identify patterns, anomalies, or potential relationships. Statistical analysis employs mathematical models to derive quantitative insights, offering a deeper understanding of the underlying characteristics of data. Machine learning, a cutting-edge facet of data analysis, leverages algorithms to predict future trends and behaviors based on historical data patterns.

The overarching goal of data analysis is to extract actionable insights, reveal hidden patterns, and uncover meaningful trends within the data. This broad scope ensures that data analysis is a versatile and dynamic tool that can cater to the multifaceted demands of decision-makers across diverse industries.

Purpose

The purpose of BI and data analysis is to transform raw data into actionable insights that guide strategic decisions. By leveraging these practices, organizations can enhance performance, improve efficiency, and stay competitive in dynamic markets.

Business Intelligence

BI plays a crucial role in organizations by focusing on monitoring and reporting KPIs, tracking business goals, and supporting strategic decision-making. It acts as a real-time monitoring tool, providing stakeholders with a comprehensive view of KPIs, facilitating the identification of areas for improvement and success.

BI tools also play a vital role in tracking progress toward organizational goals, ensuring that the business remains aligned with its strategic objectives. Additionally, BI provides structured and summarized views of business data through dashboards and reports, offering clarity for decision-makers at various levels within the organization.

Data Analysis

Data analysis is inherently exploratory and investigative. It goes beyond the surface, aiming to identify patterns, correlations, anomalies, and trends within datasets. The primary purpose of data analysis is to uncover insights that might not be immediately apparent through traditional observation.

By utilizing statistical methods, machine learning algorithms, and visualization techniques, data analysis reveals hidden stories within the data. It provides a nuanced understanding of the underlying factors influencing business outcomes, offering decision-makers the necessary insights to respond effectively to challenges and opportunities presented by their data landscape.

Tools and Technologies

Tools and technologies in BI and data analysis serve as the backbone for transforming data into actionable insights. From advanced analytics platforms to visualization tools, these resources enable organizations to efficiently process, analyze, and present data for informed decision-making.

Business Intelligence

BI relies on a spectrum of sophisticated tools and technologies designed to streamline the process of data interpretation and decision support. Prominent among these are tools such as Tableau, Power BI, and QlikView. These tools are renowned for their proficiency in visualization, reporting, and dashboard creation. They empower users to transform complex datasets into intuitive visuals, facilitating a more accessible and comprehensive understanding of key business metrics. With drag-and-drop interfaces and interactive features, BI tools enable stakeholders to explore data dynamically, fostering a data-driven culture within organizations.

Data Analysis

Data analysis, being a versatile discipline, harnesses an array of tools that cater to different aspects of the analytical process. This toolkit spans from ubiquitous spreadsheet software such as Excel to more sophisticated programming languages such as Python and R. Widely adopted in the data analysis realm, tools such as Jupyter Notebooks provide an interactive environment for code execution and documentation.

Python libraries, such as Pandas, further enhance the capabilities of data analysts by offering powerful data manipulation and analysis tools. The flexibility of data analysis tools allows practitioners to tailor their approach to the specific requirements of each analytical task, ensuring a comprehensive and customizable exploration of datasets.

Time Frame

The time frame in BI and data analysis defines the period over which data is collected, analyzed, and reported. Understanding and selecting appropriate time frames is crucial for aligning insights with business objectives and ensuring timely decision-making.

Business Intelligence

The time frame for BI implementation varies depending on the complexity of the organizational requirements and the chosen BI tools. The initial setup and deployment of BI solutions like Tableau, Power BI, and QlikView may typically range from a few weeks to a couple of months. This phase involves tasks such as data integration, establishing connections to relevant data sources, and configuring visualization dashboards.

Ongoing utilization and refinement, however, are continuous processes, with organizations consistently adapting and expanding their BI implementations as their data needs evolve. Regular updates and maintenance ensure that BI systems remain aligned with changing business dynamics, providing timely and relevant insights to stakeholders.

Data Analysis

The time frame for data analysis is inherently dynamic and influenced by the complexity of the analysis, the size of the dataset, and the specific tools and methodologies employed. EDA in tools such as Excel can yield rapid insights, often within hours or days. For more sophisticated analyses using programming languages such as Python and R, the time frame may extend to weeks, particularly when handling extensive datasets or implementing advanced machine learning models. The iterative nature of data analysis means that the process evolves over time, with ongoing refinement and validation of the results. The time invested in data analysis is a strategic investment, ensuring the accuracy and reliability of insights derived from the data.

Each of these time frames underscores the importance of considering the nuanced nature of BI and data analysis processes, acknowledging the initial setup, continuous refinement, and adaptability to changing data landscapes.

Integration

Integration in BI and data analysis involves combining data from multiple sources to create a unified view for more comprehensive insights. This process ensures consistency, enhances data accuracy, and enables seamless collaboration across various business systems and teams.

Business Intelligence

BI represents a holistic approach to data utilization, where integration extends beyond the mere incorporation of data analysis techniques. In BI systems, data analysis serves as a pivotal element, particularly in the context of deriving insights from historical data trends. By seamlessly integrating data analysis within the BI framework, organizations can enhance their capacity to reveal patterns, correlations, and valuable trends. This integration ensures that BI facilitates real-time decision-making and leverages historical data to provide a comprehensive understanding of the business landscape. The amalgamation of BI and data analysis empowers stakeholders with a multifaceted toolset to navigate the complexities of data-driven decision-making.

Data Analysis

While fundamentally integral to BI, data analysis maintains a distinct identity as a fundamental component within the broader analytical landscape. In the context of integration, data analysis plays a critical role by providing in-depth insights that form the backbone of BI systems. This integration ensures that the data analysis functions synergistically with other elements of BI, contributing to the creation of actionable insights.

Data analysis involves not only a stand-alone process but also an interconnected element that fortifies the foundation of BI systems. The integration of data analysis within BI is instrumental in transforming raw data into meaningful information, fostering a comprehensive and strategic approach to decision-making within organizations.

In summary, while business intelligence provides a structured and summarized view of business data, data analysis involves a more in-depth exploration of data to extract actionable insights. The two processes often complement each other, with BI providing the necessary framework for presenting information and data analysis, offering a detailed examination of underlying patterns and trends. Both are integral components of a comprehensive data-driven decision-making strategy within organizations.

UNVEILING THE ANALYTICAL LANDSCAPE

This section explores the transformative journey of data analysis, delving into its evolution, diverse techniques, and the ethical considerations that shape its application. This section highlights how data analysis has become a cornerstone for extracting insights and driving informed decision-making in today's complex business environment.

Evolution of Data Analysis

The evolution of data analysis has been marked by significant shifts in methodologies, tools, and approaches, driven primarily by technological advancements and changing business needs. Initially, data analysis was largely manual and relied heavily on descriptive statistics and basic visualization techniques. With the advent of computers and digital data storage, the field underwent a transformative phase, enabling analysts to handle larger datasets and perform more sophisticated analyses. The introduction of statistical software packages further democratized data analysis, allowing analysts to leverage complex algorithms and models with relative ease.

As businesses began to recognize the potential value hidden within their data, the demand for more advanced analytical techniques grew, leading to the rise of predictive analytics, machine learning, and AI. These technologies have revolutionized data analysis, enabling organizations to uncover actionable insights, forecast future trends, and make data-driven decisions with unprecedented accuracy and efficiency.

Moreover, the evolution of data analysis has been fueled by the proliferation of big data and the increasing interconnectedness of digital ecosystems. With the exponential growth of data volumes generated by online transactions, social media interactions, and IoT devices, traditional data analysis techniques have become inadequate for handling the sheer scale and complexity of modern datasets. This necessitated the development of new approaches and tools capable of processing, analyzing, and deriving insights from massive datasets in real time.

As a result, technologies like Hadoop, Spark, and cloud computing emerged, enabling organizations to store, process, and analyze vast amounts of structured and unstructured data more efficiently and cost-effectively. The evolution of data analysis continues to unfold as organizations explore emerging technologies such as edge computing, quantum computing, and advanced analytics techniques like deep learning, promising even greater capabilities for extracting value from data in the years to come.

Data Analysis: Techniques, Insights, and Ethics

Data analysis encompasses a broad array of techniques and methodologies aimed at extracting meaningful insights from datasets to inform decision-making processes. Techniques employed in data analysis range from simple descriptive statistics and visualizations to more advanced methods such as regression analysis, clustering, and machine learning algorithms. Each technique serves a specific purpose, with descriptive statistics offering a summary of data characteristics, while predictive modeling techniques enable forecasting future trends based on historical data. Moreover, EDA techniques allow analysts to delve into the data without preconceived hypotheses, uncovering unexpected insights and generating new research questions.

The insights derived from data analysis play a crucial role in guiding decision-making processes across diverse domains, including business, healthcare, finance, and public policy. By analyzing data, organizations can gain a deeper understanding of customer preferences, market trends, operational inefficiencies, and emerging risks, enabling them to make informed strategic decisions and drive performance improvements. For instance, in healthcare, data analysis techniques can be used to identify patient cohorts at higher risk of developing specific diseases, enabling targeted interventions and personalized treatment plans. Similarly, in finance, data analysis can help identify investment opportunities, assess market risks, and optimize portfolio performance based on historical market data and predictive models.

The ethical implications of data analysis have become increasingly salient in recent years as the ubiquity of data collection and analysis raises concerns about privacy, bias, and transparency. Ethical considerations in data analysis encompass issues such as informed consent, data anonymization, fairness, and accountability. Analysts must be mindful of the potential impact of their analyses on individuals and communities, ensuring that data-driven decisions do not perpetuate discrimination or harm vulnerable populations.

Moreover, transparency and reproducibility are essential principles in data analysis, as stakeholders should have access to the data, methods, and assumptions underlying analytical findings to assess their validity and reliability. By adhering to ethical guidelines and best practices, data analysts can harness the power of data analysis to drive positive social change and contribute to the advancement of knowledge while minimizing potential risks and harms.

NAVIGATING ANALYTICAL CHALLENGES

Before delving into the foundations and basics of data analysis, it is essential to equip analysts with the tools to navigate the challenges inherent in the analytical journey. In this section, we identify the complexities and hurdles that analysts may encounter, providing insights into effective strategies for overcoming these obstacles.

Handling Outliers and Missing Data

Analysts frequently encounter outliers and missing data, posing challenges that can undermine the accuracy and reliability of their analyses. Implementing effective techniques to identify and address outliers, alongside adopting strategies to manage missing data, is paramount in ensuring the integrity of the analytical process. By diligently handling outliers and missing data, analysts lay the foundation for conducting robust and dependable analyses that yield meaningful insights.

Addressing Data Biases

In the realm of data analysis, unraveling the intricacies of data biases is paramount for analysts seeking reliable insights. By comprehending how biases can subtly influence results, analysts can implement methods to detect and mitigate these biases effectively, thereby upholding the integrity of the analysis. Ultimately, this concerted effort toward addressing data biases fosters a more accurate representation of the underlying data, enabling more informed decision-making processes.

Managing Limitations of Analytical Tools

Acknowledging the inherent limitations of analytical tools is essential for analysts. Developing a nuanced understanding of these strengths and weaknesses enables analysts to navigate potential constraints effectively. By providing insights into recognizing and managing these limitations, analysts can make informed choices, optimizing their analytical approaches for more accurate and impactful results.

With these challenges in mind, analysts can approach the foundational chapters with a practical understanding of the nuances involved in data analysis. Analysts will be well-prepared to apply these insights in real-world scenarios as we transition to the core elements of data analysis foundations, from the definition and historical evolution to data types, sources, and collection methods. This prelude sets the stage for a comprehensive exploration of the multifaceted landscape of data analysis, combining theoretical knowledge with practical acumen to ensure a holistic understanding of the analytical process.

CHAPTER 17

DATA ANALYSIS: FUNDAMENTALS AND ANALYTICS

This chapter lays the groundwork for understanding the essential principles and methodologies that drive effective data analysis. It explores foundational concepts and advanced analytical approaches that empower businesses to derive actionable insights from their data.

DATA ANALYSIS ESSENTIALS

This section introduces foundational concepts that are critical to understanding how organizations extract meaningful insights from raw data. It explores the evolution, types, sources, collection methods, and preparation techniques that form the backbone of effective data analysis.

Essence and Evolution of Data Analysis

The essence of data analysis lies in transforming raw data into actionable insights that drive informed decision-making. Its evolution reflects the growing complexity of datasets and the adoption of advanced methodologies to meet modern analytical demands.

Decoding Data Analysis

Data analysis serves as the cornerstone of informed decision-making within organizations, encompassing a comprehensive set of techniques and methods aimed at scrutinizing, cleansing, transforming, and modeling data to extract valuable insights. At its core, data analysis involves the systematic examination of datasets, going beyond mere observation to uncover meaningful patterns, correlations, and trends that might elude casual observation. It transforms raw data into actionable information, enabling decision-makers to make well-informed choices.

The importance of data analysis lies in its ability to provide a deeper understanding of business operations, customer behaviors, and market dynamics. By employing statistical methods, machine learning algorithms, and visualization tools, data analysis not only reveals hidden stories within the data but also empowers organizations to gain a competitive edge by responding strategically to the evolving landscape.

Historical Context and Evolution

The historical evolution of data analysis traces back to the early days of statistical methods, where pioneers such as Francis Galton and Karl Pearson laid the groundwork for quantitative analysis. Over time, technological advancements have propelled data analysis from manual and time-consuming processes to the sophisticated, technology-driven methodologies employed in contemporary settings. The advent of computers and powerful software has revolutionized the scale and scope of data analysis, enabling analysts to handle vast datasets and implement intricate algorithms.

The evolution of data analysis mirrors the growing reliance on data-driven decision-making across diverse industries. From the basic tabulation of figures to complex predictive modeling, the journey of data analysis reflects its adaptation to the changing needs of organizations and the increasing complexity of available data sources. Understanding this historical context is pivotal for understanding the trajectory of data analysis and its pivotal role in the modern organizational landscape.

Data Types and Sources

Understanding the types and sources of data is fundamental to effective analysis, as it determines the methods and tools used to extract meaningful insights. A comprehensive approach to both structured and unstructured data ensures a holistic view of the information landscape.

Types of Data

Data, in its various forms, can be broadly categorized into qualitative and quantitative types, each offering unique insights into different aspects of the information landscape. Qualitative data involves nonnumeric information, often described as categorical or textual in nature. This can include subjective attributes such as colors, feelings, or opinions. Qualitative data is rich in context, providing a deeper understanding of the nuances within a given dataset. Alternatively, quantitative data involves numerical information that can be measured and analyzed statistically. This type of data is inherently objective, allowing for precise measurements and quantitative comparisons.

The duality of qualitative and quantitative data provides analysts with a comprehensive toolkit, enabling them to explore both the narrative depth and the numerical precision inherent in diverse datasets. Effectively harnessing these data types is essential for conducting thorough and well-rounded analyses that capture the intricacies of the underlying information.

Sources of Data

Data originates from various sources, and understanding the nature of these sources is fundamental for effective analysis. Primary data is collected firsthand, often through surveys, interviews, or experiments, and is tailored to the specific needs of the researcher. It is original and directly obtained from the source, providing a high degree of relevance and specificity. In contrast, secondary data is preexisting information gathered by someone other than the analyst. This data may include sources such as research papers, government reports, or datasets collected for different purposes. Analyzing both primary and secondary data sources allows for a comprehensive examination of a phenomenon.

Additionally, data comes in structured and unstructured formats. Structured data is organized in a predefined manner, typically stored in databases or tables, facilitating easy analysis. Unstructured data, such as text documents, images, or social media posts, lacks a predefined structure and presents challenges in terms of organization and analysis. Navigating these diverse sources and types of data is crucial for data analysts to unlock the full potential of their datasets and derive meaningful insights.

Data Collection and Cleaning

Effective data collection and cleaning are vital for ensuring the accuracy and reliability of analytical outcomes. These processes transform raw data into a refined form, ready for meaningful analysis and decision-making.

Methods of Data Collection

Data collection is a critical phase in the analytical process, involving the systematic gathering of information to address specific research questions or objectives. Various methods are employed to collect data, each of which is suited to different contexts and types of information. Surveys and questionnaires are commonly used to gather self-reported data, allowing participants to express their opinions or provide information on specific topics. Interviews offer a more interactive approach, enabling researchers to delve deeper into responses and clarify ambiguities. Observational methods involve direct observation of subjects in their natural environment, providing a firsthand account of behaviors or phenomena.

For quantitative data, experiments are designed to manipulate variables and measure their effects. Additionally, data can be collected from existing records and documents, a method often referred to as document analysis. The choice of data collection method depends on the research objectives, the nature of the data, and the resources available, highlighting the need for careful consideration and planning in this foundational phase of analysis.

Data Cleaning and Preprocessing Techniques

Once data is collected, it often requires cleaning and preprocessing to ensure its quality, accuracy, and suitability for analysis. Data cleaning involves identifying and correcting errors or inconsistencies in the dataset. This may include addressing missing values, outliers, or inaccuracies resulting from data entry mistakes. Data preprocessing goes beyond cleaning and involves transforming the data to enhance its suitability for analysis. Techniques such as normalization or standardization may be applied to ensure uniformity in the scale of numerical variables. Categorical variables might be encoded to numerical values to facilitate analysis.

Feature engineering, another aspect of preprocessing, involves creating new features from existing ones to enhance the predictive power of models. These techniques aim to refine the dataset, making it more amenable to analysis and modeling. Data cleaning and preprocessing are iterative processes, often requiring collaboration between domain experts and data analysts to make informed decisions about the most appropriate methods for enhancing data quality and analytical outcomes.

Exploratory Data Analysis

Overview

Exploratory data analysis (EDA) is a crucial phase in the analytical journey that involves systematically examining and understanding the characteristics of a dataset. Its primary goal is to gain insights into the underlying patterns, relationships, and trends within the data before formal modeling or hypothesis testing. It serves as a comprehensive and interactive approach to data analysis, allowing analysts to formulate hypotheses, identify potential outliers, and assess the distribution of variables.

EDA is not confined to specific statistical techniques but encompasses a holistic examination of the dataset, combining statistical methods, graphical representations, and domain knowledge. By providing a preliminary understanding of the data, EDA guides subsequent analytical decisions and helps refine research questions. Overall, the aim is to unearth key features and nuances within the dataset, paving the way for more focused and informed analyses in the later stages of the data analysis process.

Techniques to Summarize and Visualize data

EDA employs a diverse set of techniques to summarize and visualize data, enhancing the understanding of its inherent structures. Descriptive statistics offer a quantitative summary of key features, including measures of central tendency (mean, median, mode) and variability (range, standard deviation). Visualizations play a pivotal role in EDA, providing intuitive insights into the distribution and patterns within the data. Histograms depict the frequency distribution of a variable, offering a visual representation of its shape.

Box plots highlight the distribution's central tendency to spread and identify potential outliers. Scatter plots reveal relationships between two variables, aiding in the identification of trends or correlations. EDA may also involve the use of heat maps, pie charts, and other graphical representations to reveal patterns that might not be immediately apparent. By combining these techniques, analysts can construct a comprehensive narrative of the dataset, laying the groundwork for subsequent in-depth analyses and modeling.

STATISTICAL FOUNDATIONS AND HYPOTHESIS TESTING

Statistical foundations and hypothesis testing provide the framework for making data-driven decisions. By analyzing patterns and testing assumptions, these methods help validate insights and establish confidence in analytical conclusions.

Statistical Foundations

Statistical foundations form the backbone of data analysis, enabling the interpretation and summarization of data. Understanding key concepts and probability distributions is crucial for extracting meaningful insights and making informed decisions.

Basic Statistical Concepts

Foundational data analysis is a robust understanding of basic statistical concepts that provide a quantitative summary of data. Mean, median, and mode are measures of central tendency, representing the average, middle, and most frequent values in a dataset, respectively. The mean is sensitive to extreme values, making it essential to grasp the overall distribution. Median, the middle value, is resistant to outliers and is useful in skewed datasets. Mode identifies the most recurring value, shedding light on the dataset's prominent characteristics.

The standard deviation measures the spread or dispersion of data points around the mean. A low standard deviation indicates that the values are closely clustered around the mean, while a high standard deviation suggests greater variability. Collectively, these concepts offer comprehensive insight into the central tendencies and variability within a dataset, forming the bedrock for subsequent statistical analyses.

Role of Probability Distributions

Understanding probability distributions is paramount in data analysis, as they model the likelihood of different outcomes. Common distributions include the normal distribution, which is symmetric and bell-shaped, facilitating various statistical analyses. Other distributions, such as the binomial distribution for binary outcomes or the Poisson distribution for rare events, cater to diverse scenarios. Probability distributions are integral in hypothesis testing, where analysts assess the likelihood of observing a particular result by chance.

Z-scores, derived from the normal distribution, aid in standardizing values for comparison. The relevance of probability distributions extends to inferential statistics, guiding decisions about the generalizability of findings from a sample to a population. A solid grasp of these statistical foundations enables analysts to make informed decisions, interpret results accurately, and lay the groundwork for more advanced analyses in the data analysis process.

Hypothesis Testing

Hypothesis testing provides a structured framework for making data-driven decisions by evaluating assumptions and drawing conclusions. Its significance and systematic steps ensure analytical rigor and reliability in interpreting results.

Significance of Hypothesis Testing

Hypothesis testing is a fundamental statistical method employed in data analysis to evaluate conjectures about population parameters. At its core, hypothesis testing involves formulating a null hypothesis (H0) that assumes no effect or no difference and an alternative hypothesis (H1) that posits an effect or difference. Analysts then collect and analyze sample data to determine whether there is enough evidence to reject the null hypothesis in favor of the alternative. This process is akin to a courtroom trial, where the null hypothesis is presumed to be innocent until the evidence suggests otherwise.

The significance level, denoted by alpha (α), determines the threshold for considering evidence significant. If the p-value, which represents the probability of obtaining observed results under the assumption that the null hypothesis is true, is less than α, the null hypothesis is rejected. Hypothesis testing is integral in drawing meaningful conclusions from data guiding decision-makers in various fields to adopt or reject specific courses of action based on statistical evidence.

Steps of Hypothesis Testing

Hypothesis testing unfolds through a systematic sequence of steps, each contributing to the robustness of the analysis. The process begins with the formulation of clear and concise null and alternative hypotheses, setting the stage for subsequent analyses. Data collection follows, with analysts gathering information to test these hypotheses. Statistical techniques are then applied to assess the evidence against the null hypothesis, calculating the p-value as a measure of significance. If the p-value is less than or equal to the predetermined alpha level, the null hypothesis is rejected, suggesting that the observed results are unlikely to occur by chance alone.

Interpretation of results involves translating statistical findings into meaningful insights for decision-makers. The type of hypothesis test employed depends on the nature of the data and the research question. Overall, hypothesis testing provides a structured approach to inference, enabling analysts to draw reliable conclusions and make data-driven decisions in a variety of domains.

CORRELATION AND REGRESSION ANALYSIS

Correlation and regression analysis are essential techniques for exploring relationships between variables, providing insights into patterns and predictive trends. These methods empower businesses to make informed decisions based on data-driven connections.

Relationships Between Variables

Understanding the relationships between variables is a cornerstone of data analysis, providing valuable insights into how changes in one variable might affect another. Correlation and regression analyses are powerful tools for exploring and quantifying these relationships. Correlation measures the degree of association between two variables, indicating whether and how they change together. The correlation coefficient, typically denoted by "r," ranges from -1 to 1, with positive values signifying a positive correlation, negative values indicating a negative correlation, and zero representing no correlation.

This statistical metric is crucial for identifying patterns and dependencies within datasets. Analysts use correlation analysis to discern connections between variables, enabling them to grasp the intricate Web of relationships that contribute to a comprehensive understanding of the data landscape. While correlation reveals associations, regression analysis takes the next step, offering a predictive model to quantify and understand these relationships more precisely.

Exploring Correlation and Regression Analysis

Correlation and regression analyses are indispensable techniques for delving deeper into the dynamics of variables. Correlation, as a measure of association, serves as an initial exploration, providing a snapshot of how variables move in relation to each other. Correlation alone does not imply causation. This is where regression analysis steps in to provide a more nuanced perspective. Regression establishes a functional relationship between variables, allowing analysts to predict the value of one variable based on the value of another.

The regression equation, often represented as Y = a + bX, shows the relationship between the dependent variable (Y) and the independent variable (X). The coefficients "a" and "b" are crucial in understanding the slope and intercept of the regression line, offering insights into the strength and direction of the relationship. Regression analysis goes beyond mere association, providing a framework for making predictions and understanding the underlying patterns that drive the observed correlations. It is a vital tool for decision-makers seeking to forecast outcomes and make informed choices based on the interplay of variables.

CHAPTER 18

DATA ANALYSIS: ADVANCED INSIGHTS

T his chapter examines sophisticated techniques and methodologies that go beyond foundational analysis, enabling deeper exploration of data patterns. These insights empower organizations to uncover hidden opportunities and optimize decision-making processes.

DATA VISUALIZATION

Role in Analysis

Data visualization plays a pivotal role in data analysis by translating complex datasets into visual representations that are easily understandable and interpretable. The human brain is inherently wired to process visual information more efficiently than raw data, making visualization a powerful tool for conveying insights and patterns hidden within the numbers. Visualization enhances the communicative power of data analysis, allowing analysts to present findings in a compelling and accessible manner, even to audiences without a background in statistics. Through graphical representations, trends, correlations, and outliers become immediately apparent, facilitating a quicker and more intuitive understanding of the underlying information.

Data visualization is instrumental in decision-making processes within organizations. Clear visualizations enable stakeholders to swiftly grasp key takeaways, fostering a more informed decision-making culture. Whether it is identifying market trends, evaluating the success of a business strategy, or understanding customer behaviors, effective data visualization transforms data into a strategic asset. In a world inundated with information, the ability to distill complex data into visually compelling narratives is a competitive advantage, empowering organizations to stay agile and responsive to changing dynamics.

Techniques

Techniques for effective data visualization encompass a range of approaches. Choosing the right visualization type depends on the nature of the data and the insights sought. Bar charts and line graphs are effective for comparing values and trends, while pie charts are suitable for illustrating proportions. Heatmaps can reveal patterns and correlations in large datasets, and scatter plots are invaluable for exploring relationships between variables.

The judicious use of color, size, and other visual elements enhances the clarity and interpretability of visualizations. Furthermore, storytelling through visualization involves structuring visualizations into a narrative flow, guiding the audience through the data story, and ensuring that the insights are conveyed in a coherent and compelling manner. Ultimately, mastering tools and techniques for data visualization empowers analysts to unlock the full potential of their data and communicate findings effectively.

MACHINE LEARNING

This section explores the transformative role of machine learning in data analysis, highlighting its capacity to uncover complex patterns and generate predictive insights. By leveraging these advanced techniques, organizations can enhance their analytical capabilities and drive data-driven innovation.

Basic Concept

At its core, machine learning represents a paradigm shift in computer science, where systems are designed not to follow explicit instructions but to learn from data. This transformative field encompasses various fundamental concepts that underpin its functioning. Supervised learning, a foundational concept, involves training models on labeled datasets, teaching them to make predictions or decisions based on input data and corresponding output labels. In contrast, unsupervised learning explores data without predefined outcomes, seeking to identify patterns or structures within the information.

Reinforcement learning introduces the concept of agents who learn through interactions with an environment, receiving rewards for correct actions and penalties for errors. These learning paradigms are driven by the utilization of features, which are the distinctive attributes or variables used by algorithms to make predictions. Models, representing the algorithms themselves, are crafted to generalize patterns from training data to new, unseen data.

In machine learning, critical concepts include training and testing datasets, where the former is used to train the model, and the latter evaluates its performance. Evaluation metrics such as accuracy, precision, recall, and F1 score gauge the effectiveness of machine learning models. The field is dynamic and continually evolving, with ongoing advancements in deep learning, neural networks, and NLP pushing the boundaries of what machines can comprehend and achieve. As machine learning concepts continue to mature, they contribute significantly to the development of intelligent systems that can automate decision-making and learn from experience.

Machine Learning in Data Analysis

Machine learning has emerged as a powerful catalyst for innovation within the field of data analysis, offering a diverse array of applications that transform raw data into actionable insights. Predictive modeling is a prominent technique for forecasting future trends or outcomes based on historical data patterns. It is particularly valuable in sectors such as finance for predicting market trends, healthcare for diagnosing diseases, and marketing for anticipating consumer behavior.

Classification and clustering algorithms play a pivotal role in organizing and categorizing data into distinct groups or classes, facilitating a deeper understanding of patterns and relationships. NLP, a subset of machine learning, is instrumental in enhancing language-related tasks. It empowers computers to understand, interpret, and generate human-like language, contributing to applications such as sentiment analysis, chatbots, and language translation.

In the realm of data analysis, machine learning facilitates anomaly detection, uncovering irregularities in datasets that may indicate fraudulent activities or unusual patterns. Recommendation systems leverage machine learning to analyze user behavior and preferences, offering personalized suggestions on platforms such as streaming services or e-commerce sites.

As machine learning algorithms continue to advance, their applications in image and speech recognition become increasingly sophisticated, automating tasks that were once dependent on human expertise.

In essence, the integration of machine learning into data analysis processes enhances the efficiency, scalability, and extraction of meaningful insights from complex datasets.

DATA ANALYSIS TOOLS

This section discusses the software and libraries that empower analysts to process and visualize data effectively. These tools streamline complex workflows, enabling users to derive meaningful insights with efficiency and precision

Popular Data Analysis Tools

In data analysis, the choice of tools significantly influences the efficiency and depth of insights that analysts can derive from datasets. One of the most widely used tools is Excel, which is known for its user-friendly interface and spreadsheet capabilities. It is particularly favored for tasks involving data manipulation, basic statistical analysis, and the creation of visualizations. Its formula-based approach allows users to perform calculations, filter data, and generate summary statistics effortlessly.

Python, a versatile programming language, has gained immense popularity in data analysis due to its extensive libraries and frameworks. Pandas, a Python library, provides powerful data structures and tools for data manipulation and analysis. Combined with NumPy and SciPy for numerical operations and statistical functions and scikit-learn for machine learning tasks, Python offers a comprehensive ecosystem for data analysts and scientists.

R, another programming language, is specifically designed for statistical computing and data analysis. Renowned for its statistical packages and visualization capabilities, R is favored in academic and research settings. Its vast array of packages, such as ggplot2 for creating intricate visualizations, makes it a robust choice for analysts working with complex datasets.

In addition to programming languages, integrated development environments (IDEs) such as Jupyter Notebooks facilitate interactive and collaborative data analysis, allowing analysts to weave together code, visualizations, and narrative explanations. The amalgamation of these tools provides data analysts with a diverse toolkit, catering to different stages of the analysis process and accommodating various preferences and skill levels.

Data Visualization Tools and Libraries

Data visualization is a cornerstone of effective data analysis, which translates complex datasets into visually comprehensible representations. A plethora of tools and techniques exist for creating impactful and insightful data visualizations. Among the most widely used tools is Tableau, known for its user-friendly interface and robust visualization capabilities, facilitating dynamic data exploration. It allows users to create interactive dashboards and reports, making them accessible to a broader audience, including those without programming backgrounds. Similarly, Power BI empowers users to generate compelling visualizations and reports by seamlessly integrating with various data sources. These tools provide a bridge between raw data and meaningful insights, allowing users to experiment with different visualization types and formats.

Several other tools and libraries specialize in this crucial aspect of analysis. Matplotlib, a popular plotting library for Python, offers a versatile range of 2D and 3D plots, catering to a broad spectrum of visualization needs. Its integration with NumPy arrays makes it a go-to choice for those working in Python. Seaborn, built on top of Matplotlib, focuses on enhancing aesthetics and statistical summaries, providing an additional layer of abstraction for creating appealing visualizations with minimal code.

The interplay of these visualization tools extends beyond static images. Interactive libraries such as Plotly facilitate the creation of dynamic visualizations, enhancing the user experience and allowing for the exploration of data from multiple perspectives. GIS tools, such as QGIS, enable the integration of spatial data into visualizations, adding another dimension to the analytical process.

As data visualization continues to evolve, the integration of diverse tools and libraries empowers analysts to choose the most suitable platform for conveying insights to diverse audiences, whether they are technical stakeholders, decision-makers, or the general public.

ADVANCED ANALYTICS

This section explores cutting-edge methodologies and tools that enable organizations to derive deeper insights from complex datasets. By leveraging techniques like time series analysis and advanced interpretation, it empowers decision-makers to predict trends and make informed, strategic decisions.

Harnessing Big Data for Advanced Analysis

Big data represents a paradigm shift in the volume, velocity, and variety of data that organizations now encounter. It encompasses massive datasets that exceed the processing capabilities of traditional databases and analytical tools. The impact of big data on data analysis is profound, necessitating new approaches and technologies to extract meaningful insights.

Unlike traditional datasets, big data often includes unstructured information, such as text, images, and videos, in addition to structured data. This diversity requires sophisticated tools and techniques to harness the full potential of the information. Technologies such as Hadoop and Spark have emerged as key players in the big data landscape, offering distributed computing frameworks that can handle vast amounts of data across clusters of computers.

The impact of big data extends beyond the technical realm, influencing decision-making processes and strategic planning. Organizations now have the ability to analyze large-scale data in near real-time, enabling timely responses to market trends, customer behaviors, and emerging opportunities. Machine learning algorithms, a subset of advanced analytics, play a crucial role in extracting insights from big data. These algorithms can identify patterns, make predictions, and automate decision-making processes.

The integration of big data analytics has become a competitive advantage for organizations seeking to innovate, adapt, and thrive in an increasingly data-driven business environment. As the volume of data grows exponentially, harnessing big data effectively remains a cornerstone of modern data analysis.

Advanced Analytics Techniques in Data Analysis

Advanced analytics techniques represent the frontier of data analysis, encompassing a spectrum of sophisticated methodologies that go beyond traditional statistical approaches. A key component of advanced analytics is machine learning, a field of AI that focuses on creating algorithms that can learn from and make predictions or decisions based on data. Machine learning models, ranging from decision trees to neural networks, play a pivotal role in uncovering patterns and relationships within datasets, automating complex tasks, and enabling predictive modeling. Predictive modeling, another facet of advanced analytics, involves creating models that forecast future outcomes based on historical data.

Moreover, advanced analytics includes techniques such as clustering and segmentation, which group similar data points together, aiding in the identification of patterns and trends. Time-series analysis, which is essential for understanding data that evolves over time, is crucial in various domains, including finance, healthcare, and environmental science. These advanced techniques empower analysts to extract deeper insights, make accurate predictions, and optimize decision-making processes.

As organizations embrace the era of big data, advanced analytics has become integral to unlocking the true value of data. Advanced analytics techniques contribute significantly to the evolution of data analysis in the modern landscape, whether by predicting customer preferences, optimizing supply chain logistics, or identifying potential risks.

Time Series Analysis

Time series analysis is a specialized field within data analysis that focuses on understanding and extracting patterns from data points collected sequentially over time. The basics of time series data involve examining the temporal patterns and dependencies present in the dataset. Such data commonly arises in various domains, including finance, economics, climate science, and manufacturing, where observations are recorded at regular intervals. The fundamental challenge lies in unraveling the underlying structure and trends within the temporal dimension. Time series data often exhibits characteristics such as seasonality, trends, and cyclic patterns.

Analyzing time series data involves employing a variety of statistical and machine-learning techniques to uncover insights and make predictions about future values. Descriptive statistics, such as moving averages and exponential smoothing, provide a snapshot of the data's behavior over time. Time series decomposition separates the data into its constituent components, such as trend and seasonality, facilitating a more granular analysis. Additionally, autoregressive integrated moving average (ARIMA) models and machine learning algorithms, such as recurrent neural networks (RNNs) and long short-term memory (LSTM) networks, offer advanced methods for forecasting future values based on historical patterns.

The applications of time series analysis are vast, ranging from predicting stock prices and demand forecasting to climate modeling and anomaly detection. Analysts can extract valuable insights, improve decision-making processes, and anticipate future trends in dynamic environments by mastering the basics of time series data and leveraging appropriate analytical techniques.

Data Interpretation and Reporting

Data interpretation and reporting are pivotal aspects of the data analysis process, emphasizing the need to bridge the gap between raw analytical outcomes and actionable insights for stakeholders. Once the analysis is complete, interpreting the results becomes a strategic endeavor, requiring a nuanced understanding of the context, domain, and objectives. Analysts must not only comprehend the statistical or machine learning findings but also discern their practical implications for decision-makers. This involves connecting the dots between data patterns, trends, and the broader business or research questions at hand.

Effective interpretation goes beyond mere numerical summaries, delving into the story that the data tells. Analysts employ domain knowledge, statistical reasoning, and critical thinking to distill complex findings into digestible narratives. Clear, concise, and relevant interpretations enhance the value of the analysis, providing actionable insights that guide decision-makers. Equally important is the art of communication—translating these insights into comprehensible reports and presentations.

Strategies for effective reporting involve choosing appropriate visualization techniques, structuring information logically, and tailoring the communication style to the audience's level of expertise. The goal is to empower stakeholders to make informed decisions based on the analysis. Whether presenting to executives, clients, or colleagues, the report should convey not only the "what" of the analysis but also the "so what" and "now what." This strategic approach to data interpretation and reporting ensures that the results of rigorous analysis translate into tangible value for the organization or research initiative.

CHAPTER 19

AI in *BI* and *Data Analysis*

UNDERSTANDING AI

AI has emerged as a transformative force in the realm of business intelligence and data analysis, revolutionizing the way organizations derive insights and make informed decisions. This chapter provides an in-depth exploration of the role of AI in BI and data analysis, covering its definition, historical context, and significance in shaping the future of data-driven decision-making.

Definition of AI

At its core, AI represents a groundbreaking advancement in computer science, encompassing a spectrum of technologies and methodologies aimed at imbuing machines with the ability to simulate human-like intelligence. At the heart of AI lies the pursuit of developing computer systems that can autonomously perform tasks traditionally associated with human cognition, including learning from experience, reasoning through complex problems, solving intricate puzzles, and perceiving and interpreting the world around them.

Objective

AI technologies strive to replicate human intelligence by leveraging sophisticated algorithms and computational models, allowing machines to adaptively respond to dynamic and unpredictable situations. By equipping machines with the capability to process vast amounts of data and extract meaningful insights, AI facilitates the automation of tasks that were once exclusive to human operators, revolutionizing industries and reshaping the way we interact with technology.

Integration

The integration of AI with various technologies and industries is reshaping business operations, offering unparalleled capabilities in data processing, pattern recognition, and decision-making. This integration not only enhances efficiency and accuracy but also drives innovation and problem-solving across sectors. From healthcare to finance, manufacturing to transportation, AI's integration is revolutionizing operations, propelling progress, and reshaping industries. As organizations leverage AI technologies, they unlock new avenues for growth and advancement, fueling a wave of unprecedented opportunities and discoveries.

INTERCONNECTED LANDSCAPE: AI, BI, AND DATA ANALYSIS

This section highlights the seamless integration of artificial intelligence, business intelligence, and data analysis, showcasing how these domains collectively drive smarter decision-making and innovative strategies. This synergy transforms raw data into actionable insights, fostering a dynamic and competitive edge for organizations.

Data-Driven Decision-Making

In the interconnected landscape of AI, BI, and data analysis, organizations harness advanced technologies to derive actionable insights from data, driving informed decision-making and strategic outcomes. AI plays a pivotal role in augmenting traditional BI and data analysis practices, revolutionizing the way organizations extract value from their data assets.

AI-powered BI systems leverage machine learning algorithms to analyze vast datasets, uncovering hidden patterns and correlations that might elude traditional analytical approaches. By integrating AI into BI workflows, organizations can automate data processing tasks, accelerate decision-making processes, and unlock unprecedented efficiencies in data analysis.

Moreover, AI enhances the predictive capabilities of BI systems, enabling organizations to forecast future trends, anticipate customer behavior, and identify emerging opportunities with greater accuracy. Through the integration of AI-driven predictive analytics models, businesses can proactively adapt strategies, mitigate risks, and capitalize on market trends, staying ahead of the competition in dynamic environments.

Furthermore, AI-driven data analysis techniques empower organizations to derive deeper insights from their data, enabling them to optimize processes, enhance customer experiences, and drive innovation. By harnessing the power of AI in conjunction with BI and data analysis, organizations foster a culture of data-driven decision-making, where stakeholders can access timely and accurate insights to inform strategic choices and drive sustainable growth.

In summary, the interconnected landscape of AI, BI, and data analysis represents a paradigm shift in how organizations leverage data for decision-making. By embracing AI-powered BI and data analysis solutions, organizations unlock new possibilities for innovation, agility, and competitiveness in today's data-driven world.

Historical Context and Evolution of AI in BI

The historical evolution of AI in business intelligence can be traced back to the early development of expert systems and rule-based reasoning, which aimed to automate decision-making processes. During this period, basic algorithms were utilized to encode human expertise and decision rules into computer systems, enabling them to perform fundamental tasks such as data classification and inference. While these early AI systems laid the groundwork for BI automation, their effectiveness was constrained by the rigidity of rule-based approaches and their inability to scale effectively to handle large and complex datasets.

The landscape of AI in BI underwent a significant transformation with the introduction of machine learning, neural networks, and deep learning technologies. These advancements marked a new era where AI systems could learn from data, adapt to changing environments, and make increasingly accurate predictions. Machine learning algorithms, such as decision trees and support vector machines, empowered BI systems to uncover intricate patterns and correlations within data, facilitating predictive analytics and forecasting. Moreover, the emergence of neural networks and deep learning architectures revolutionized BI by enabling AI systems to process unstructured data types, like images, text, and audio, with unprecedented precision and efficiency. As AI continues to progress, it promises to enhance BI capabilities further, driving innovation and unlocking new opportunities for organizations seeking to harness the power of data-driven decision-making.

Exploring AI's Role in BI and Data Analysis

AI's role in BI and data analysis is transformative, reshaping how organizations extract insights from data. By integrating AI algorithms, tasks such as data preparation, analysis, visualization, and decision support are streamlined, empowering organizations to make informed decisions and gain a competitive edge in dynamic business environments. Furthermore, AI automation extends beyond data analysis to routine activities like data cleansing and visualization, enhancing operational efficiency and freeing up human resources for strategic initiatives. AI-powered decision support systems provide intelligent recommendations, enabling confident, data-driven decisions.

Moreover, AI enables advanced analytics techniques such as predictive modeling and prescriptive analytics, forecasting future outcomes and providing actionable recommendations to optimize processes and mitigate risks. This proactive approach empowers organizations to anticipate market shifts, identify opportunities, and stay ahead of the competition.

As organizations continue to integrate AI into their BI and data analysis initiatives, they position themselves at the forefront of innovation, unlocking new opportunities and driving business growth in an increasingly data-driven world. AI's multifaceted impact across various domains significantly transforms how organizations derive insights from data, streamlining processes, identifying correlations, anomalies, and patterns efficiently to drive competitive advantage.

As AI technologies evolve, their potential to revolutionize BI and data analysis remains unparalleled, driving innovation and enabling organizations to extract maximum value from their data assets.

BI AND DATA ANALYSIS TRANSFORMATION WITH AI

This section explores how artificial intelligence reshapes business intelligence and data analysis, enhancing efficiency, accuracy, and predictive capabilities. By leveraging AI-driven tools, organizations can uncover deeper insights and make proactive, data-informed decisions.

Application of AI Technologies in BI

The application of AI technologies in BI represents a transformative advancement in data-driven decision-making. Traditionally reliant on static reports and predefined queries, BI systems now incorporate advanced analytics powered by AI. This integration allows organizations to extract actionable insights from vast and complex datasets in real time, enhancing decision-making capabilities significantly.

AI-powered BI solutions utilize machine learning algorithms to detect patterns, trends, and anomalies in data, enabling businesses to make more accurate and swift data-driven decisions. Furthermore, AI technologies streamline BI operations by automating repetitive tasks such as data cleansing, classification, and visualization. This automation not only saves time but also empowers analysts to focus on more strategic initiatives, driving further innovation within organizations.

In addition to improved operational efficiency, the application of AI in BI unlocks new possibilities for predictive analytics and prescriptive insights. AI-driven predictive models facilitate forecasting future trends, anticipating customer behavior, and identifying potential risks and opportunities. Moreover, AI-powered prescriptive analytics provide actionable recommendations to optimize business processes and capitalize on emerging opportunities, ultimately driving growth and competitiveness in today's data-centric landscape.

The Impact of AI on Data Processing

The impact of AI on data processing speed and accuracy is profound, revolutionizing the way organizations handle vast amounts of data with unprecedented efficiency and precision. AI-powered algorithms, leveraging advanced machine learning and deep learning techniques, enable organizations to process massive datasets at remarkable speeds, far surpassing the capabilities of traditional data processing methods. By harnessing parallel processing and distributed computing architectures, AI systems can analyze complex data structures in real time, providing near-instantaneous insights for informed decision-making and operational optimization.

Furthermore, AI enhances data processing accuracy by minimizing human error and bias, ensuring organizations can trust the integrity and reliability of their data-driven insights. Through sophisticated algorithms and predictive analytics models, AI systems can identify patterns, trends, and anomalies within data with precision, enabling organizations to uncover hidden insights and opportunities that may have otherwise gone unnoticed. Moreover, AI-driven data processing systems continuously learn and adapt from new data inputs, refining algorithms and improving accuracy over time. As organizations increasingly rely on AI for data processing tasks, they benefit from enhanced operational efficiency, improved decision-making, and a competitive edge in today's data-driven business landscape.

The integration of AI into data processing workflows enables organizations to achieve new levels of agility and scalability in handling data-intensive tasks. AI-powered data processing systems can dynamically adjust resources and scale operations in response to changing data volumes and processing requirements, ensuring optimal performance and efficiency at all times. Additionally, AI-driven automation stream-lines data processing workflows, reducing manual intervention and accelerating time-to-insight for critical decisions. As organizations lev-erage AI to augment their data processing capabilities, they unlock new opportunities for innovation, growth, and competitive differentiation in an increasingly data-driven world.

AI Integration with BI Tools and Platforms

The integration of AI with BI tools and platforms signifies a substantial leap forward in the realm of data-driven decision-making. This inte-gration seamlessly incorporates AI algorithms and techniques into BI environments, thereby amplifying the efficiency, accuracy, and depth of insights garnered from data analysis processes. AI-powered BI tools leverage machine learning, NLP, and predictive analytics to automate data processing tasks, unearth concealed patterns and provide actiona-ble real-time insights. Consequently, organizations can streamline their BI workflows, diminish manual effort, and expedite decision-making by promptly delivering pertinent information to stakeholders.

Furthermore, this integration empowers organizations to tap into unprecedented levels of intelligence from their data reservoirs, facilitat-ing more informed and strategic decision-making endeavors. AI-driven BI solutions offer advanced functionalities such as predictive mode-ling, anomaly detection, and personalized recommendations, enabling organizations to proactively anticipate trends, mitigate risks, and capital-ize on emerging opportunities. With AI's adaptive capabilities, BI tools can adjust to evolving data landscapes, learn from user interactions, and continually enhance their analytical prowess, furnishing organizations with a competitive edge in today's dynamic business landscape.

Moreover, the integration of AI with BI tools and platforms has ush-ered in a new era of democratized data-driven insights within organi-zations, empowering users across all levels to access and harness data for decision-making purposes. AI-powered BI solutions provide intui-tive interfaces, natural language querying functionalities, and personal-ized dashboards, enabling nontechnical users to delve into data, derive insights, and extract actionable recommendations sans specialized technical knowledge. This democratization of data access and analysis nurtures a culture of data-driven decision-making across organizations, facilitating effective collaboration among stakeholders from diverse departments and propelling business outcomes collaboratively. As organizations embrace this inclusive approach to data analysis fueled by

AI, they foster innovation, agility, and competitiveness in today's rapidly evolving business landscape.

AI-Driven Innovations in Data Analysis

AI-driven innovations in data analysis are pervasive across industries, exemplifying the transformative potential of AI in unlocking insights and steering business outcomes. In healthcare, for instance, AI-powered diagnostic systems utilize machine learning algorithms to scrutinize medical imaging data, aiding healthcare professionals in pinpointing diseases like cancer with unparalleled precision. Similarly, in finance, AI-driven predictive analytics models sift through extensive financial data to spot fraudulent activities, mitigate risks, and fine-tune investment strategies. These instances underscore how AI empowers organizations to harness data analysis for bolstered decision-making, risk mitigation, and operational streamlining.

Moreover, AI-driven advancements in data analysis transcend conventional sectors, reshaping industries like retail and e-commerce. Recommendation engines fueled by AI algorithms scrutinize customer browsing and purchase histories to deliver tailored product suggestions, amplifying sales and customer satisfaction. Additionally, AI-powered sentiment analysis tools dissect social media data to grasp customer preferences, trends, and sentiments, enabling retailers to tailor marketing strategies and product assortments accordingly. These illustrations underscore how AI-driven data analysis equips organizations with actionable insights from diverse data sources, optimizing processes and enriching customer experiences in today's data-centric landscape.

Furthermore, the fusion of AI into data analysis workflows propels organizations toward heightened agility and scalability in managing data-intensive tasks. AI-powered data analysis tools adeptly adapt to evolving data landscapes, assimilate insights from user interactions, and continually refine their analytical capabilities over time. This iterative learning process empowers organizations to stay abreast of market dynamics, unearth novel insights, and spearhead innovation in a swiftly evolving business milieu. As organizations embrace AI-driven data analysis, they position themselves at the vanguard of technological progress, propelling growth and competitiveness in today's digital domain.

Benefits of AI Adoption in BI

The potential benefits of incorporating AI into BI practices are manifold, offering a paradigm shift in how organizations extract insights from their data. A notable advantage lies in the improved efficiency and automation of BI operations. Through the integration of AI algorithms into BI tools and platforms, organizations can streamline processes such as data cleansing, classification, and visualization, minimizing manual intervention and expediting decision-making. Additionally, AI-driven BI solutions empower organizations to swiftly process vast datasets, extracting actionable insights in real time and facilitating prompt, informed decision-making by stakeholders.

Another pivotal benefit of AI adoption in BI lies in its capacity to unveil concealed insights and patterns within data. AI algorithms, including machine learning and predictive analytics, excel at discerning correlations, anomalies, and trends that may elude human analysts. Leveraging AI-driven data analysis techniques enables organizations to delve deeper into their operations, customer behaviors, and market dynamics, thereby enabling proactive trend anticipation, risk mitigation, and opportunity exploitation. Moreover, AI-powered BI solutions continually refine their analytical capabilities over time, adapting to evolving data inputs and furnishing organizations with a competitive edge in today's dynamic business environment.

Furthermore, the fusion of AI with BI facilitates the democratization of data-driven insights throughout enterprises. Empowering users across all levels with self-service BI tools augmented by AI fosters a culture of data-driven decision-making and innovation. Employees from diverse departments can independently access and analyze data, unearthing actionable insights and collectively driving business outcomes. Moreover, AI-driven BI solutions offer user-friendly interfaces and natural language querying functionalities, democratizing data analysis for nontechnical users, and expediting decision-making processes. As organizations embrace AI-powered BI solutions, they not only enhance operational efficiency and decision-making but also cultivate a culture of data-driven innovation and collaboration across the enterprise.

LEVERAGING AI FOR SMARTER DECISION-MAKING

This section delves into how AI revolutionizes data-driven decision-making by enhancing accuracy, enabling real-time insights, and providing a strategic edge through advanced analytics and predictive capabilities. Each sub-section explores a unique facet of AI's transformative impact on organizational decision processes.

Role of Data-Driven Decision Making

Data-driven decision-making plays a pivotal role in modern businesses, guiding strategic choices and operational processes across various domains. At its core, data-driven decision-making involves leveraging data analytics and insights to inform and validate business decisions. By harnessing data from internal and external sources, organizations can gain a comprehensive understanding of their operations, market dynamics, and customer behavior, enabling them to make informed choices that drive growth and competitiveness. Moreover, data-driven decision-making fosters a culture of accountability and transparency within organizations, as decisions are grounded in empirical evidence rather than subjective opinions or intuition.

One significant benefit of data-driven decision-making is its ability to enhance operational efficiency and effectiveness. By analyzing historical data and performance metrics, organizations can identify inefficiencies, streamline processes, and optimize resource allocation. Moreover, predictive analytics and forecasting techniques enable organizations to anticipate future trends and outcomes, enabling them to proactively address challenges and capitalize on opportunities. This proactive approach to decision-making not only minimizes risks but also maximizes returns, driving sustainable growth and profitability in today's dynamic business environment.

Furthermore, data-driven decision-making enables organizations to gain a competitive edge by fostering innovation and agility. By continuously monitoring and analyzing data, organizations can identify emerging trends, market opportunities, and customer preferences, enabling them to adapt their strategies and offerings accordingly. Moreover, data-driven insights empower organizations to experiment with new ideas and initiatives, iterate quickly based on feedback, and pivot as needed to stay ahead of the competition. In essence, data-driven decision-making enables organizations to navigate uncertainty with confidence, seize opportunities for innovation, and drive long-term success in a rapidly evolving marketplace.

The Vital Role of AI in Data-Driven Insights

The importance of AI in generating actionable insights cannot be overstated in today's data-driven landscape. AI technologies, powered by advanced algorithms and machine learning models, have revolutionized the way organizations extract value from their data. One of the key roles of AI in this context is its ability to sift through vast volumes of data, both structured and unstructured, to uncover patterns, correlations, and trends that may not be readily apparent to human analysts. By leveraging AI-driven analytics, organizations can gain deeper insights into their operations, customers, and market dynamics, enabling them to make more informed decisions.

Moreover, AI enhances the accuracy and relevance of insights by eliminating human bias and error. Unlike traditional analytics approaches, which may be influenced by subjective interpretations or limited sample sizes, AI-driven analytics rely on objective data-driven algorithms to analyze information impartially and objectively. This results in more accurate and reliable insights that stakeholders can trust when making critical business decisions. Additionally, AI enables organizations to analyze data in real time, providing timely insights that empower stakeholders to take immediate action and respond swiftly to changing market conditions or emerging opportunities.

Furthermore, AI augments human capabilities by automating repetitive tasks and surfacing insights that human analysts may overlook. Through advanced machine learning and NLP techniques, AI systems can identify patterns and anomalies within data, highlight key trends, and generate actionable recommendations tailored to specific business objectives. This not only accelerates the decision-making process but also frees up valuable human resources to focus on more strategic tasks, such as interpreting insights, devising strategies, and driving innovation. In essence, the importance of AI in generating actionable insights lies in its ability to transform raw data into meaningful intelligence that drives business growth, innovation, and competitive advantage in today's data-driven economy.

AI: Enhancing Decision Accuracy

AI plays a pivotal role in enhancing decision-making accuracy across various domains by leveraging advanced algorithms and data-driven insights. One of the key ways in which AI improves decision-making accuracy is through predictive analytics. By analyzing historical data and identifying patterns, AI algorithms can forecast future trends and outcomes with remarkable accuracy. This enables organizations to anticipate changes in market conditions, customer behavior, and operational performance, empowering stakeholders to make informed decisions based on data-driven predictions rather than relying solely on intuition or past experience.

Moreover, AI enhances decision-making accuracy by minimizing human bias and error. Traditional decision-making processes may be influenced by cognitive biases or subjective judgments, leading to sub-optimal outcomes. AI-driven decision support systems rely on objective data-driven algorithms to analyze information impartially and identify optimal courses of action. By removing human bias from the decision-making process, AI ensures that decisions are based on empirical evidence and logical reasoning, resulting in more accurate and reliable outcomes.

Furthermore, AI improves decision-making accuracy by augmenting human expertise with machine intelligence. Through techniques such as machine learning and NLP, AI systems can analyze vast amounts of data, extract relevant insights, and provide recommendations tailored to specific business objectives. This not only enhances the quality of decisions but also accelerates the decision-making process, enabling organizations to respond swiftly to changing market dynamics and emerging opportunities. By harnessing the power of AI to augment human decision-making capabilities, organizations can achieve greater accuracy, efficiency, and competitiveness in today's fast-paced business environment.

AI for Real-Time Decisions

Real-time decision-making has become increasingly critical in today's fast-paced business environment, where organizations must respond swiftly to changing market conditions and customer demands. AI-powered business intelligence tools play a crucial role in enabling real-time decision-making by providing timely insights and recommendations based on up-to-date data. Through advanced analytics techniques such as machine learning and NLP, AI-driven BI systems can process large volumes of data in real time, identifying trends, anomalies, and patterns as they emerge. This empowers organizations to make informed decisions quickly and effectively, gaining a competitive edge in dynamic markets.

One of the key advantages of AI-powered BI for real-time decision-making is its ability to automate data processing and analysis tasks. Traditional BI systems often require manual intervention to collect, cleanse, and analyze data, resulting in delays and inefficiencies. AI-driven BI solutions can automate these processes, enabling organizations to access real-time insights without human intervention. This not only accelerates the decision-making process but also ensures that insights are based on the most up-to-date and accurate data available, improving the quality and relevance of decisions.

Furthermore, AI-powered BI facilitates proactive decision-making by enabling organizations to anticipate future trends and outcomes in real time. Through predictive analytics and forecasting techniques, AI systems can analyze historical data and identify patterns that indicate potential future events or changes. This enables organizations to take preemptive action to capitalize on opportunities or mitigate risks before they fully materialize. By harnessing the power of AI for real-time decision-making, organizations can stay ahead of the curve, adapt to changing market dynamics, and drive sustainable growth in today's rapidly evolving business landscape.

AI IMPLEMENTATIONS IN DECISION-MAKING PROCESSES

This section highlights real-world applications of AI in decision-making, showcasing its transformative potential across diverse industries. Through detailed case studies, it illustrates how AI enhances operational efficiency, reduces costs, and drives strategic outcomes by addressing complex challenges in risk management, supply chain optimization, predictive maintenance, and customer service.

Case Study 1: Enhanced Risk Management

A leading multinational bank sought to improve its risk management processes to mitigate financial losses and ensure regulatory compliance. Leveraging AI technologies, the bank implemented a sophisticated risk assessment system capable of analyzing vast amounts of financial data in real time. Using machine learning algorithms, the system identified patterns indicative of potential risks, such as fraudulent activities, credit defaults, and market fluctuations. By continuously monitoring transactional data and market indicators, the AI system provided timely insights to decision-makers, enabling proactive risk mitigation strategies.

The implementation of AI-powered risk management solutions led to tangible benefits. The bank experienced a significant reduction in fraudulent transactions and credit defaults, resulting in millions of dollars in cost savings. Moreover, the AI system enhanced decision-making accuracy by providing actionable insights based on real-time data analysis, enabling the bank to adapt quickly to changing market conditions and regulatory requirements. Overall, the successful integration of AI in decision-making processes bolstered the bank's risk management capabilities, ensuring financial stability and maintaining customer trust.

Case Study 2: Optimized Supply Chain Management

A leading retail chain faced challenges in optimizing its supply chain to meet customer demands efficiently while minimizing operational costs. To address these challenges and enhance its decision-making processes, it deployed an AI-driven supply chain management solution. Using predictive analytics and machine learning algorithms, the AI system analyzed historical sales data, customer preferences, and market trends to forecast demand accurately. Additionally, the system optimized inventory levels, transportation routes, and procurement processes to streamline operations and reduce inefficiencies.

The implementation of AI-powered supply chain management solutions yielded significant improvements. The retail chain experienced a notable reduction in stockouts and excess inventory, leading to improved customer satisfaction and increased sales revenue. Moreover, the AI system optimized logistics operations, resulting in faster delivery times and reduced transportation costs. By leveraging AI to inform decision-making processes, the company gained a competitive edge in the retail market, driving operational efficiency and enhancing overall business performance.

Case Study 3: Predictive Maintenance in Manufacturing Company

A leading manufacturer of industrial machinery, implemented AI-powered predictive maintenance solutions to optimize maintenance processes and minimize downtime. By leveraging historical equipment data and sensor readings, the AI system identified patterns indicative of potential equipment failures before they occurred. Through machine learning algorithms, the system continuously analyzed data in real-time, predicted maintenance needs, and scheduled proactive interventions to prevent costly breakdowns.

The implementation of AI-driven predictive maintenance resulted in significant improvements in the company's equipment reliability and operational efficiency. By proactively addressing maintenance issues, the company reduced unplanned downtime by 30% and increased equipment uptime by 20%. This not only improved overall productivity but also enhanced customer satisfaction by ensuring timely delivery of products. Additionally, the AI system enabled the company to optimize maintenance schedules and resource allocation, resulting in cost savings and improved resource utilization.

Case Study 4: Customer Service at a Financial Institution

A leading financial institution implemented AI-driven customer service solutions to enhance the efficiency and effectiveness of its customer support operations. The company automated routine customer inquiries and streamlined the resolution process for common issues such as account inquiries, transaction disputes, and loan applications by deploying chatbots powered by NLP and machine learning algorithms. The chatbots were trained on historical customer interactions and continuously improved their responses based on user feedback and real-time data.

The implementation of AI-powered customer service solutions resulted in significant benefits for the company. By automating routine inquiries, the company reduced average response times by 40% and improved overall customer satisfaction ratings by 25%. Moreover, the chatbots enabled the company to handle a greater volume of customer inquiries without increasing staffing levels, resulting in cost savings and improved operational efficiency. Additionally, the AI system provided valuable insights into customer preferences and behavior, enabling the company to personalize interactions and tailor offerings to individual customer needs. Overall, the successful implementation of AI in customer service helped the company deliver a superior customer experience while driving operational excellence and cost savings.

HOW AI ENHANCES DATA ANALYSIS

AI enhances data analysis by leveraging predictive analytics and advanced machine learning tools to uncover actionable insights, forecast trends, and drive informed decision-making. This section explores the transformative role of AI in data-driven strategies, emphasizing its capacity to optimize outcomes and reveal hidden patterns.

Power of AI-Driven Insight Generation

AI-driven insight generation represents a paradigm shift in the way organizations derive value from their data. At its core, this approach leverages AI and machine learning algorithms to analyze vast volumes of data and extract meaningful insights that drive informed decision-making. Unlike traditional analytics methods, which may rely on manual data processing and analysis, AI-driven insights generation automates these processes, enabling organizations to uncover hidden patterns, correlations, and trends with unprecedented speed and accuracy.

One of the key advantages of AI-driven insight generation is its ability to handle complex and unstructured data sources. Traditional analytics tools may struggle to process unstructured data such as text, images, and sensor readings, limiting their ability to derive insights from diverse data sources. AI algorithms, however, excel at processing unstructured data, leveraging techniques such as NLP, computer vision, and deep learning to extract valuable insights from a wide range of data formats. This enables organizations to gain a more comprehensive understanding of their operations, customers, and market dynamics, facilitating more informed decision-making.

Furthermore, AI-driven insights generation enables organizations to move beyond descriptive analytics toward predictive and prescriptive insights. By analyzing historical data and identifying patterns, AI algorithms can forecast future trends, anticipate potential outcomes, and recommend optimal courses of action. This empowers organizations to proactively address emerging challenges, capitalize on opportunities, and drive innovation.

Moreover, AI systems can continuously learn and adapt from new data inputs, refining their analytical models and improving the quality and relevance of insights over time. As organizations increasingly adopt AI-driven insights generation, they gain a competitive edge by harnessing the power of data to drive strategic decision-making and achieve business objectives.

Harnessing Predictive Analytics with AI

Predictive analytics with AI represent a powerful approach for forecasting future outcomes and trends based on historical data and statistical algorithms. At its core, predictive analytics leverages machine learning and AI techniques to analyze large datasets, identify patterns, and make predictions about future events. Unlike traditional analytics methods, which focus on descriptive analysis of past data, predictive analytics enables organizations to gain actionable insights into future trends, risks, and opportunities, empowering them to make informed decisions and take proactive measures to achieve their goals.

One of the key benefits of predictive analytics with AI is its ability to uncover hidden patterns and correlations within data that may not be apparent to human analysts. By applying advanced machine learning algorithms, predictive analytics systems can identify complex relationships between variables and predict future outcomes with a high degree of accuracy. This enables organizations to anticipate market trends, customer behavior, and operational performance, facilitating strategic decision-making and competitive advantage.

Moreover, predictive analytics with AI enables organizations to move beyond traditional forecasting methods by incorporating real-time data and dynamic variables into their predictive models. By continuously analyzing incoming data streams and updating their predictions in real time, predictive analytics systems can adapt to changing conditions and provide up-to-date insights into evolving trends and patterns.

This agility and responsiveness enable organizations to stay ahead of the curve, mitigate risks, and capitalize on opportunities in today's fast-paced business environment. As organizations increasingly embrace predictive analytics with AI, they unlock new possibilities for optimizing operations, enhancing customer experiences, and driving business growth.

Power of Prescriptive Analytics in BI

Exploring prescriptive analytics in BI unveils a proactive approach to decision-making that goes beyond descriptive and predictive analytics. Prescriptive analytics leverages advanced AI and machine learning algorithms to not only forecast future outcomes but also recommend optimal courses of action to achieve desired objectives. By analyzing historical data, current conditions, and various decision variables, prescriptive analytics models generate actionable insights that can guide organizations in making informed decisions and executing strategies with the highest probability of success.

One of the key advantages of prescriptive analytics in BI is its ability to provide organizations with actionable recommendations based on data-driven insights. Unlike descriptive analytics, which focuses on analyzing past data, and predictive analytics, which forecasts future outcomes, prescriptive analytics goes a step further by recommending specific actions to achieve desired outcomes. These recommendations are derived from complex algorithms that consider multiple variables, constraints, and objectives, enabling organizations to make strategic decisions that maximize value and mitigate risks.

Furthermore, prescriptive analytics in BI empowers organizations to optimize processes, allocate resources efficiently, and respond proactively to changing market conditions. Prescriptive analytics models enable organizations to identify the most effective strategies for achieving their goals by simulating various scenarios and evaluating the potential impact of different decisions. Moreover, prescriptive analytics facilitates continuous improvement by enabling organizations to learn from past decisions, adjust strategies in real time, and drive innovation across all aspects of their operations. As organizations increasingly embrace prescriptive analytics in BI, they gain a competitive edge by leveraging data-driven insights to drive strategic decision-making and achieve business objectives.

Impact of AI Recommendation Systems

The importance of AI-powered recommendation systems in various industries cannot be overstated, as they play a crucial role in enhancing customer experiences, driving sales, and fostering brand loyalty. These systems leverage sophisticated algorithms and machine learning techniques to analyze vast amounts of data, including user preferences, behavior, and purchase history, to generate personalized recommendations tailored to individual preferences and needs. By delivering relevant and timely suggestions to users, AI-powered recommendation systems enable organizations to engage customers effectively, increase conversion rates, and maximize revenue opportunities.

Moreover, AI-powered recommendation systems offer significant benefits to organizations by improving operational efficiency, optimizing inventory management, and reducing marketing costs. By automatically suggesting products or services that are likely to resonate with customers, these systems streamline the decision-making process and guide users toward desired outcomes. Additionally, recommendation systems help organizations better understand customer preferences and market trends, enabling them to make data-driven decisions and adapt their strategies in real time to meet changing consumer demands, transforming the way organizations interact with customers and drive business growth in today's digital economy.

As AI continues to evolve and become more sophisticated, recommendation systems will play an increasingly integral role in shaping consumer behavior, influencing purchasing decisions, and driving competitive advantage in the marketplace.

Case Studies: The Impact of AI on Business Performance

Case studies showcasing the impact of AI-driven insights on business performance illustrate the transformative power of AI in driving strategic decision-making and achieving organizational goals. For instance, a retail giant leveraged AI-powered analytics to analyze customer data and identify purchasing patterns, enabling them to personalize marketing campaigns and product recommendations. By tailoring their offerings to individual preferences and needs, the company experienced a significant increase in sales and customer satisfaction, leading to improved business performance and competitive advantage in the market.

In another case study, a financial services firm utilized AI-driven insights to optimize investment strategies and mitigate risks in its portfolio management. By analyzing market trends, economic indicators, and historical data, the firm was able to identify lucrative investment opportunities and adjust its asset allocation accordingly. As a result, they achieved higher returns on investments and minimized losses during market downturns, ultimately driving profitability and enhancing shareholder value.

Furthermore, a healthcare organization employed AI-driven analytics to improve patient outcomes and operational efficiency. It gained valuable insights into disease patterns, treatment effectiveness, and resource utilization by analyzing electronic health records, medical imaging data, and clinical notes. This enabled them to streamline healthcare delivery, reduce wait times, and enhance the quality of care provided to patients. As a result, the organization achieved better health outcomes, reduced costs, and improved overall business performance, demonstrating the significant impact of AI-driven insights on driving positive outcomes across various industries.

AI APPLICATIONS IN BI

AI applications in BI demonstrate transformative potential by enhancing decision-making and operational efficiency across various business functions. The subsections explore specific applications, including predictive analytics in marketing, customer segmentation, sales forecasting, and supply chain optimization, highlighting how AI drives strategic insights and improves performance.

AI Revolutionizes Marketing Analytics

The application of AI in marketing analytics has revolutionized the way organizations understand and engage with their target audiences. One prominent application is in customer segmentation, where AI algorithms analyze vast amounts of data to identify distinct customer segments based on demographics, behavior, and preferences. By segmenting customers more accurately, organizations can tailor their marketing efforts to specific audience segments, delivering personalized experiences that resonate with individual preferences and needs. This leads to higher engagement rates, increased conversions, and, ultimately, improved ROI in marketing campaigns.

Another key application of AI in marketing analytics is predictive analytics, where machine learning algorithms forecast future trends and behaviors based on historical data. By analyzing past interactions, purchase history, and demographic information, AI models can predict which customers are most likely to convert, churn, or respond to particular offers. This enables organizations to allocate resources more effectively, target high-value prospects, and optimize marketing spend for maximum impact. Additionally, predictive analytics empowers organizations to anticipate market trends, identify emerging opportunities, and stay ahead of the competition in today's dynamic business environment.

Furthermore, AI-powered recommendation systems have become increasingly prevalent in marketing analytics, particularly in e-commerce and content recommendation platforms. These systems leverage machine learning algorithms to analyze user behavior and preferences and recommend products, services, or content that are likely to resonate with individual users. Organizations can enhance the customer experience, increase engagement, and drive sales by delivering personalized recommendations. Additionally, recommendation systems help organizations better understand customer preferences and behavior, enabling them to refine their offerings and marketing strategies over time for improved effectiveness and customer satisfaction.

AI-Powered Customer Segmentation and Personalization

AI-powered customer segmentation and personalization have become indispensable tools for marketers seeking to enhance engagement, drive conversions, and build long-term relationships with their audience. With AI algorithms analyzing vast amounts of customer data, organizations can identify distinct segments based on demographics, behavior, purchase history, and other relevant factors. This enables marketers to create more targeted and relevant marketing campaigns tailored to each segment's unique preferences and needs, leading to higher response rates and improved ROI.

Moreover, AI-powered customer segmentation allows organizations to go beyond traditional demographic-based segmentation and uncover more nuanced customer insights. By leveraging advanced machine learning techniques, AI models can identify hidden patterns and correlations within data, revealing previously unrecognized segments and affinities. This enables marketers to develop highly granular audience profiles and deliver hyper-personalized experiences that resonate with individual customers on a deeper level, fostering stronger brand loyalty and advocacy.

Furthermore, AI-driven personalization enables organizations to deliver seamless and consistent experiences across multiple touchpoints throughout the customer journey. By analyzing real-time interactions and historical data, AI algorithms can dynamically adjust content, offers, and recommendations based on individual preferences and behaviors. This level of personalization not only enhances the customer experience but also increases engagement and conversion rates, driving business growth and competitive advantage in today's crowded marketplace. As AI continues to evolve, its role in customer segmentation and personalization will only become more central to successful marketing strategies.

AI for Sales: Forecasting and Revenue Prediction

AI-driven sales forecasting and revenue prediction have become invaluable tools for businesses seeking to optimize their sales strategies, allocate resources effectively, and drive revenue growth. AI algorithms can generate accurate forecasts of future sales performance by analyzing historical sales data, market trends, customer behavior, and other relevant factors. These forecasts enable organizations to anticipate demand, identify growth opportunities, and align their sales efforts with strategic objectives, ultimately maximizing revenue potential.

Moreover, AI-powered sales forecasting goes beyond traditional methods by leveraging advanced machine learning techniques to uncover hidden patterns and correlations within data. By considering a multitude of variables and their interdependencies, AI models can provide more nuanced and accurate predictions, even in complex and dynamic business environments. This enables organizations to make data-driven decisions with greater confidence, reducing uncertainty and minimizing the risk of overestimating or underestimating sales projections.

Furthermore, AI-driven revenue prediction enables organizations to gain insights into key revenue drivers and factors influencing revenue performance. By analyzing various metrics such as customer acquisition costs, lifetime value, churn rates, and pricing elasticity, AI algorithms can identify opportunities to optimize pricing strategies, improve customer retention, and maximize revenue streams. This enables organizations to adapt their sales and marketing tactics in real time, capitalizing on emerging trends and market dynamics to drive sustainable revenue growth. As AI technology continues to evolve, its role in sales forecasting and revenue prediction will only become more crucial in helping businesses achieve their financial goals.

AI Revolutionizes Supply Chain Management

The use of AI in supply chain optimization has revolutionized the way businesses manage their logistics, inventory, and operations. By harnessing AI algorithms, organizations can analyze vast amounts of data from various sources, including sales forecasts, inventory levels, supplier performance, and transportation routes. This enables them to optimize their supply chain processes, minimize costs, and improve efficiency. AI-driven demand forecasting, for example, enables organizations to predict customer demand more accurately, reducing the risk of stockouts or excess inventory and ensuring that the right products are available at the right time.

Furthermore, AI-powered predictive analytics allows organizations to identify potential bottlenecks or disruptions in the supply chain before they occur. By analyzing historical data and external factors such as weather patterns, market trends, and geopolitical events, AI algorithms can anticipate potential risks and provide recommendations for mitigating them. This proactive approach enables organizations to respond quickly to changes in demand or supply conditions, minimizing disruptions and maintaining operational continuity.

Moreover, AI-driven optimization techniques enable organizations to streamline their supply chain processes and make data-driven decisions to improve overall performance. AI algorithms can optimize inventory levels, warehouse layouts, transportation routes, and production schedules to maximize efficiency and reduce costs. By automating routine tasks and providing real-time insights, AI empowers organizations to make faster and more informed decisions, enabling them to adapt to changing market conditions and stay ahead of the competition. As AI technology continues to advance, its role in supply chain optimization will become increasingly critical in helping businesses achieve greater agility, resilience, and competitiveness in the global marketplace.

CASE STUDIES: REAL-WORLD AI APPLICATIONS IN BI

The following three real-world case studies provide compelling examples of how AI applications are transforming business intelligence practices across various industries.

Case Study 1: Recommendation System

Amazon, a leading e-commerce company, implemented AI-powered recommendation systems to enhance customer engagement and drive sales. By analyzing vast amounts of customer data, including browsing history, purchase behavior, and demographic information, the AI algorithms were able to generate personalized product recommendations in real time. As a result, the company saw a significant increase in conversion rates and customer satisfaction, ultimately leading to higher revenue and market share.

Case Study 2: Optimization of Inventory Management

Walmart, a multinational retail corporation, leveraged AI-driven predictive analytics to optimize its inventory management processes. By analyzing historical sales data, seasonal trends, and external factors such as weather forecasts and economic indicators, the AI algorithms were able to generate accurate demand forecasts for each product category and location. This enabled the company to optimize inventory levels, reduce stockouts and excess inventory, and improve overall supply chain efficiency. As a result, the company reduced carrying costs, improved cash flow, and enhanced customer satisfaction by ensuring the availability of products when and where they were needed.

Case Study 3: Patient Outcome Improvement

The Mayo Clinic, a healthcare organization, utilized AI-powered data analytics to improve patient outcomes and reduce costs. By analyzing electronic health records, medical imaging data, and patient demographics, AI algorithms were able to identify patterns and correlations that could indicate potential health risks or predict patient outcomes. This enabled healthcare providers to personalize treatment plans, identify high-risk patients for proactive interventions, and optimize resource allocation for better healthcare delivery. As a result, the organization improved patient care, reduced hospital readmissions, and lowered healthcare costs, demonstrating the transformative impact of AI applications in BI across diverse sectors.

ENHANCING DATA ANALYSIS WITH AI ALGORITHMS

The section examines the transformative role of machine learning and deep learning techniques in modern data analysis. It explores key applications, approaches, and challenges associated with leveraging these algorithms to unlock actionable insights and drive data-driven decision-making.

Machine Learning Algorithms in AI

Machine learning algorithms are at the heart of AI systems, enabling computers to learn from data and make predictions or decisions without explicit programming. These algorithms can be broadly categorized into three main types: supervised learning, unsupervised learning, and reinforcement learning.

Supervised learning algorithms learn from labeled data, where the correct output is provided for each input example, allowing the algorithm to learn the mapping between inputs and outputs. Common supervised learning algorithms include linear regression, decision trees, support vector machines, and neural networks.

Contrastingly, unsupervised learning algorithms learn from unlabeled data, seeking to find patterns or structures within the data without explicit guidance. Clustering algorithms, such as K-means and hierarchical clustering, are commonly used in unsupervised learning to group similar data points together based on their features or attributes. Dimensionality reduction techniques, such as principal component analysis (PCA) and t-distributed stochastic neighbor embedding (t-SNE), are also examples of unsupervised learning algorithms used to reduce the complexity of high-dimensional data.

Reinforcement learning algorithms learn by interacting with an environment and receiving feedback in the form of rewards or penalties based on their actions. These algorithms aim to determine the optimal policy or strategy for maximizing the cumulative rewards over time. Reinforcement learning has been successfully applied in various domains, including robotics, gaming, and autonomous systems. Examples of reinforcement learning algorithms include Q-learning, deep Q-networks (DQN), and policy gradient methods. Overall, machine learning algorithms play a crucial role in AI systems, enabling computers to learn from data and make intelligent decisions or predictions across a wide range of applications and domains.

Supervised versus Unsupervised Learning in BI

In the landscape of BI, machine learning algorithms play a pivotal role in extracting valuable insights from data. Each of the two primary approaches to machine learning, supervised learning, and unsupervised learning, offer distinct advantages and applications in BI contexts. In supervised learning, the algorithm learns from input-output pairs to make predictions or classify new data. This approach is particularly useful in scenarios where the desired outcome is known, such as predicting customer churn or classifying transactions as fraudulent or legitimate. By leveraging historical data with known outcomes, supervised learning algorithms can generalize patterns and relationships to accurately predict unseen data.

In unsupervised learning the algorithm aims to identify hidden patterns or structures within the data without explicit guidance. This approach is valuable in BI for tasks such as clustering similar customer segments or identifying anomalies in financial transactions. Unsupervised learning algorithms, such as clustering and anomaly detection, enable organizations to explore the inherent structure of their data and uncover insights that may not be immediately apparent. By allowing the data to speak for itself, unsupervised learning empowers organizations to discover novel patterns and trends that can inform strategic decision-making and drive business growth.

In BI applications, the choice between supervised and unsupervised learning depends on the nature of the problem and the availability of labeled data. While supervised learning offers more precise predictions when labeled data is abundant, unsupervised learning excels in scenarios where the data is largely unlabeled or when the objective is to uncover hidden structures within the data. By understanding the strengths and limitations of both approaches, organizations can effectively leverage machine learning in BI to extract actionable insights and gain a competitive edge in today's data-driven landscape.

The Power of Deep Learning

Deep learning, a subset of machine learning, has gained significant traction in recent years due to its remarkable ability to tackle complex tasks with unprecedented accuracy. At the core of deep learning are artificial neural networks, which are computational models inspired by the structure and function of the human brain. These networks consist of interconnected layers of neurons, each layer responsible for extracting and transforming features from the input data. Deep learning architectures, characterized by multiple layers of neurons, enable the network to learn hierarchical representations of the data, capturing intricate patterns and relationships that may be difficult to discern with traditional machine learning methods.

One of the key advantages of deep learning is its ability to automatically learn representations from raw data, eliminating the need for manual feature engineering. By leveraging hierarchical representations, deep learning models can extract meaningful features directly from the input data, such as images, text, or audio signals. This capability enables deep learning to excel in tasks such as image recognition, NLP, and speech recognition, where the data may be high-dimensional and complex. Through the iterative process of forward and backward propagation, deep neural networks learn to optimize their parameters to minimize prediction errors, iteratively refining their representations and improving their performance over time.

The success of deep learning can be attributed to several factors, including the availability of large-scale labeled datasets, advances in computational power, and innovations in neural network architectures. With the advent of deep learning frameworks such as TensorFlow and PyTorch, researchers and practitioners can easily build, train, and deploy complex neural network models at scale. Moreover, the proliferation of deep learning applications across various industries, from healthcare and finance to automotive and entertainment, underscores the transformative potential of this technology. As deep learning continues to evolve, fueled by ongoing research and development efforts, it promises to revolutionize how we solve complex problems and interact with intelligent systems in the digital age.

Machine Learning in Data Organization

Machine learning techniques are widely employed in data classification and clustering tasks, offering powerful tools for organizing and categorizing large datasets based on patterns and similarities within the data. In data classification, machine learning algorithms learn from labeled data to classify new, unseen instances into predefined categories or classes. Supervised learning algorithms, such as support vector machines (SVM), decision trees, and neural networks, are commonly used for classification tasks. These algorithms analyze the features of the input data and learn decision boundaries that separate different classes, enabling them to accurately classify new data points based on their characteristics. Applications of data classification range from spam email detection and sentiment analysis to medical diagnosis and fraud detection.

In contrast, data clustering involves grouping similar data points together into clusters or segments based on their intrinsic characteristics or relationships. Unsupervised learning algorithms, such as k-means clustering, hierarchical clustering, and Gaussian mixture models, are frequently used for clustering tasks. These algorithms partition the data into clusters based on similarity measures, such as distance or density, without prior knowledge of class labels. Data clustering has applications in customer segmentation, market analysis, anomaly detection, and pattern recognition. By identifying natural groupings within the data, clustering algorithms provide valuable insights into the underlying structure and organization of the dataset, facilitating decision-making and problem-solving in various domains.

The applications of machine learning in data classification and clustering are diverse and span numerous industries and domains. From identifying customer segments for targeted marketing campaigns and optimizing inventory management in retail to detecting fraudulent transactions and analyzing genomic data in healthcare, machine learning techniques play a pivotal role in extracting actionable insights from large and complex datasets. As organizations continue to collect and analyze vast amounts of data, the adoption of machine learning in data classification and clustering becomes increasingly essential for unlocking valuable information, driving innovation, and gaining a competitive edge.

Challenges in Machine Learning Implementation

Implementing machine learning solutions poses several challenges and requires careful consideration to ensure successful deployment and integration into existing systems. One primary challenge is data quality and availability. Machine learning algorithms rely heavily on high-quality, labeled training data to learn patterns and make accurate predictions. Obtaining sufficient and clean data can be difficult, especially in domains where data collection is expensive, time-consuming, or subject to privacy concerns. Ensuring data integrity, completeness, and relevance is crucial for the effectiveness of machine learning models.

Another challenge is model complexity and interpretability. As machine learning models become more sophisticated, they often become black boxes, making it a challenge to understand the underlying mechanisms driving their predictions. This lack of interpretability can hinder trust and acceptance of machine learning solutions, especially in high-stakes domains where transparency and accountability are paramount. Balancing model complexity with interpretability is essential, and organizations must strive to develop models that not only perform well but also provide insights into how decisions are made.

Additionally, scalability and deployment are significant considerations in machine learning implementations. Building and training machine learning models can require substantial computational resources and expertise. Scaling machine learning solutions to handle large datasets or real-time applications can be technically challenging and resource-intensive. Moreover, deploying machine learning models into production environments requires careful planning to ensure compatibility with existing systems, performance optimization, and ongoing maintenance.

Addressing these challenges and considerations requires a holistic approach involving collaboration between data scientists, domain experts, and IT professionals to overcome technical, organizational, and ethical hurdles in machine learning implementation.

AI IN BI: BENEFITS AND CHALLENGES

This section explores the transformative advantages AI brings to business intelligence, such as enhanced efficiency and predictive capabilities, while also addressing the hurdles like data privacy concerns and implementation complexities that organizations must navigate.

Benefits of AI Adoption in BI and Data Analysis

The adoption of AI in BI and data analysis brings forth a multitude of benefits that significantly enhance organizational decision-making processes and operational efficiency. One primary advantage is the ability of AI-powered systems to analyze vast amounts of data with unprecedented speed and accuracy. By leveraging advanced machine learning algorithms, AI enables organizations to extract valuable insights from complex datasets, uncovering hidden patterns, trends, and correlations that may not be apparent through traditional analytics methods. This capability empowers decision-makers with timely and relevant information, enabling them to make data-driven decisions more confidently and precisely.

Another key benefit of AI adoption in BI and data analysis is the automation of repetitive tasks and processes. AI-powered systems can streamline data preparation, cleansing, and analysis processes, reducing manual effort and freeing up valuable human resources for more strategic endeavors. By automating routine tasks, organizations can accelerate decision-making processes, improve operational efficiency, and allocate resources more effectively. Additionally, AI-driven automation minimizes the risk of human error, ensuring data accuracy and reliability, which are crucial for making informed decisions and driving business success.

Furthermore, AI adoption in BI and data analysis facilitates the implementation of predictive and prescriptive analytics capabilities, enabling organizations to anticipate future trends and outcomes and prescribe actionable recommendations. By leveraging predictive modeling techniques, AI systems can forecast market trends, customer behavior, and operational performance with greater accuracy and confidence. This enables organizations to proactively identify opportunities, mitigate risks, and optimize business strategies to achieve their objectives.

Additionally, AI-powered prescriptive analytics provides decision-makers with intelligent recommendations for optimizing processes, mitigating risks, and driving business growth, further enhancing the value derived from BI and data analysis initiatives. Overall, the benefits of AI adoption in BI and data analysis are far-reaching, empowering organizations to gain deeper insights, make more informed decisions, and drive innovation and growth in today's competitive business landscape.

AI Integration Challenges in BI Infrastructure

Implementing AI in the BI infrastructure presents several challenges that organizations must address to maximize the effectiveness and success of their AI initiatives. One significant challenge is the complexity of integrating AI technologies into existing BI systems and infrastructure. Organizations often grapple with legacy systems, disparate data sources, and siloed data repositories, making it challenging to deploy AI solutions seamlessly. Moreover, ensuring interoperability and compatibility between different AI tools and BI platforms requires careful planning and coordination to avoid integration bottlenecks and data inconsistencies.

Another challenge in implementing AI in BI infrastructure is the scarcity of skilled talent and expertise. The development and deployment of AI-powered BI solutions require specialized knowledge in data science, machine learning, and AI algorithms, which are in high demand but low supply. Organizations may struggle to find qualified data scientists and AI engineers capable of designing and implementing AI models that meet their specific business needs. Additionally, the rapid pace of technological innovation in AI necessitates continuous learning and upskilling among existing BI professionals to stay abreast of the latest developments and best practices in AI-driven BI.

Furthermore, data privacy and security concerns pose significant challenges in implementing AI in BI infrastructure. AI-powered BI systems rely on vast amounts of sensitive data, including customer information, financial data, and proprietary business insights. Ensuring the privacy and security of this data throughout the AI lifecycle, from data acquisition and processing to model training and deployment, is paramount to compliance with regulatory requirements and protection against data breaches and cyber threats.

Organizations must implement robust data governance frameworks, encryption protocols, and access controls to safeguard sensitive data and mitigate the risks associated with AI-driven BI initiatives. Addressing these challenges requires a holistic approach that combines technical expertise, organizational buy-in, and a commitment to ethical and responsible AI practices.

AI Integration in Established BI Systems

Integrating AI into existing BI systems requires careful consideration of several key factors to ensure successful implementation and maximize benefits. First, compatibility and interoperability are crucial aspects. AI solutions should seamlessly integrate with the existing BI infrastructure, databases, and analytics tools without disrupting current operations. Compatibility ensures smooth data flow and minimizes the need for extensive system overhauls, saving both time and resources.

Second, data quality and governance are paramount. AI relies heavily on data, and BI systems are no exception. Ensuring data accuracy, completeness, and consistency is essential for AI algorithms to generate reliable insights. Additionally, establishing robust data governance frameworks guarantees compliance with regulatory requirements and mitigates the risks associated with data privacy and security breaches.

Finally, user adoption and training are vital for successfully integrating AI into BI systems. Employees need to understand how AI-powered analytics enhance decision-making processes and contribute to organizational objectives. Comprehensive training programs should be implemented to empower users with the necessary skills to leverage AI-driven insights effectively. Moreover, fostering a culture that embraces AI innovation encourages widespread adoption and fosters continuous improvement in BI practices. By addressing these considerations, organizations can unlock the full potential of AI integration with existing BI systems, driving informed decision-making and gaining a competitive edge in today's data-driven landscape.

Data Privacy and Security in AI Implementations

Addressing data privacy and security concerns is paramount when implementing AI solutions. One key consideration is implementing robust encryption techniques to protect sensitive data throughout its lifecycle, from collection to analysis. Encryption ensures that even if data is intercepted, it remains unintelligible to unauthorized users. Additionally, adopting stringent access controls and authentication mechanisms limits access to data to only authorized personnel, reducing the risk of unauthorized use or breaches.

Furthermore, depending on the jurisdiction and industry, organizations must prioritize compliance with relevant data privacy regulations such as GDPR, CCPA, and HIPAA. This involves conducting thorough data privacy impact assessments to identify and mitigate potential risks to individuals' privacy rights. Additionally, implementing transparency measures, such as providing clear disclosures about data usage and obtaining informed consent from users, fosters trust and demonstrates a commitment to ethical AI practices.

Moreover, continuous monitoring and auditing of AI systems are essential for promptly detecting and responding to potential security threats or breaches. By leveraging AI-driven anomaly detection and threat intelligence solutions, organizations can proactively identify suspicious activities and take corrective actions to safeguard data integrity and maintain user trust. Ultimately, a proactive approach to addressing data privacy and security concerns with AI ensures that organizations can harness its transformative potential while upholding the highest standards of data protection and ethical conduct.

Resistance to AI Adoption

Overcoming resistance to AI adoption in business requires a multifaceted approach that addresses various concerns and fosters organizational buy-in. First, education and awareness-building efforts are crucial. Many employees may fear AI's potential to automate their jobs or view it as a threat to job security. Providing comprehensive training programs and transparent communication about the benefits of AI, such as enhancing productivity, streamlining processes, and enabling more informed decision-making, can alleviate fears and skepticism. Moreover, highlighting successful case studies and real-world examples of AI implementation in similar industries can illustrate its potential to drive positive outcomes and inspire confidence among stakeholders.

Second, involving employees in the AI adoption process empowers them to become advocates for change rather than passive recipients. Soliciting feedback, ideas, and concerns from frontline staff ensures that their voices are heard and that their perspectives are considered in the decision-making process. Additionally, fostering a culture of experimentation and continuous learning encourages employees to embrace AI technologies as tools that augment their capabilities rather than threats to their roles. By engaging employees as partners in the AI journey, organizations can cultivate a sense of ownership and commitment to its success, driving greater acceptance and adoption.

Finally, addressing concerns about ethical implications and ensuring transparency in AI algorithms and decision-making processes are essential for building trust. Establishing clear guidelines and governance frameworks for responsible AI use, including principles of fairness, accountability, and transparency, demonstrates a commitment to ethical AI practices. Furthermore, implementing mechanisms for monitoring and auditing AI systems to detect and mitigate biases or unintended consequences reinforces trust and credibility. By prioritizing ethical considerations and transparency, organizations can mitigate resistance to AI adoption and foster a culture of trust and innovation conducive to successful implementation.

CHAPTER 20

AI IN BI AND DATA ANALYSIS: RISKS, ETHICS, AND FUTURE

RISKS

Bias and Fairness

Organizations must implement rigorous processes for ongoing monitoring and auditing of AI algorithms to detect and address biases in real time, ensuring that decisions are made equitably and transparently. This proactive approach not only mitigates the risk of biased outcomes but also fosters a culture of accountability and continuous improvement in AI-driven BI and data analysis practices. Organizations can build trust with stakeholders and uphold ethical standards by prioritizing fairness and addressing bias concerns comprehensively, fostering a more inclusive and equitable data-driven ecosystem.

Organizations must conduct thorough bias assessments to identify and mitigate biases in AI algorithms, including biases related to data selection, preprocessing, and algorithmic decision-making. Implementing fairness-aware machine learning techniques and bias detection algorithms helps ensure that AI-driven BI systems produce equitable outcomes for all individuals. Moreover, transparency and accountability are essential for addressing bias and fairness concerns in AI-driven BI. Organizations must provide clear explanations of how AI algorithms make decisions, including the factors considered and the rationale behind outcomes. Additionally, establishing mechanisms for auditing and monitoring AI systems enables organizations to detect and rectify biases in real time.

Additionally, organizations should prioritize diversity and inclusivity not only within AI development teams but also among stakeholders involved in the decision-making process. This diverse representation ensures that a wide range of perspectives is considered, helping to identify and mitigate biases more effectively. Ultimately, organizations can enhance stakeholder trust, uphold ethical standards, and promote equitable outcomes in AI-driven BI and data analysis initiatives by fostering a culture of inclusivity and addressing bias and fairness concerns.

Accuracy and Reliability

Organizations must continuously refine and optimize AI algorithms to enhance accuracy and reliability over time, adapting to changing data patterns and business requirements. This iterative approach ensures that AI-driven BI systems evolve to meet the evolving needs of the organization, delivering increasingly accurate and reliable insights for informed decision-making. By prioritizing accuracy and reliability, organizations can maximize the value of AI-driven BI and data analysis, driving business growth and innovation with confidence in the reliability of their insights.

Organizations must implement rigorous validation and testing procedures to assess the accuracy and reliability of AI algorithms, including benchmarking against ground truth data and conducting sensitivity analyses to evaluate algorithmic robustness. Additionally, organizations should establish mechanisms for monitoring and validating AI-driven insights in real time, enabling proactive detection and correction of errors or anomalies. Moreover, transparency and interpretability are essential for addressing accuracy and reliability issues in AI-driven BI. Organizations must clearly explain how AI algorithms generate insights, including the underlying assumptions, limitations, and uncertainties.

Additionally, establishing mechanisms for validating AI-driven insights against domain knowledge and expert judgment helps ensure the accuracy and reliability of findings. Furthermore, fostering a culture of data literacy and critical thinking among users enables organizations to evaluate and interpret AI-driven insights effectively. By prioritizing accuracy and reliability in AI-driven BI, organizations can confidently make informed decisions and derive actionable insights, driving business success and innovation.

Overreliance

Overreliance on automation poses a significant risk in the realm of BI and data analysis driven by AI. While automation can streamline processes, enhance efficiency, and generate insights at scale, an excessive dependence on automated systems may lead to complacency and oversight. Organizations may overlook the importance of human oversight and critical thinking, blindly accepting AI-generated insights without proper validation or contextual understanding. This overreliance on automation can result in erroneous conclusions, missed opportunities, and even reputational damage if flawed insights are acted upon without scrutiny.

Moreover, overreliance on automation can exacerbate the potential impact of AI biases and inaccuracies. AI algorithms, while powerful, are not infallible and may inadvertently perpetuate biases or generate inaccurate conclusions, especially in complex or ambiguous scenarios. Organizations that rely too heavily on automated decision-making processes risk amplifying existing biases or overlooking critical nuances that require human judgment and intervention. Furthermore, an overreliance on automation may lead to a lack of accountability and transparency in decision-making processes, as stakeholders may struggle to understand or challenge AI-driven insights, resulting in decreased trust in the reliability and fairness of BI and data analysis outcomes.

Organizations must strike a balance between automation and human involvement to mitigate the risks associated with overreliance on automation in AI-driven BI and data analysis. While automation can augment human capabilities and improve efficiency, human oversight and critical thinking remain indispensable. Organizations should establish robust validation processes, encourage interdisciplinary collaboration between data scientists, domain experts, and business stakeholders, and foster a culture that values skepticism and inquiry. By integrating human judgment with AI-driven automation, organizations can enhance the reliability, fairness, and accountability of BI and data analysis processes, thereby minimizing the risks associated with overreliance on automation.

Interpretability and Transparency

Interpretability and transparency challenges present significant hurdles in the adoption of AI for BI and data analysis. While AI algorithms can deliver powerful insights and predictions, the inner workings of these algorithms are often complex and opaque, making it difficult for stakeholders to understand how decisions are made. A lack of interpretability can hinder trust and acceptance of AI-driven insights, especially in high-stakes scenarios where decisions impact business strategies or customer interactions. Furthermore, regulatory requirements, such as the right to explanation under GDPR, mandate transparency in AI decision-making, adding another layer of complexity for organizations seeking to leverage AI in BI and data analysis.

Addressing interpretability and transparency challenges requires organizations to prioritize explainability in AI models and decision-making processes. This involves developing AI algorithms that not only deliver accurate predictions but also provide clear explanations of how those predictions are generated. Techniques such as model-agnostic interpretability methods, feature importance analysis, and visualization tools can help illuminate the factors driving AI-driven insights, enabling stakeholders to understand and trust AI decisions. Moreover, organizations must establish mechanisms for documenting and communicating AI-driven insights, ensuring transparency in decision-making processes. Organizations can enhance stakeholder trust, facilitate regulatory compliance, and promote accountability in decision-making by promoting interpretability and transparency in AI-driven BI and data analysis.

Achieving interpretability and transparency in AI-driven BI and data analysis is not without its challenges. Complex AI algorithms, such as deep learning models, may inherently prioritize accuracy over interpretability, making it difficult to explain their decisions clearly. Additionally, the trade-offs between model complexity and interpretability must be carefully balanced, as overly simplistic models may sacrifice predictive performance for interpretability.

Furthermore, ensuring transparency in AI decision-making processes requires organizations to address issues such as algorithmic bias and data privacy while maintaining compliance with regulatory requirements. Despite these challenges, organizations that prioritize interpretability and transparency in AI-driven BI and data analysis can reap significant benefits, including improved decision-making, stakeholder trust, and regulatory compliance.

Employment

The potential impact of AI on employment and workforce dynamics is a critical aspect of AI risks in BI and data analysis. While AI technologies have the potential to automate routine tasks, streamline processes, and augment human capabilities, they also pose challenges related to job displacement and changes in workforce skill requirements. As AI-driven automation becomes more prevalent in BI and data analysis, certain roles may become obsolete or significantly transformed, particularly those involving repetitive, rule-based tasks. This could lead to job displacement for workers in traditional BI and data analysis roles, necessitating reskilling or upskilling to remain relevant in the evolving labor market.

Moreover, the widespread adoption of AI in BI and data analysis may reshape workforce dynamics by creating demand for new skill sets and job roles. As organizations increasingly rely on AI-driven insights to inform decision-making, there is a growing need for data scientists, machine learning engineers, and AI specialists capable of developing, implementing, and maintaining AI algorithms. Additionally, roles that require human-centric skills such as critical thinking, problem-solving, and creativity may become increasingly valuable in complementing AI-driven automation. Organizations must anticipate these shifts in workforce demand and invest in training programs to equip employees with the skills needed to thrive in an AI-driven workplace.

Furthermore, the potential impact of AI on employment extends beyond individual job roles to broader socioeconomic implications. There is a risk of widening inequality if certain segments of the workforce are disproportionately affected by job displacement or lack access to opportunities for reskilling. Additionally, ethical considerations such as fairness, diversity, and inclusion must be prioritized to ensure that AI-driven automation benefits all members of society equitably. By proactively addressing these challenges and embracing responsible AI adoption, organizations can mitigate the risks associated with AI's impact on employment and workforce dynamics while maximizing innovation, productivity, and economic growth opportunities.

Security

Security risks in AI-driven BI and data analysis are critical challenges that organizations must address comprehensively to safeguard sensitive information and maintain trust among stakeholders. With the rise in data breaches and cyberattacks, protecting data integrity and confidentiality is paramount. AI algorithms often rely on vast datasets containing sensitive information, making them lucrative targets for malicious actors.

Organizations must implement robust security measures throughout the AI lifecycle to mitigate security risks. This includes employing encryption techniques, access controls, and authentication mechanisms to protect data integrity and prevent unauthorized access. Regular security audits, penetration testing, and employee training programs are essential for proactively detecting and mitigating security vulnerabilities.

Additionally, organizations should remain vigilant against emerging cybersecurity threats and vulnerabilities specific to AI-driven BI systems. This requires staying informed about evolving threats and implementing appropriate countermeasures to safeguard against potential breaches. By prioritizing security measures and adopting a proactive approach to cybersecurity, organizations can minimize the risk of data breaches and cyberattacks, thereby preserving the integrity of their AI-driven BI systems and maintaining trust among stakeholders.

Privacy

Addressing privacy concerns in AI-powered BI is essential for maintaining trust and compliance with data protection regulations. One crucial aspect is data anonymization and pseudonymization techniques, which help mitigate privacy risks by removing or obfuscating personally identifiable information from datasets used in AI-driven BI analysis. By anonymizing data at the source and implementing strict access controls, organizations can safeguard individuals' privacy while still deriving valuable insights from their data. Additionally, employing differential privacy methods, which inject noise into query responses to protect sensitive information, further enhances privacy protection in AI-powered BI systems.

Furthermore, adopting privacy-by-design principles ensures that privacy considerations are integrated into the entire lifecycle of AI-powered BI solutions, from design and development to deployment and maintenance. This approach involves conducting comprehensive privacy impact assessments to identify and mitigate privacy risks associated with AI algorithms and data processing practices. By embedding privacy controls and safeguards into AI-powered BI systems from the outset, organizations can proactively address privacy concerns and demonstrate a commitment to responsible data stewardship. Moreover, providing transparency about data usage and privacy practices, such as through privacy policies and user consent mechanisms, fosters trust and empowers individuals to make informed decisions about their data.

Finally, implementing robust data governance frameworks and regulatory compliance measures is essential for ensuring that AI-powered BI systems adhere to privacy regulations such as GDPR, CCPA, and HIPAA. This involves establishing clear policies and procedures for data collection, storage, sharing, and processing, as well as mechanisms for obtaining and managing user consent. Regular audits and assessments of AI-powered BI systems help verify compliance with privacy regulations and identify areas for improvement. By prioritizing privacy protection and compliance, organizations can mitigate privacy risks, build trust with stakeholders, and unlock the full potential of AI-powered BI to drive informed decision-making and business innovation.

Regulatory/Compliance

Regulatory and compliance challenges represent a critical aspect of AI implementation in BI and data analysis. As AI technologies continue to evolve rapidly, regulatory frameworks struggle to keep pace, leading to uncertainties and ambiguities regarding compliance requirements. Organizations must navigate a complex landscape of regulations governing data privacy, security, and ethical use, such as the GDPR, CCPA, and sector-specific regulations such as the HIPAA. Failure to comply with these regulations can result in severe penalties, legal liabilities, and reputational damage, making regulatory compliance a top priority for organizations leveraging AI in BI and data analysis.

Furthermore, the global nature of data and AI-driven insights complicates compliance efforts, as organizations must contend with varying regulatory requirements across different jurisdictions. Data localization requirements, cross-border data transfer restrictions, and differing definitions of personal data pose significant challenges for organizations operating in multiple regions. Additionally, the lack of standardized guidelines for AI development and deployment further exacerbates compliance complexities as organizations struggle to interpret and implement regulatory requirements effectively. To address these challenges, organizations must adopt a proactive approach to regulatory compliance, conduct comprehensive assessments of regulatory risks, and establish robust governance frameworks prioritizing data protection, transparency, and accountability.

Legal

Legal considerations are a critical aspect of AI adoption for businesses, given the increasing scrutiny and evolving landscape of laws and regulations governing AI technologies. Organizations must navigate a complex Web of legal frameworks, including data protection regulations such as GDPR or CCPA and sector-specific regulations such as those governing healthcare (HIPAA) and finance (e.g., Sarbanes-Oxley Act). Failure to comply with these regulations can result in severe penalties, including fines, legal liabilities, and reputational damage.

Furthermore, legal considerations extend beyond compliance with existing regulations to encompass risk management and liability issues associated with AI adoption. As AI systems become more autonomous and decision-making processes increasingly automated, legal liability and accountability questions become more complex. Organizations must clarify the roles and responsibilities concerning AI systems, including defining who is accountable for AI-driven decisions and outcomes.

Additionally, businesses should consider potential legal risks, such as data breaches, algorithmic biases, intellectual property infringements, and contractual disputes, and implement measures to mitigate these risks, such as robust cybersecurity protocols, bias detection algorithms, and contractual clauses addressing AI-related liabilities. By proactively addressing legal considerations in AI adoption, organizations can minimize legal risks, ensure ethical AI use, and build trust with stakeholders in an increasingly AI-driven world.

ETHICS

This section discusses the critical importance of ethical principles in AI, including fairness, transparency, and accountability, while addressing challenges like bias and regulatory compliance. Through its subsections, it explores the ethical dilemmas, practices, and frameworks essential for ensuring responsible and equitable AI deployment in business intelligence and data analysis.

Ethical Dilemmas

As AI algorithms become increasingly integrated into decision-making processes, organizations must grapple with ethical dilemmas related to bias, fairness, accountability, and transparency. Ensuring that AI systems adhere to ethical principles and societal values is essential for maintaining trust with stakeholders and upholding organizational integrity. By embedding ethical considerations into AI development and deployment practices, organizations can mitigate regulatory and compliance risks while fostering a culture of responsible AI use that prioritizes fairness, transparency, and accountability in BI and data analysis initiatives.

Ethical and societal concerns surrounding AI, such as bias, fairness, accountability, and transparency, are increasingly being addressed through regulatory initiatives and guidelines. For instance, the European Union's proposed Artificial Intelligence Act aims to regulate AI technologies by establishing requirements for transparency, accountability, and risk assessment. Similarly, regulatory bodies and industry groups world-wide are developing guidelines and standards to promote ethical AI practices and mitigate potential risks. Organizations must stay abreast of these developments and incorporate ethical considerations into their AI strategies to ensure compliance and uphold responsible AI use.

Ethical AI Practices

The importance of ethical AI practices in business cannot be overstated in today's data-driven landscape. Ethical AI ensures that businesses harness the transformative power of AI while upholding principles of fairness, transparency, and accountability. By prioritizing ethical considerations, organizations build trust with stakeholders, including customers, employees, regulators, and the public. This trust is foundational for long-term success, as it fosters positive relationships, enhances brand reputation, and mitigates the risk of regulatory scrutiny or public backlash.

Moreover, ethical AI practices are essential for mitigating biases and promoting inclusivity. AI algorithms are only as unbiased as the data they are trained on, and without careful consideration, they can inadvertently perpetuate or amplify existing biases. By implementing ethical data collection, processing, and analysis guidelines, businesses can mitigate biases and ensure that AI systems produce fair and equitable outcomes for all stakeholders. Inclusivity in AI not only aligns with ethical principles but also expands market reach and enables businesses to better serve diverse customer bases.

Furthermore, ethical AI practices are essential for navigating legal and regulatory landscapes. As governments worldwide introduce increasingly stringent regulations governing data privacy, security, and AI use, businesses that prioritize ethical AI practices are better positioned to comply with regulatory requirements and mitigate legal risks. Proactively integrating ethical considerations into AI development and deployment processes not only safeguards against potential fines or penalties but also demonstrates a commitment to responsible corporate citizenship. Ultimately, by embracing ethical AI practices, businesses can unlock the full potential of AI while fostering trust, inclusivity, and compliance in the digital age.

Bias

The ethical implications of AI bias in data analysis are profound, reflecting broader societal concerns about fairness, equity, and justice. AI algorithms are trained on vast datasets that may contain inherent biases reflecting historical injustices, systemic discrimination, or societal prejudices. When left unaddressed, these biases can perpetuate or even exacerbate inequalities, leading to discriminatory outcomes in areas such as hiring, lending, criminal justice, and healthcare. Consequently, the deployment of biased AI systems not only undermines trust in technology but also perpetuates societal injustices, exacerbating existing disparities and marginalizing vulnerable populations.

Addressing AI bias requires a multifaceted approach that encompasses data collection, algorithm design, and decision-making processes. Organizations must prioritize diversity and inclusivity in their datasets to mitigate biases, ensuring representation across different demographic groups. Moreover, employing techniques such as fairness-aware machine learning and algorithmic auditing enables organizations to proactively detect and mitigate biases in AI algorithms. Additionally, fostering transparency and accountability in AI decision-making processes, including disclosing how decisions are made and providing avenues for recourse or appeal, promotes trust and ensures that AI systems uphold ethical standards.

Furthermore, regulatory frameworks and industry standards play a crucial role in governing AI bias and promoting ethical practices. Governments and regulatory bodies worldwide are increasingly introducing legislation and guidelines to address AI bias and promote fairness and accountability in AI deployment. Compliance with these regulations not only mitigates legal risks but also reinforces organizational commitments to ethical AI practices. Moreover, industry collaboration and knowledge-sharing initiatives enable stakeholders to exchange best practices, tools, and methodologies for addressing AI bias collectively. Ultimately, by acknowledging and actively mitigating AI bias, organizations can harness the transformative potential of AI while upholding ethical principles and promoting fairness and equity in society.

Fairness and Transparency

Ensuring fairness and transparency in AI-driven decision-making is imperative for fostering trust and accountability in today's increasingly automated world. Fairness requires that AI systems treat all individuals fairly and without discrimination, regardless of race, gender, ethnicity, or any other protected characteristic. Iti's important to note that transparency entails providing clear explanations of how AI algorithms make decisions, including the factors considered and the reasoning behind outcomes. By prioritizing fairness and transparency, organizations can mitigate the risk of biased or discriminatory decisions and promote confidence among stakeholders in AI-driven processes.

To achieve fairness in AI-driven decision-making, organizations must address biases that may be present in both data and algorithms. This involves conducting comprehensive bias assessments to identify and mitigate biases at every stage of the AI development lifecycle, from data collection and preprocessing to algorithm training and deployment. Implementing fairness-aware machine learning techniques and incorporating fairness constraints into algorithm design enables organizations to mitigate biases and proactively ensure equitable outcomes for all individuals. Moreover, ongoing monitoring and auditing of AI systems are essential for detecting and addressing biases in real-world contexts, enabling organizations to continuously refine and improve the fairness of their AI-driven decision-making processes.

Transparency is equally critical for promoting trust and accountability in AI-driven decision-making. Providing clear explanations of how AI algorithms reach decisions, including the features or variables considered and the relative importance assigned to them, enhances interpretability and enables stakeholders to understand and scrutinize AI-driven outcomes. Additionally, organizations should establish mechanisms for documenting and communicating AI-driven decisions, such as decision logs or audit trails, to promote accountability and facilitate regulatory compliance. Organizations can build trust with stakeholders, uphold ethical standards, and mitigate risks associated with biased or opaque decision-making processes by prioritizing fairness and transparency in AI-driven decision-making.

FUTURE OF AI IN BI AND DATA ANALYSIS

In the dynamic landscape of BI and analytics, staying abreast of the latest trends is crucial for organizations aiming to derive actionable insights and maintain a competitive edge. From the integration of advanced technologies such as AI to evolving approaches in data visualization and privacy governance, the realm of BI is witnessing transformative shifts. The following sub-sections delve into prominent trends shaping the current BI and analytics landscape, unraveling the innovative methodologies and technologies that are reshaping the way businesses harness data for informed decision-making.

Current Trends and Developments in AI for BI

The evolving landscape of AI within BI is fundamentally altering how organizations interpret and leverage data for strategic decision-making and competitive advantage. AI-powered analytics platforms are seamlessly integrating into BI solutions, revolutionizing data analysis by automating tasks, extracting insights from complex datasets, and enabling real-time decision-making. This integration is not merely about historical analysis; it emphasizes predictive modeling, empowering organizations to anticipate future trends and automate decision-making processes with increasing accuracy and efficiency.

Moreover, advancements in NLP and conversational AI are democratizing access to BI insights. Users can now interact with analytics platforms using voice commands or text queries, making BI more accessible to nontechnical users. This shift toward intuitive data analysis fosters a deeper engagement with data-driven insights, enhancing decision-making processes across all levels of an organization.

Augmented analytics, another significant trend, combines AI and machine learning techniques with traditional BI processes to enhance data analysis capabilities. By automating data preparation, identifying relevant insights, and generating actionable recommendations, augmented analytics platforms empower organizations to derive maximum value from their data. Furthermore, these platforms promote data democratization by providing self-service analytics tools to business users, reducing dependence on IT departments for data analysis tasks, and fostering a culture of data-driven decision-making.

The emphasis on real-time analytics, especially through streaming analytics, underscores the importance of immediate insights in today's fast-paced business environment. Live data dashboards enable users to access the most current information, facilitating timely decision-making and agility in response to evolving market dynamics.

In conclusion, the integration of AI into BI processes marks a significant shift in how organizations harness the power of data. By leveraging AI-powered analytics platforms, organizations can gain deeper insights, optimize operations, and drive innovation in a data-driven world. Ethical considerations must underpin these initiatives to ensure responsible AI adoption and maintain trust with stakeholders. Ultimately, the transformative potential of AI in BI lies in its ability to empower organizations to make smarter, more informed decisions that drive sustainable growth and competitive advantage.

Predictions for the Future of AI-Driven Data Analysis

Predicting the future of AI-driven data analysis involves envisioning a landscape where AI continues to play an increasingly integral role in shaping how organizations harness data to drive insights and innovation. One key prediction is the continued proliferation of AI-powered analytics platforms that seamlessly integrate advanced machine learning algorithms with traditional BI tools. These platforms will evolve to offer more sophisticated capabilities, including real-time predictive analytics, anomaly detection, and prescriptive recommendations, enabling organizations to extract deeper insights from their data and respond to changing market dynamics with agility and precision.

Moreover, the future of AI-driven data analysis is likely to be characterized by the democratization of data science and analytics capabilities. As AI technologies become more accessible and user-friendly, organizations of all sizes and across industries will empower business users with self-service analytics tools that enable them to explore, visualize, and interpret data independently. This democratization of data analysis will democratize decision-making, enabling employees at all levels to leverage data-driven insights to inform strategic initiatives, drive innovation, and optimize performance. Additionally, NLP and conversational AI advancements will further democratize access to insights by enabling users to interact with AI-driven analytics platforms through voice commands or text queries, making data analysis more intuitive and accessible to nontechnical users.

The future of AI-driven data analysis is intricately linked with ongoing advancements in AI research and technology, which are poised to drive innovation and expand the horizons of what organizations can achieve with their data. Breakthroughs in fields such as deep learning, reinforcement learning, and explainable AI will pave the way for the development of more robust and transparent AI algorithms capable of tackling increasingly complex data analysis tasks. This emphasis on explainable AI is gaining significance, highlighting the importance of transparent models and interpretable algorithms in ensuring that AI-driven decisions are understandable and also trusted by users. By promoting transparency and accountability, Explainable AI enhances the reliability of AI-driven insights, fostering trust and confidence among stakeholders.

Furthermore, interdisciplinary collaborations between data scientists, domain experts, and business stakeholders will drive the co-creation of AI-driven solutions tailored to specific industry needs and business objectives. By embracing these predictions for the future of AI-driven data analysis, organizations can position themselves at the forefront of innovation, staying ahead of the curve and unlocking the full potential of data to drive business success and innovation in the years to come.

Emerging Technologies Shaping the Future

Emerging technologies are reshaping the BI and data analysis landscape, promising to revolutionize how organizations harness and derive insights from their data. One such technology is AI, which continues to evolve rapidly and plays a pivotal role in enhancing BI capabilities. AI-powered algorithms enable organizations to automate data analysis processes, uncover hidden patterns, and generate predictive insights, empowering decision-makers to make informed choices with greater accuracy and efficiency. As AI technologies mature, they are expected to become increasingly sophisticated, enabling organizations to extract deeper insights and drive innovation across various industries.

Another emerging technology shaping the future of BI and data analysis is edge computing, which involves processing data closer to its source rather than relying solely on centralized cloud infrastructure. This decentralized approach enables organizations to analyze data in real time, reducing latency and enabling faster decision-making. With the proliferation of IoT devices generating vast amounts of data at the edge of the network, edge computing is becoming increasingly important for organizations seeking to leverage data-driven insights in near real-time. By combining edge computing with advanced analytics techniques, organizations can unlock new opportunities for optimizing operations, improving customer experiences, and driving innovation.

Furthermore, blockchain technology is poised to revolutionize data analysis by enhancing data integrity, security, and transparency. Its decentralized and immutable ledger enables organizations to record and verify transactions securely, ensuring the integrity and traceability of data throughout its lifecycle. With significant implications for BI and data analysis, particularly in industries such as finance, supply chain management, and healthcare, where data integrity and security are paramount, blockchain offers a solution to enhance trust in data.

Leveraging blockchain technology allows organizations to streamline auditing processes, facilitate secure data sharing and collaboration across networks, and explore the potential of smart contracts to automate and enforce data-related agreements within analytics scenarios. As these emerging technologies mature and converge, they have the potential to transform BI and data analysis, enabling organizations to derive actionable insights and drive strategic decision-making with unprecedented speed, accuracy, and efficiency.

Strategies to Stay Ahead in the AI Revolution

In the rapidly evolving landscape of the AI revolution, businesses can implement several strategies to maintain a competitive edge and stay ahead of the curve. First and foremost, investing in talent acquisition and development is crucial. By hiring skilled professionals with expertise in AI, machine learning, and data science, organizations can build a strong foundation for effectively leveraging AI technologies. Additionally, providing ongoing training and upskilling opportunities for existing employees ensures that the workforce remains equipped with the latest knowledge and capabilities to harness AI tools and techniques. Furthermore, fostering a continuous learning and innovation culture encourages employees to experiment with new AI applications and methodologies, driving organizational growth and adaptability in the face of technological advancements.

Another key strategy for businesses to stay ahead in the AI revolution is to prioritize data-driven decision-making. By leveraging AI-powered analytics tools and platforms, organizations can extract actionable insights from vast amounts of data, enabling them to make informed decisions more accurately and efficiently. The implementation of advanced analytics techniques such as predictive modeling, NLP, and anomaly detection empowers businesses to proactively anticipate market trends, identify opportunities, and mitigate risks. Moreover, adopting a holistic approach to data management, including data governance, quality assurance, and privacy protection, ensures that organizations can derive maximum value from their data assets while maintaining compliance with regulatory requirements.

Furthermore, embracing collaboration and partnerships with AI solution providers and technology partners is essential for businesses to stay ahead in the AI revolution. By collaborating with industry experts and leveraging their specialized knowledge and resources, organizations can accelerate the development and deployment of AI solutions tailored to their specific needs and objectives. Additionally, participating in industry consortia, research initiatives, and open-source communities facilitates knowledge sharing and innovation, enabling businesses to stay abreast of emerging technologies and best practices in AI. By embracing collaboration and fostering a culture of innovation, businesses can position themselves as leaders in the AI revolution and drive sustainable growth and competitiveness in their respective markets.

INDEX